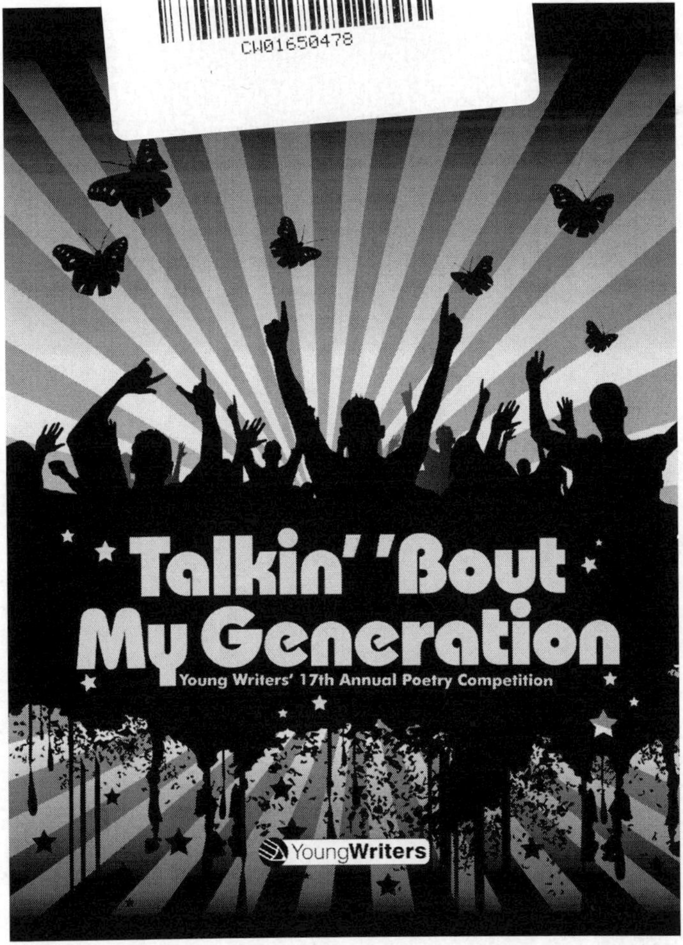

West Midlands Poets

Edited by Allison Jones

YoungWriters
First published in Great Britain in 2008 by:
Young Writers
Remus House
Coltsfoot Drive
Peterborough
PE2 9JX
Telephone: 01733 890066
Website: www.youngwriters.co.uk

SB ISBN 978-1 84431 498 0

Foreword

This year, the Young Writers' *Talkin' 'Bout My Generation* competition proudly presents a showcase of the best poetic talent selected from thousands of up-and-coming writers nationwide.

Young Writers was established in 1991 to promote the reading and writing of poetry within schools and to the young of today. Our books nurture and inspire confidence in the ability of young writers and provide a snapshot of poems written in schools and at home by budding poets of the future.

The thought, effort, imagination and hard work put into each poem impressed us all and the task of selecting poems was a difficult but nevertheless enjoyable experience.

We hope you are as pleased as we are with the final selection and that you and your family continue to be entertained with *Talkin' 'Bout My Generation West Midlands Poets* for many years to come.

Contents

St Martin's Catholic School, Stoke Golding

The Poems

My School

School is great,
But breaks are better,
I have all the best of friends,
Teachers and us in the classroom,
'Get to work,' they say.

Friends in school are the best ever,
Always there for me,
That's why I don't mind coming to school,
There goes the bell for break and lunch,
We go out to have our brunch.

School is OK,
Break, lunch and PE are the best,
Homework, school, homework,
I guess . . .
That is what school is all about!

Kate Irish (11)
Bishop Perowne CE College, Worcester

My Poem

I love school
It's so fun
Doing PE, have to run
I love school
When it's break time
I play football till half-past nine
I love school
Wait for the bell
Hope next lesson is maths as well
I love school, lots of friends
Hope to see them, it all depends.

Nicholas Macpherson (12)
Bishop Perowne CE College, Worcester

On The Day I Was Born

On the day I was born,
The sea was rushing onto the rocks violently,
Trees being pushed side to side in the mild wind,
River jumping, pounding onto the muddy bank.
The scientists adding new potions into test tubes,
Planets being discovered spinning around and around,
Factories inventing new types of candy and chocolate,
The wind swooping and whizzing around the cities,
Armies training and getting prepared for war,
Children skipping, playing and squabbling over the last carton of milk,
The Earth rotating, gravitating towards the sun.

Hannah Russell (12)
Bishop Perowne CE College, Worcester

School

There are lots of different subjects,
Like English, drama and RE,
Maths, history and French
And my worst subject, PE.
Writing in English,
Acting in drama,
Bible studies in RE,
In history, Tutankhamun,
In maths, doing fractions,
In French, the basic steps,
In PE we're doing football,
I wonder what we'll do next
This is what they teach in school,
Though there are lots of things I do,
Sometimes it's work,
Sometimes it's play,
But learning's always new.

Joeli Boxall (11)
Bishop Perowne CE College, Worcester

My Family

My mum is like a flower and as gentle as a mouse
My dad is like a football player and as good as one too
My sister is like a sporty queen and as fast as an Olympic runner
My rabbit is like a cuddly bear and as cute as a puppy
My fish are like a swarm of bees and as quick as a flash of lightning
My dog is like a brick but as funny as a joker
And I am like a poetry writer and as funny as a clown!

Christopher Guinivan (11)
Bishop Perowne CE College, Worcester

My Family

My mum
Is a bit different,
She has a secret hobby,
She skydives!
She skydives in the day
And she skydives at night.
Sometimes she gives people a terrible fright!

I'm James,
I'm a bit different.
I have a secret hobby,
I collect stick insects!
I train them to do stunts.
Unfortunately, they are forever escaping,
So Mum's always on the hunt!

My dad;
My dad is a bit . . . normal!
He is really into cricket
And never misses a game.
He hogs the telly when a match is on,
Which can be a real pain!

James Whitehouse (11)
Bishop Perowne CE College, Worcester

School, Teachers And Pupils

School,
School, the final frontier,
School, a place to fear,
School, a place that some people dislike,
School, activities of fun and enjoyment.

Teachers,
Teachers, secret alien spies,
Teachers, like little annoying flies,
Teachers, tell you time for work not play,
Teachers, just there to spoil the day.

Pupils,
Pupils, some are friend and some are foe,
Pupils, some weep and some have woe,
Pupils, to play and have fun with,
Pupils, the thing in the day that makes me,
Smile.

John Hewitt (12)
Bishop Perowne CE College, Worcester

School Poem

S afe and warm place to be,
C aring people in the school,
H appy environment to be in,
O pinions spread round the room,
O utings all year round,
L ovely food in the canteen.

Natalie Jenkins (11)
Bishop Perowne CE College, Worcester

The Argument

She didn't walk to school with me today,
She walked with someone else.
I didn't share my cookie with her,
I shared with Katy instead.
She didn't stand next to me,
She whispered with Anne instead.

She moved my chair an inch,
I moved hers a centimetre.
She drew a tiny line on my work,
I drew a tiny one on hers.
She took my rubber,
I took her pencil.
She swung her PE bag at me,
She did something too small to mention, so did I.
She came round to my house today, we had a good time.

Bethany Cheyne (11)
Bishop Perowne CE College, Worcester

Killer School

The school was dark, the school was grey
Teachers stalking you like prey
Seeing if you are chewing gum
So they can take it off you and make you glum
Class is scary, class is frightening
Teacher's eyes going back and forth like lightning.

Look in their eyes and at their glare
They'll do nothing more than give you a scare
Go to the head teacher's office, do not strain
Because it's most likely you'll never be seen again!

Qasim Hussain (11)
Bishop Perowne CE College, Worcester

The First Day At Bishops

The sky was dull, dark and cloudy
The children were loud, excited and scared
The tutors were busy, friendly and calm
The parents were proud, worried and happy
The lessons were nothing, we had none
The information was overloading people's brains

The school was big, alive and weird
The bag was full, heavy and new
The day was long, exhausting and gone.

Lia Mariano (11)
Bishop Perowne CE College, Worcester

Lessons

As I get to the gates
It's half-past eight
I must get a move on
Before I am late
I attend registration
Before my first lesson
Then on to RE
Maths and English and finally PE
As the day comes to an end
It's nearly three
Time to go home
Ready for my tea.

Tayla Macdonald (11)
Bishop Perowne CE College, Worcester

When The Bell Goes!

My favourite part of school
Is when the bell goes
The corridors fill with noise
As everybody rushes
To get out to the playground
Going left, going right
Me and my friends
Try to be first in the line
For the canteen
So we can get our food first
Still with break to spare
We're never there on time though
We're only near the front
When it's music upstairs
Because we're really close
Finally we get outside
We laugh and run and talk
Before we have to go inside
And lessons start again
Watching the clock until it is 3
And everyone goes home
Knowing tomorrow they'll be back again
Wondering if they'll make it through
Another day at school.

Thea Green (11)
Bishop Perowne CE College, Worcester

My Friends

A mazing, the bestest friend ever
M agnificent, she is never nasty, never
Y oung and kind and that's just fine

J oyful, Amy is the best and she shines
E verlasting, that's what our friendship is
F unny and if you say an idea, she never doubts
F riendly, never ever makes you feel left out
R eliable, you can always trust her
I maginative and creative in more ways
E ager to do what she wants to do
S upportive, helps me in all I do.

Sophie Upfield (11)
Bishop Perowne CE College, Worcester

A Lifetime

The sea was calm
The birds were cheeping
Flowers were blooming
Trees were gently swaying
Factories were cheering
Making and baking
Whilst I was waking.

Annabella Beesley (11)
Bishop Perowne CE College, Worcester

My Friends Poem

F riends are cool
R unning around having fun
I n and out of my friends' houses
E verybody loves to play
N ever want to stop
D oing things like football and more
S houting and screaming.

Joe Birbeck (12)
Bishop Perowne CE College, Worcester

School Is Fun!

School was fun today, we did a lot
We learnt how to cook a hot pot.
After lunch we went to gym,
Did some cartwheels and then a spin.
Back to class, French and maths,
Homework was given to our class.
Now the bell has gone,
It's time to go home.
Hallelujah and off we go!

Lauren Scott (11)
Bishop Perowne CE College, Worcester

Friends

F riends are funny, kind and caring
R unning, shouting, gossiping and more
I nseparable, sleepovers and big phone bills!
E nglish, science, French or maths
N ever ever apart
D ecisions about what to wear
S tupid fallouts always happen, but good friends always make up.

Claire Reynolds (11)
Bishop Perowne CE College, Worcester

Homework

As I come home from school to play
I realise I haven't finished the day.
My homework is sitting on my desk,
Like a gnome humming in an evil tone.
But then I grab my shoes and go to play,
Before I know it, it's the next day
And I've forgotten all about my work!

Louis Woodhouse (11)
Bishop Perowne CE College, Worcester

The Animals In My Generation

My mum had a fish whose name was called Squish,
But my dad wanted him on a dish.
He loved to splash about,
So I saved it with a wish.

My dad had a rabbit who had a dirty habit,
Not the type that monks wear,
But one that makes my dad swear.

My grandma had a cat called Sam,
Who wouldn't eat out of a can.
Only the best for Sam,
Boiled beef and ham.
When all the food was eaten by Sam,
With a full tummy he would fall asleep
And would dream of ham.

My grandad had a dog,
Who acted like a hog.
When he used to bark at the neighbours,
They would say, 'Hark!'
He used to bark at owls in the dark.

My great grandma had a tortoise,
Who was passed down through choice,
He was one hundred and five years old
And how differently they compare,
It would be quite fair
To see the nation through to my generation.

Artemis Jones (12)
Dodderhill School, Droitwich

My Family Through The Generations

My family are loopy,
They've all gone mad,
So read my poem and you'll know
Why this is so bad.

My great grandad is always asleep,
He's always such a bore,
But when it comes to my great grandma,
She snores and snores and snores.

Now for my great aunt,
Well, she's just plain silly
And as for my grandma,
She loves saying people are willy nilly.

My grandad, he's just really stupid,
He's absolutely off his rocker,
But my auntie, oh dear, what shall I say?
She enjoys breaking into my school locker.

My uncle loves all types of sports,
It's his favourite thing,
My mum adores to clean the house,
Well, it's a bit embarrassing.

My baby brother's cute,
We call him Little Ben,
And me, I'm bonkers,
Why do you think I'm writing this then?

Molly Everitt (11)
Dodderhill School, Droitwich

Through The Eyes Of A Baby

When I was born I was completely amazed!
All this new atmosphere and setting and all this noise!
I looked around slowly and what did I see?
All these people smiling and staring at me.
At first I screamed and gurgled loudly,
After I'd calmed down,
I smiled and gazed around rather proudly.
Soon enough I started getting angry, just like I imagined I would,
But no, the humans did not do anything,
They just laughed and rocked me off to sleep.
Soon I would not stop crying,
I carried on and on.
They quickly got tired and gave up
And just wouldn't stop singing this one song.
They gave me toys to play with
And a bottle with milk in.
But I shook them about
And threw them straight out of my baby cot.
I talk to Ben the dog, he understands me you know,
I just sigh and huff and roll my eyes.
He just chases flies.
Yes, he understands me and so do you, I hope.
I just want some peace, some quiet time,
Somewhere I can be by myself.
Never.
It will never happen, oh no,
Without all this prodding, poking and playing!
I soon discover something,
I actually quite like my mum,
The way she cuddles me, me, me!
Yes, I know I'm sweet,
It just comes naturally.

Chloe Drage (11)
Dodderhill School, Droitwich

Through The Eyes Of An Abandoned Dog

It's not fair,
I get kicked, shouted at,
I want someone kinder to care for me,
I get locked up, no freedom.

I hardly get anything to eat at all,
Sometimes I just eat the grass because I'm so hungry,
I get driven to a lonely beach,
All alone, no one to love me.

The wind is hard and cold,
It's getting dark now,
I don't know what to do,
All I hear is the waves crashing.

I . . . I think I can see someone,
The figure is getting closer,
I think it's a girl,
She starts to run towards me.

I climb into the car,
It is a long drive,
Finally we stop,
We are at a dogs' home.

I love it here,
They love me and are kind to me,
I like it here with the other dogs,
I hope I stay here forever and ever.

Emily Roberts (11)
Dodderhill School, Droitwich

A World For The Future

My dream is to be a show jumper
I have the best pony in the world
She helps me out
Connie was my first show jumper
She started my dream - my wish

The pony was not the only thing that helped me out
It was my teacher, Mandy, and don't
Forget my mum's support, we go out
Every weekend to get my four double clears
In BSJA show jumping - British Novice

I haven't all my clears
I only need two more
My mum and I can't count on Jess
She doesn't always go so well
Sometimes she goes really well, others she
Stops and we get eliminated

The young lady who inspired me
Was the one and only Ellen Whittaker
She rides in her own special way
And she sits quietly on her horse, Lacrano
She has a cousin called Robert and
Her uncle is called John
The Whittaker generation is huge
I hope one day I will be like one
Of the Whittakers.

Heidi Fellows (11)
Dodderhill School, Droitwich

Through The Eyes Of An Abandoned Foal

My owner abandoned me not long ago,
She used to say my white coat was aglow.
After a while she liked me less and less,
All because my coat was muddy and a mess.
We used to go to the woods to ride,
Through the trees and woods we'd glide.
Then one day we rode off the track,
She said she'd be one minute, but never came back.
I assumed she would be back very soon,
But then the sun left and out came the moon.
Days and nights passed
And I got hungry and thirsty fast.
A girl came through the woods one day,
With her friend who had come to stay.
She and her friend came over to me,
And led me out of the woods full of trees.
She took me down to the house on the farm,
Where her mum got me food and told me to be calm.
The little girl looked after me,
I thought, *I'll never be lonely again, you'll see!*
So I guess this shows some people really care,
Even if you do have muddy, messy hair!

Abigail Smith (11)
Dodderhill School, Droitwich

Looking Through The Mirror To The Future

I look through the mirror with despair
To find the future waiting there
My dark side tries to drag me in
To the scary future within
Future, past, now and then . . .
Choose which one you want to commence

She drags me in, which is very hard
Because I have my own personal guard
Tries and tries to pull me in
But I won't let her win
Future, past, now and then . . .
Choose which one you want to commence

I finally get pulled through
And then am startled with a big boo
I see the world differently now
Because robots have shown us how
Future, past, now and then . . .
Choose which one you want to commence

Now I am trapped
And the thunder clapped
But how can I get home
The robots all have a groan
Future, past, now and then . . .
Choose which one you want to commence

The mirror hole closes
As all the robots doze
Now I can't get back
To the rest of my pack
Future, past, now and then . . .
Choose which one you want to commence.

Emily Brazier (12)
Dodderhill School, Droitwich

It Is 2050

It is 2050
The sky is dark and black
There are no healthy things around
Everyone is fat

It is hot
It is stuffy
There are no healthy things around
Everyone is fat

There is no snow in winter
It's just much darker
There are no healthy things around
Everyone is fat

I have heard there was once a blue sky
And that the water and air was not polluted
There are no healthy things around
Everyone is fat

When I was little I saw a flightless bird
My father said, 'It's a penguin.' I've never seen one since
There are no healthy things around
Everyone is fat

Some people call winter the dark season
Because it's like night
There are no healthy things around
Everyone is fat

I wish I lived back in 2007
There was snow, there was ice
There were all four seasons
But now there are no healthy things around
Everyone is fat.

Emily Webster (12)
Dodderhill School, Droitwich

The World Of Animals

I wish the world was not so evil
Think of the animals, think of their homes,
Think of the trees, do you know how they feel?
Think of the owls, think of the birds.

I wish the world was not so cruel,
Think of the animals, think of their homes,
Think of the clouds all fluffy and white,
Think of the sun all round and hot.

I wish the world was not so destructive,
Think of the animals, think of their homes,
Think of the fires, think of the bangs,
Think of the men all dead and red.

I wish the world was not so harsh,
Think of the animals, think of their homes,
Think of the babies coming into our world,
Think of the children all happy and sad.

I wish the world was not so heartless
Think of the animals, think of their homes,
Think of the world all dying and black,
Why did they make the world so cruel?

Beth Young (11)
Dodderhill School, Droitwich

Bang, Bang

Bang, bang, they shot him down,
Bang, bang, he hit the ground,
Bang, bang, the gangsters shot him down.
On the floor, blood all around,
That is where he was found.
Bang, bang.

His hoodie big and brown,
His bike on the ground,
Right in the centre of town,
Oh, what a bad sound.
The crying will always last.
Bang, bang.

The gangsters shot him down, down.

His friends shouted out,
His family joined the crowd.
'That's our boy,' they shouted out.
'That's our boy on the ground.'
Bang, bang.

Katie Fletcher (13)
Dodderhill School, Droitwich

Glory On My Land

Back in the time when the dinosaurs were around,
I used to see glory on all my land,
The ground was so flat, as flat as my hand,
I used to see glory on all my land.
When I breathe I feel so free,
The fresh air around my knees.
I hear the birds go tweet, tweet, tweet,
But now I hear horns going beep, beep, beep.
I wish it could be the way it used to be,
I loved it back then, oh how I loved it back then.
Why are there lots of crimes,
Bullets, knives, bombs, planes, Twin Towers?
Why? Why? Why?
Nothing was like this back then.
It makes me cry thinking of them.
My life is now better than it used to be,
I still see glory on all my land,
I still see glory on all my land.

Heather Young (11)
Dodderhill School, Droitwich

My Poem

My name is Jack
The world looks so dead
The trees are rotting
The sun is not out

The world looks so dead

The grass is not green
The clouds are grey
The flowers are not bursting
And hopefully it's the end of the day
So I can't see what is now

The world looks so dead

With these strange people everywhere
The animals have changed too
With these strange machines making ice melt
Polar bears stranded, dying, the water around them

The world looks so dead

This is my story.

April Allen (11)
Dodderhill School, Droitwich

The Endangered Species

As I jump through the waves
I wonder why the water always seems warmer
When my pod and I look for food
There are never any fish around

All my family are always dying
Because they get caught in fishing nets
They throw us back in the water
All hurt and bleeding

We have no time to grieve
We are too busy swimming miles
To get to warmer seas
Why, why, why do people treat us like this?

We are used for show and entertainment
People love us then
But when it comes to saving us
Nobody loves us then

Can you guess what animal I am?
I'm the endangered dolphin
We are an endangered species
Like the pink and bottlenose
So please help us.

Holly Jones (12)
Dodderhill School, Droitwich

Martha

(Inspired by the book 'Abomination')

I'm sitting alone,
With no one to play with,
All alone, rejected.

I sit down in class,
And my classmates ignore me,
So, I am different, but why?

I've forgotten my pencil,
I look around, one to spare?
But no one responds, they do not care.

At break time they poke,
Surround me, jeer and laugh,
I seem to be brave - I hope.

I hide in the toilet,
They can't find me here I thought,
They found me, I was cornered, I had been caught.

At home time they chase me,
All up the hill to my home,
What have I done, what's the point?

There is a new boy in class, he might be my friend,
Alas, he has joined the bullies,
Now the horror will never end.

Libby Gandhi (12)
Dodderhill School, Droitwich

Destroyed

The world a desolate wasteland,
The people savage or ill.
What could have happened here,
That makes us want to kill?

A hundred years really changed things,
From good to bad to worse.
And it's us, the twenty-first century,
Who have made this curse.

All we hold dear will be destroyed,
Just because we're careless.
But if we hadn't polluted,
Then there could be fairness.

Of course the savages do try,
To bring back what we had.
The world is just a desert now,
It's our fault and it's sad.

There is something that we can do,
To keep the world just right.
If we walk, not take the car,
And switch off every light.

The world a green, fresh paradise,
The people so content.
'Cause we've looked after Mother Earth,
Her resources aren't spent.

Hannah Morris (13)
Dodderhill School, Droitwich

My World

My world,
Hate and despair,
Yet some people care,
For our world and life.

My world,
Should help others,
Sisters and mothers,
Together they help.

My world,
Expanding, growing,
Yet never stopping,
To make the future.

My world,
We must stand strong,
Haven't for so long,
For now, is our time.

My world,
Doesn't need war,
If people just saw,
That good can happen.

My world,
Where hope can live,
If people just give,
Some time for others.

Nikki Foulkes (12)
Dodderhill School, Droitwich

In My Future

In my future,
My world would be different.
No war, no enemies,
Just peace and unity.

In my future,
My world would be different.
No hate or despair,
Just friends who care.

In my future,
My world would be different.
No people who judge,
Just people who welcome.

In my future,
My world would be different.
No poverty or hunger,
Just happiness and joy.

In my future,
My world would be different.
No global warming,
Just fresh, clean air.

In my future,
My world would be different.
No fear or anger,
Just thoughtfulness and love.

In my future,
My world would be different.
No stealing or jealousy,
Just kindness and generosity.

Charlotte Jacob (12)
Dodderhill School, Droitwich

Through The Eyes Of An Abandoned Animal

He would laugh and joke
And prod and poke
But I can't work out why.

He staggered through the door
And fell to the floor
Lying in a pool of drink.

He kicked me out
And started to shout
I knew he didn't care.

I'm cold and wet
I need a vet
But no one's here to care.

I'm hurt and confused
I feel unwanted and abused
But no one's here to care.

I was hit, kicked and beaten too
When all I ever did was give love to you
But no one's here to care.

If I could speak
The truth would leak
But no one's here to care.

Then suddenly she came
I hid behind the bin in shame
What if she would hurt me?

She wrapped me up
Called me her pup
Now someone's here to care.

She plays with me an awful lot
And I've been renamed Spot
She is my person who cares!

Sophie Holliday (13)
Dodderhill School, Droitwich

Talkin' 'Bout My Generation

Talkin' about my generation
We all get blamed for doing wrong

Hoodies, caps,
It's all our fault

Muggers, robbers, even murderers
That's what people say we are

Talking about my generation
We aren't muggers, murderers or killers

Some of us raise money for charity
Baking cakes and jumble sales

Others go to nursing homes to cheer people up
We're not all bad

If you could see this
You would know so much more

Just a few don't care
There are more of us who do.

Bethany Barnes (12)
Dodderhill School, Droitwich

Colours Are The World

C olours are everything
O range and blue
L ight or dark
O chre and blue
U nderneath the colours
R ed is a sparkling apple
S apphire is pure and blue

A zure is as deep a colour as the sky above
R oses are pink, but sometimes red
E els are grey and electrifying

T ime has changed the colour of the world
H eaven is white, Hell is red
E co is green

W ater is green and blue
O ceans contain many fish
R are species are slowly dying
L ives are being lost
D eath is happening all around me.

Rebecca Peake (12)
Dodderhill School, Droitwich

The Challenger

The lion stood powerful, but still.
Protective, with an unmistakable roar,
Sunlight danced off his mane of gold
And his pride, respectful of his will,
Watched as everything cowered around him.
    This lion protects his pride and home
    And no other has yet challenged him.
    But danger lurks and is about to come
    In a form of one who will not rest till he's gone.
That lion, is in the distance,
Quietly creeping, advancing with an army.
Coat, dark gold, in dusty light,
He calls his allies to support the fight.
    Darkness came and with it,
        Attack!
        Roars,
        Claws.
    Blood on the paws of the magnificent cat.
A bitter end for one so vile,
Who threatened his family pride.
    Victorious, but wounded, he rose from the pile
    Of death and devastation.
King of the jungle, the victor stood still,
Protective with an unmistakable roar,
The sunlight danced off his future generations.
        Safe,
        Unchallenged,
        To grow and explore.

Jessamy Reece (12)
Dodderhill School, Droitwich

The Life Of A Sofa

I'm the old, tatty sofa
No one wants me
I'm stuck at the back of a furniture store
I wish someone would take me home with them.

At night it's cold
And all my friends
Are back with people who love them
I wish someone would take me home with them.

If I don't get sold soon
I'll be put on the bonfire
I try so hard to get sold
I wish they'd take me home with them.

Hang on, someone's coming in
A lovely happy family
Please buy me, please buy me
I wish they'd take me home with them.

They sit on me
'Oh, how comfy!'
The lady says
I wish someone would take me home with them.

Next thing I know, I'm on the van
Then I'm in a home, finally
I love it here
See, someone did take me home with them.

Amelia Fox (12)
Dodderhill School, Droitwich

Being Tall

I can see over tall buildings,
And touch the ceilings,
I am 6 feet 4
And I am very poor.

When I go down to the sea,
Everyone stares at me.
I am 6 feet 4
And I am very poor.

It's so annoying when I am not allowed on rides,
So I have to wait on the side.
I am 6 feet 4
And I am very poor.

At school I get teased about my height,
So I stay out of sight.
I am 6 feet 4
And I am very poor.

When I go home to my room,
I hope tomorrow doesn't come soon.
I am 6 feet 4
And I am very poor.

Alice McMahon (12)
Dodderhill School, Droitwich

Recycling

Recycling is the new craze
It's happening everywhere
On every weekday
Recycling, the craze

Purple bags, white bags
Other colours too
Left in heaps, smells, rots, rags
Recycling, the craze

Cans, tins, plastics
Cardboard, paper, boxes
There's a wide range of things
Recycling, the craze

To try and help some more
Use a compost store
Goodness can come from bad
Recycling, the craze

Help the world survive
And keep us all alive
Recycling is the key
Come and join in with me.

Lucinda White (12)
Dodderhill School, Droitwich

Today

Some people see a life of crime and bitterness,
Others see fortune and fame,
I see love, support and happiness.

The world is a changing place,
More buildings, more roads,
But if there's no sudden surge of change,
We'd be stuck in the distant past.

Walking down the street, seeing the people we meet,
Going past clothes, shoes, CDs,
But these things aren't really important.

People pass with their own opinions,
On their diet or the government,
But should be pleased, happy and smiling,
'Cause in our lives we're free.

And then there's the subject of eco,
The environment with animals and trees,
We must think of the future of our world.

There are schools, factories and jobs,
People work for a living.
Some think they work too much,
But what about the starving in the world?

Some people are pressured to look good,
But you should be you.
Everyone has their own personality.

On my way home I look around me,
There are families together,
That is exactly the way it should be.
I see love, support and happiness.

Maisie Heath (12)
Dodderhill School, Droitwich

Breakfast, Play, Zzzzzz

Here we go again, my daily harassment,
The giants are picking me up
And throwing me up and down.
I'm having a bottle shoved down my throat
And I'm getting a new nappy on.
I'm being carried down a deep staircase which never ends
And I appear in some busy room with pots and pans.
It's so uncomfortable in this hard chair,
I feel like I'm in the sky and I'm going to fall any minute.
I'm being fed this sloppy mush - yum, apple.

I'm all dressed in my pink top and blue trousers,
Oh, and my cosy, pink shoes.
I'm playing with my rattle, doing a concert for my giant friends.
I've made a tower out of my building blocks, it's nearly as tall as me!
Time for tea. Pea mush - favourite.

I'm done with tea now.
Up the staircase I go.
I've got changed now,
I'm all snug and warm in my pink bed suit.
Pink's my favourite colour you know.
In my cot, a mobile spinning above me.
I'm alone, just dreaming of what I'll do tomorrow.
What's my next hit going to be on my rattle?
How tall will my tower be?
Oh well, I'll guess I'll find out.
Zzzzzzzz . . .

Jessica Wood (13)
Dodderhill School, Droitwich

Friends

When I was young what fun I used to have
Playing with my friends and having a good laugh.
We used to go out riding with the Pony Club
Riding round the forest until we found a jump.
When Pony Club camp was on, we used to have such fun.
Playing in the morning, playing in the night
We went cross country jumping and we all fell in the mud!

Now I'm older, my friends still come around,
But we do different things
And are children messing around.

Lily Hewitt (12)
Dodderhill School, Droitwich

Peer Pressure On The Catwalk

Fashion, fashion, fashion,
That's all I have to say,
No one seems to care about
The individual way.

Pressure, pressure, pressure,
Too much overload.
You wear something the wrong way
And suddenly you're alone.

Catwalk, catwalk, catwalk,
Ain't what it seems,
Size zero's taking over
And ruining people's dreams.

Sad, sad, sad,
Underneath the mask,
Got what you wanted,
But not what you had.

Caitlin Kinsman (12)
Dodderhill School, Droitwich

Generations

This is a poem about me, my brother and sister too
About the generation that I followed after.

First let's talk about Mum and Dad
They went dippy, took a blow to head
Never been the same since.

The one set of grandparents
They live in the past
All stuck with the Spam and rationing book.

My other grandparents are mad
Think that pigs can fly
Think that my brother, sister and I
Don't get out enough.

I don't know about the generations any further
Back except that they were crazy.

Amelia Clancy (11)
Dodderhill School, Droitwich

Talkin' 'Bout My Generation

My mum always tells me to be careful
My granny says, be prepared.

My mum says you are what you eat
My granny says sweets are for the sweet.

Let go. Granny says life is an adventure
My mum always says, 'Sit still, please.'

My mum says throw that junk away
Granny says save it for a rainy day.

Mum says stop looking in the mirror
Granny says always look your best.

Mum says you should never look in a lady's purse
Granny says never say never!

Grace Hewitt (13)
Dodderhill School, Droitwich

Talkin' 'Bout My Generation

A child of seven in 2007,
Her brother's been shot, he's in a gang,
Her sister's a teenager who's an addict,
Her mum's alcoholic and is never home,
Her dad's in Iraq fighting, he might be dead.

And everyone is labelled in our little world,
Why label, why accuse, why fight?
Maybe her brother was just copying his friends,
But does he know not everyone does that?
It's just our generation is labelled.

Our world is dying, overheating,
The weather is odd, tsunamis, hurricanes, the lot,
The environment is ruined,
Maybe her sister wants to leave this world
And wants to leave a trace of her behind.

Parents, grandparents and family members,
The respect to them is nearly all gone,
Except sometimes one or two children are respectful,
Maybe her mother drinks because she is stressed,
Her two children show no respect to her.

Why does war still carry on?
Many people fought in WW1 and WW2,
So we were free from war,
Soldiers die every day and what for?
Maybe her father is fighting right now in the trenches,
Maybe if he was home, everything would be better.

And the little girl, she cares about our world,
She knows celebrities aren't real.
What made them famous?
She understands that we need to recycle,
She wishes her life away, praying for a better world,
But can her generation help her make a better world?

Kayleigh Cowie (13)
Dodderhill School, Droitwich

Talkin' 'Bout My Generation

What's a celebrity in 2007
A size zero model or a farmer in Devon?

There are soldiers at war we all admire
While we sit at home in front of the fire

There are surgeons working to save our lives
While other gangs just kill with knives

There are policemen who work day in, day out
While we complain there's none about

There are criminals on the streets today
Frightening everybody that comes their way

There was an accident on our road last night
The doctors were there even with no light

There are people living on the street
Asking for change from all they meet

Why is all this bad on Earth?
Fighting and arguing, but what's it worth?

Racism and violence and much, much more
While we watch TV and just shut the door

What's an idol in 2007?
A soldier at war or a druggie at seven?

You're told to trust no one in the world today
Be careful what you do and what you say

We all believe in different things
So let us speak and spread our wings

But I'm confused, so please tell me
What's a celebrity in 2007?

Kelly Lane (13)
Dodderhill School, Droitwich

9/11/01

(Dedicated to those who lost their lives on 11th September 2001)

I sit here now, alone with my thoughts,
I think about what I'm about to do,
I just wanted to be noticed,
I wonder if I am ready to make the ultimate sacrifice,
Am I ready?

I sit here now, alone with my thoughts,
People know not what I'm about to do,
I've been told this is my purpose,
I'm told God will reward me for my bravery and courage,
Are they right?

I sit here alone with my thoughts,
Wondering if my family will forgive me,
Thinking how the families of the dead will feel,
People will remember me and hate me for what I've done,
Is that true?

I sit here now, alone with my thoughts,
Together we are soaring through the air,
In front of us is our sure death,
Behind us will be a trail of terrible destruction,
But I should have thought of that before I decided to go,
Was I right?

God help!
I'm not ready!
I can't do this!
I need to get out before . . .

Sophie Harrison (13)
Dodderhill School, Droitwich

Talkin' 'Bout My Generation

Why do big people always assume
That all I can do is eat and poo?
Why is it they never consider
That although my body is small, my brain may be bigger?
Why is it they never agree?
Fair enough, I can't yet talk but I'm soon to be three

Why do adults always assume
That I'll scream and shout and strop in my room?
Why is it they never consider
That my life ahead may be planned and figured?
Why is it they never agree?
I have a mind of my own and I'm thirteen.

Why do children always assume
That I'll do all their washing and clean up their rooms?
Why is it they never consider
That I have a life or a potential career?
Why is it they never agree?
I'm older and wiser now I'm thirty-three.

Why do young uns always assume
That I'm old and crippled and have nothing to do?
Why is it they never consider
That I might have been fun when I was a tiddler?
Why is it they never agree?
I'm older by far now, I'm ninety-three.

Emily White (13)
Dodderhill School, Droitwich

Generation

Oh how the whole world has changed since I was a lad.
I think it was better back then in the old days.

Barely any cars on the roads, the only fumes from
my father's old mower!
Aeroplanes, which waste all the oil, were for eccentric daredevils
Factories were thought of as amazing!
Not bad for the environment.
I think it was better back in the old days.

All the ridiculous guns, bombs, tanks were not in man's mind
years ago.
The London bombings, the Twin Towers, war in Iraq.
I think it was better back in the old days.
Drug mad people were not around, alcoholics were only the rich.
Cigarettes were thought of as a way to relax, not a way to die.
Children had respect for their elders and if not be beaten!
No ASBOs given out then.
I think it was better back in the old days.

Our Prime Minister is trying his best
To cut down on the terrible things that happen
Let's give him time to work on it
After all, I don't think things can get any worse
I still think it was better in the old days.

Lydia Tainty (11)
Dodderhill School, Droitwich

Who Are They? What Have They Done?

A model, a millionaire, a footballer's wife,
Who are these people? We know their lives.
Jacuzzis and swimming pools, shopping in LA,
They get paid so much money for sitting around all day.

Why are they famous? What have they done?
Posed for a picture, it's alright for some!
A stroke of luck, it must have been,
To look like that and then to be seen.

But what about scientists trying to save the Earth?
All the working nurses, helping mums to give birth?
And then there's policemen, making everywhere safe,
All these different people, making the world a better place.

You don't see a doctor on the front of a magazine,
So why all these others? The ones called celebrities.
Like Nicole, Paris, Posh and Coleen,
Socialites and girlfriends is all they have ever been.

'I want to be famous,' is every child's dream,
But as they grow older, it's not what it seems.
Academics' voices are the ones we should hear,
Without their advice, we would not be here.

Emily Farmer (13)
Dodderhill School, Droitwich

Talkin' 'Bout My Generation

I'm all alone in the sky at night
I see some dreadful things in fact
Swearing, fighting and vandalising everything in sight
Some people in this generation just don't have the right
For some reason they just don't seem to care
Especially in the evening, they're such a nightmare
Drinking and partying until the crack of dawn
With the shortest skirts and jeans all torn
They should be at home having family time
Instead of wrecking the place and thinking it's fine
I have seen some things which I regret
It will be a couple of years before they settle down, I bet
Generations come and go
This is the worst, I should know
Maybe they are misunderstood
They will be better soon, well at least they should
I'm anxiously awaiting this time
I'm anxiously awaiting my time to shine.

Lauren Prosser (13)
Dodderhill School, Droitwich

We Don't Do That!

People always think we're bad.
Think we're gonna kick their head in
But some will and others won't.
The majority of us don't do that stuff.

Adults wear hoodies too,
Not just us.
Oh, and it doesn't mean we're gonna rob you.
We're just wearing hoodies, it's not that bad, is it?

Some kids get expelled from school
But doesn't mean we're all evil,
Because some of us are top of the class
But adults would never think that.

Most of us are quite good
We don't kick your head in, rob you or carry guns,
We go to school, learn and have lots of fun
Because we're kids, that's what we're meant to do isn't it?

Lizzy Prosser (12)
Dodderhill School, Droitwich

I See Nothing

It's my lifelong ambition
To walk to the top of the world
But when I arrive
I see nothing.

The trees around me sway
Expressing their voice
The birds perched on their branches
I see nothing.

The sun beats down from above
I walk to a tree for some shade
While the insects are having fun, playing in the grass
I see nothing.

I sit down on the soil
As a slimy snake slithers over my leg
Tears fall down my face
I see nothing.

My heart is filled with sadness
I am just a blind old man
People say I have grey hair and brown eyes
I see nothing.

I'd love to be able to see
The pleasures in the world
But I'll never be able to
I see nothing.

Rebecca Wheadon (13)
Dodderhill School, Droitwich

What About Me?

It's my big day,
I want to have fun,
Followed by paparazzi,
One by one.

They're in my back garden,
They're in my street,
They're in my house,
They're under my feet.

What about me?
It isn't fair,
I've had enough,
But they really don't care.

I'm standing at the altar,
Next to my guy,
It doesn't feel right,
I can sense a spy.

I'm out of the church,
It all went well,
We're together at last,
I can still hear the bell.

I'm very happy,
We're married at last,
Lots of paparazzi
. . . But they're in the past.

Helena Cleaver (13)
Dodderhill School, Droitwich

Days And Months

On Monday I love to dance,
On Tuesday I go swimming,
On Wednesday I chill out,
On Thursday I go to the park,
On Friday I love to party,
On Saturday I go shopping,
On Sunday I play netball.

In January I had a party,
In February I turned thirteen,
In March I broke my arm,
In April I had Easter eggs,
In May my cousin turned eighteen,
In June I moved to LA
In July I went to Disneyland.

In August I went on holiday,
In September I started high school,
In October I made new friends,
In November I hated my school,
In December I got presents,
In January I start a new school,
I love to have fun!

Georgia Whitehouse (12)
Dodderhill School, Droitwich

Starlet

How I wish I was important,
Noticed down below,
How I wish I was important,
Glowing from down below.

Dim and high,
Out of sight,
Not glowing from down below.

I'm really not important,
Just dull and all alone,
Oh, how I wish I was important,
Glowing from down below.

As I look at others, I feel sad inside,
Ugly, dim and neglected,
Pushed to the side.

I am treated as nothing,
Feeling blank inside,
I want to be treated as something,
To feel happy within.

Am I something or am I nothing?
You decide!

Sara Ekerol (13)
Dodderhill School, Droitwich

I Have A Wish

I have a wish
If I could change the world
I wish that
There was no war
We were nice to each other
Raising money for poor people
Birthdays and Christmas with presents
To make a happy life for poorer people
If parents have died
Help us to protect these children
Get a foster mum or dad
So they can eat and drink
Not be on their own
Help them to have a new family
When it is your birthday have a party
So that you can now have friends to play with
Raise money for poor people to have their first toy
Raise money for cancer
And all places that need money to help people get a better life
We should make houses for them to stay in
So they aren't living on the street
Have schools so they can get a better education
I wish that
All children could have a family
Someone to care for them
I wish that
All children got on well together
I wish that
We could raise money for cancer to make people better
I wish that
My generation could help people have better lives for everyone.

Rebecca Hardy (11)
Dodderhill School, Droitwich

Wedding Day

On a cold and frosty morning
The leaves in spring are falling
It is the gay day of Mr and Mrs Crown
Thank God that there's not one frown

The time is 6.50am
The wedding bells ring at 2pm
To Mrs Crown that time is soon
Let's hope that there's a full moon!

The groom is getting ready
For today the groom is steady
As the bride has got her own way
For today's big, long day

Wedding cars arrive
The wedding couple are alive
Ahead of them they cannot wait
This is no longer a forthcoming date!

Friends and family are there
To speak they will not dare
Because they are too excited
The wedding couple are delighted

Hooray! Hooray!
Here comes the long day
In they come
Looking stunning for some

'Let's go,' they say
This has been a nervous day
But worth having this date
As it's a cold and frosty May

The leaves in spring are falling
For it's the gay day of Mr and Mrs Crown
Thank God there's not one frown
Because this is the day of Mr and Mrs Crown.

Sophie Rees (13)
Dodderhill School, Droitwich

Bullied

I woke up late this morning,
Just to miss my mum,
But obviously not late enough,
There's no escaping her.

I got dressed and went downstairs,
She sent me straight outside,
I had nothing to eat, I was starving,
It was worse when I got to school.

The chavs of the school were waiting,
Waiting for me to arrive,
When I didn't come they went away,
Then I went inside.

At break time they dragged me out,
Took me out to the yard,
They punched me, kicked me, hit me till I bled,
Just left me there to die.

I staggered home from there,
Mum was waiting with her belt,
With all my sores and bruises,
I went upstairs to bed.

I still don't know how to solve this,
I've tried to pick up the phone,
I have also seen the adverts,
It's harder than it seems.

Lucy Fellows (13)
Dodderhill School, Droitwich

Flying

I'm at the airport all hot and bothered
We're going to New York
They've called our flight, so it's now or never
I've never flown before!

I'm shaking as I get onto the plane
This plane is very big
As we sit down the seat belt sign goes on
I've never flown before!

I'm sitting by the window, big mistake
We're told just to relax
Now I can hear the engines roaring loudly
I've never flown before!

We're going backwards, my legs like jelly
I want to get off *now*
The cabin crew are doing safety checks
I've never flown before!

We're on the runway ready for take-off
My sister holds my hand
Going very fast, everything's a blur
I've never flown before!

The plane is in the air, I'm still alive!
This is not all that bad
She smiles at me, we're heading for New York
Wow, now I've flown before!

Alix Hutchinson (13)
Dodderhill School, Droitwich

Through The Eyes Of A River

My generation is never-ending,
Though I am nature's oldest man.
I'm bursting full of life and spring,
Even I can't remember back when I began.

Icy cold and sparkling,
I'm new, fresh and clean.
As I spiral my way down the mountain,
I'm just a meandering stream.

I finally reach flat ground,
My eroding edges start to crack.
Although I look slow, I am mighty,
Like an alligator waiting for his time to snap.

I start gushing down the valley,
A waterfall hiding ahead,
I thrust to take my leap of faith
And land in the cushioned sandy bed.

The bottom of the drop is bustling,
Splashing and pushing around,
Everyone forging forward,
Longing for flatter ground.

I am reaching the end of my journey,
Time for me and the banks to part,
But don't be fooled that this is the ending,
For me this is only the start.

Felicity Newland (13)
Dodderhill School, Droitwich

My Life

When I was 2 I played with my teddies,
When I was 4 I played with my dolls,
When I was 8 I played inside,
When I was 10 I played outside.

When I was 12 I hung out with my friends,
When I was 14 I hung out on my own,
When I was 16 I shopped for clothes,
When I was 18 I danced at nightclubs.

When I was 20 I started university,
When I was 22 I finished university,
When I was 24 I studied law,
When I was 26 I ended law.

When I was 28 I became a lawyer,
When I was 30 I became a barrister,
When I was 32 I met someone new,
When I was 34 he proposed to me.

When I was 36 I had my first child,
When I was 38 I had my second child,
When I was 40 I got fired,
When I was 42 I worked at McDonald's.

When I was 44 I caught a disease,
When I was 46 I had an operation,
When I was 48 my heart stopped beating,
When I was 50 I was no longer here.

Phoebe Selby (12)
Dodderhill School, Droitwich

Talkin' 'Bout My Generation

I live in an old, spooky house,
I'm sure it has many secrets to tell.
If only, if only, I can hear its yell,
Then maybe I can start to ring the bell.

One day I went to its core,
Which is the big grandfather clock,
It stands so tall and wide,
It's hard to see both sides.

I stood at the front of the clock
And thought,
How can I talk to you, understand you?
So I started to talk away.

I asked so many questions
And each time it was the same answer;
Tick-tock, tick-tock.
So once again I was back to, *how can I talk to you?*

I didn't give up on my quest,
Each day I would return and be talking again,
Until finally, one day,
The secrets started to tick away.

My days seemed long and soon faded away,
Each secret was better than the last.
Some were about the love in the house,
Some were about heroes or dark doers.

Until one day it spoke no more,
No more secrets or even chimes.
I miss my days of sitting, looking and listening,
Maybe the next person will have the same joy as I have.

Zoe Bryson (14)
Dodderhill School, Droitwich

That's What Girls Say . . .

Mini skirts
Long tops
Lots of pink
Short dresses
Jackets
And tights
Long jeans
Flared jeans
Skinny little tight jeans
That's what girls say
Fashion is about.

Beads
And rings
Alice bands too
Bracelets
Badges
And make-up
Lots of hair dye
That's what girls say
Fashion's about.

Dolly shoes
Converse
And furry boots
Long boots
Kitten heels
And wedges
Stiletto heels
And platforms
That's what girls say
Fashion is about!

Lucy Greenhead (12)
Dodderhill School, Droitwich

Celebrity

Once I was a normal person, just like you.
Wanting all my dreams to come true.
Until one day I took a chance
And entered the audition for High School Musical One!
My mum and dad were there and I said,
'I'm going to be a celebrity.'
The following week,
I was offered the part,
My dream had come.
And my manager was called Bill.
The paparazzi drove me mad!
I didn't mind, I was a pop star, actor.
Money and fame came,
I even changed my name.
I was happy and loved going abroad,
The pictures and the photo shoots –
I never got bored.
Soon it took its toll,
Just too much and such a pain.
Now I am a normal person,
Free to be me again.

Sophie Baker (11)
Dodderhill School, Droitwich

My Sister And I

It's Monday, the first day of the holiday
My sister is at work and I am waiting.
She finally gets back. I ask, 'Can you come on the trampoline?'
But she said, 'No, not now, I've got work to do.'

I wake up on Tuesday morning and feel like baking cakes.
I get my clothes and put them on,
Go downstairs and get the mixture ready.
I mix it all together and put them in the oven.

The egg timer went and made me jump
I got them out and they looked delicious.
We got the icing on and had the leftovers.

But then on Wednesday she's in a bad mood
We have a fight 'cause she won't help.
My drawing goes wrong and I get upset
That is my sister and me.

Clemmie Kear (11)
Dodderhill School, Droitwich

The Mars Generation

Today is a time of faster, faster; power, power,
Technology improves so much, hour by hour.
So many straight white smiles, it's strange:
We've got computers and cars, soon we'll get to Mars.

But today, yeh, it's a time of spitting in alleys,
Today is a time of choking old grannies.
Neighbours get shot with guns bought online:
We've got computers and cars, can't wait to trash Mars.

Today we control, mass produce, we fool,
People are dying out there but we just moan about school.
I'm OK though cos I've got my Nike trainers;
We've got computers and cars, enough cash to buy Mars?

Today - forget tomorrow - let's blow the world to bits!
Or suffocate our link to life with 4x4 bliss.
You just can't be bothered to take a few steps:
We've got computers and cars, who cares about Mars?

In my nan's time, yeh, they had respect,
I'm not saying *we're* wrong - we're just not right yet.
People would smile real smiles in the street:
No computers or cars, or dreams of Mars.

Today, we don't care about our nation,
I'm sorry to say that's just our generation.
Was it the parents that brought us up wrong?
We've got computers and cars, those crazy dreams of Mars.

Rhiannon Allen (15)
Malvern St James School, Great Malvern

Talking About My Generation

The world is getting hotter
The ice caps are melting
It's all our fault.
In the future fish won't swim
And cows won't go moo
In the future, in the future.

The countryside's disappearing
Replaced by large buildings
Cities are multiplying
The animals are becoming extinct
In the future, in the future.

The sea level's rising
The floods are multiplying
There's snow in March
There's sun in October
A country will disappear
In the future, in the future.

No one's doing anything
It's such a shame
Does anyone care?
I bet our atmosphere will be a huge ball of fog
In the future, in the future.

Laura Jones (12)
Pershore High School, Pershore

My Generation

The trees tease the scarlet sun,
But soon there will be no more trees
And certainly no more sun!

Landfills making more pollution,
Teenagers making the new revolution.

Whizzkids on computers,
Technology is our generation.
People at the underground train station,
Mobile phones, PS2,
Which one should I choose?

Bang, bang! goes the gun,
Bang, bang! goes our sun,
Bang, bang! goes our generation!

Lauren Pleciak (12)
Pershore High School, Pershore

Talking About My Generation

Guns, wars, fighting
Hoping it all will stop
Wishing one day
They will all disappear
And all of them
Will fizz and pop
Bashing and banging
All crashing together
They are all destroyed
Forever never ever
Seen again by anyone
The fighting has come to an end
Victory has come
Never again will we watch anyone die.

Alexandra Baird (12)
Pershore High School, Pershore

Talking About My Generation

In my generation
There are lots of things to do
Like playing on the computer
And even PS2s
In my generation
There are lots of things to do
Like going on my mobile phone
And that's why my parents moan
In my generation
There are lots of things to do
Like watching my TV
All night in my room
But people don't care
That all the green grass
Really isn't there
And what they're doing to our generation
Isn't very fair
And all the land around us
Is slowly, slowly, slowly
Slowly decreasing
And as I travel to the cinema
I realise we should care
That what's happening to our generation
It might not be there
In the future
Because we don't care.

Megan Roberts (13)
Pershore High School, Pershore

Talking About My Generation

Teenagers, teenagers, dreaming in day
Teenagers, teenagers, vandals at night
Looking, looking, looking to fright.

But some teens aren't the same,
They're good, they're not to blame
It's the bad ones, they're a shame.

But most of them are crazy
Maybe just plain lazy
Walking home is a daunting task
Are they dangerous? Don't ask.

Driving home you're also scared
Fear also being shared
A crash, a bang, drunk driver
You can bet a fiver
It was a teen
That's how short my life has been.

Bill Hemming (12)
Pershore High School, Pershore

My Generation

My generation is different,
Different,
Different from my parents,
My grandparents
And even my great grandparents,
Different,
In my generation there is gun crime,
Murder,
Abduction,
My generation is different,
Of course there are good things,
We help one another,
But sometimes everyone is out for themselves,
My generation is different,
In my generation everyone is equal,
All humans anyway,
In my generation everyone is free,
My generation is different,
Different . . .

Eleanor Hennerley (12)
Pershore High School, Pershore

My Generation

A flame on the end of a stick,
What is this world coming to?
Smoking, what a horrible habit,
What is this world coming to?
Bullying, who came up with that?
What is this world coming to?
Punching, kicking, calling people names,
What is this world coming to?
Drinking alcohol, it needs to stop,
What is this world coming to?
Slow down, driving can kill,
What is this world coming to?
Drugs, let's stop bringing them here,
What is this world coming to?
Carbon dioxide, stop giving off that,
What is this world coming to?
Racism, we don't need that,
What is this world coming to?
We are all the same and that is that,
What is this world coming to?

Now then, is this what you want the future to be?
No!
Then let's get it sorted sooner rather than later!

Oliver Wilcox (13)
Pershore High School, Pershore

My Generation

Bang! Another life goes,
His blood like rubies, surrounds him,
His black skin, clammy and cold, through which blood did flow,
Shot dead because he went out with a white girl called Kim.

Violence on every street,
Kids, lining up for their joint,
Police scared on their beat,
Politicians ignoring the point.

Racism, that's a big issue,
Playing with guns, kids think that's fun,
Another family needing, every second, a new tissue,
All because of young people and guns.

ASBOs being handed out left and right,
Young kids nicking stuff out of a shop,
Gangs of kids, itching for a fight,
It's only another pool of blood for someone to mop.

Mark Grimes (13)
Pershore High School, Pershore

Life In Darkness

From my moment of birth,
Since my life began,
All I've ever seen is black.

Living in a big dark hole,
With no one to see,
That is normal to me.

My life as an infant was slow,
Slow and steady, like a snail I heard,
Everything took it's time.

Years passed, a child I became,
A long pole placed in my hand,
A dog of yellow stationed at my side.

And then, school,
What a place! I felt like everyone else,
The best time of my life.

Another school along the line,
True friends I now possessed,
Life was fun and my yellow dog, such a help.

Such fun I had with my yellow dog,
Slowly, he was getting old
And school life, wow!

A job I thought I needed next,
But oh, how I was wrong!
So daft of me to think that I had a chance.

So home I went,
To sulk,
A place where I was not understood.

My friends were gone,
No one was around, just my yellow dog and me
And a lady I called C.

My yellow dog, he left soon after,
I could not believe,
Why?

Old I grew and that was that,
Because nothing could change,
I thought such a waste.

My life in darkness,
Never ended,
Because that was me.

And now, no more,
I am gone,
So that is the end of darkness for me.

Faye Tomkotowicz (12)
St Egwin's CE Middle School, Evesham

Fast Nation

Fast food, fast life, fast nation,
Does injustice lie in this creation?
Are we becoming
A vast abomination,
Or is this merely
My own imagination?

And why this greed
That nothing can feed?
Always it dwells in the rich,
Callous for those in need
And uncaring for where other lives lead.

They care not for poverty,
They that hold sovereignty,
Caring for only their good,
While they live like royalty,
Showing no loyalty,
Never doing what they should.

Rory Sinclair (12)
St Egwin's CE Middle School, Evesham

Acts Of God?

The world is a strange and mysterious place,
people and animals co-existing together.
Different colours and different race,
all affected by the weather.

Tornadoes twirl and twist,
ripping across the countryside,
spewing out everything in their paths.

Raging rivers burst their banks
and flood the entire area with brown, dirty water,
which washes away people's possessions, homes
and in some cases, their lives.

Then drought.
The intense heat drains life from the Earth.
It stunts growth and scorches crops.
Starving children cry endless tears,
hoping, praying that they will find food and water
even though they may never discover any in the dry,
humid landscape.

The colossal waves of a tsunami cause destruction,
devouring villages, towns and cities like a monster on a rampage.
Is this extreme weather caused by Man, or is it an act of God?

Sophia Fraser (12)
St Egwin's CE Middle School, Evesham

A Poppy For A Soldier

His brow was covered in sweat
As he staggered towards the shelter,
His head spinning,
The pain was incomprehensible.

Mud was smudged across his cheeks
And every muscle within his body was weak,
The impact of the bullet had been like a storm
And the inky blackness of death was seeping into his head.

It hurt even more when he tried to stay alive,
The struggle was unbearable,
His body was screaming for this to stop,
His knees buckled.

A part of his mind wanted him to carry on
But slowly doubt took over his control,
He stared at the distorted, wet mud
And saw a single poppy, its red leaves the only colour.

This struck him like a beam of light,
One single glint of solace,
Among a field of depression
And that's what kept him alive.

Paul Retallick (12)
St Egwin's CE Middle School, Evesham

Misunderstood

They keep going on at me all the time,
Why couldn't you have and why can't you be?
I wish they would stop,
I don't understand.
I'm just misunderstood.

I try to be more like them, I really do,
If only they would listen,
Then they might comprehend
Why I can't be like them or do what they do.
Why am I misunderstood?

Old people sneer, they don't want me near
Just because I push a buggy,
They assume I'm an underage mum,
When that is not true.
I'm just misunderstood.

In the pram sleeps my baby sister,
Left to me to care for.
Mum and Dad are bored with her now.
I know how it feels, it happened to me.
Why am I misunderstood?

Hanging around on the streets at night,
Police want to know why I'm there.
They offer to take me back to my house
But I lie and say no one's at home.
I'm just misunderstood.

I had already been home, but the door was locked.
I could hear loud music, I knew they were in.
I wish they would love me and let me in.
I wish they were there whenever I needed them.
Why am I misunderstood?

Bridie O'Brien (12)
St Egwin's CE Middle School, Evesham

Last Night's News

As I look out my window
Remembering last night's news
I think about how fortunate I am
To have a proper home.

All the clean water,
All the fresh food,
All the TVs and computers,
All the things I take for granted -
Could I live without them?

I wonder how they feel,
Being sick forever,
I wonder what they do
For twelve hours every day.

All the little children,
No proper nutrients,
Their little bodies riddled with disease,
Staring at a camera with desperation in their eyes.

How horrid is life in Africa?
Why don't we give money?
Can't we help in any way?
How many times have I seen
The same video on the news?

Africa has a special place in my heart,
It is a beautiful and spectacular part of our world.
Without help from us,
The people will not be around for much longer,
So why do we hesitate to help?

Michelle Stevenson (12)
St Egwin's CE Middle School, Evesham

Drugs, Olympics And Me

Drugs, Olympics and me.
Three words never to mix up,
Or could they?
A faraway dream becoming reality,
With a price.

I can get there,
I am nearly there.
But progress is slow,
Training is hard.
Is there a quicker way?

Then I find a way. *Drugs.*
It's quicker, yes,
But is it better?
The temptation is there,
But to risk everything, my sport?

And now to be told I will never get to the top,
Without drugs. I'm not fast enough, not agile enough.
If I did, what sort of role model would I be,
As the one everyone looks up to,
Only to crumble so fast under the expectations?
Would that be right?

I think of myself
And what it would be like as a shamed athlete.
To cheat or not?
I don't.
I want to get there fairly,
To the Olympics without a dirty conscience.

I am content with second, when I wasn't before.
I realised my dream, I worked for it, no short cuts.
To hear the crowds,
Like a rumble of thunder cheering me on
Is enough.

Alice Morrey (13)
St Egwin's CE Middle School, Evesham

Hearing

My world is quiet,
My life is silent
And still I carry on
Living day after day,
Waiting, just waiting
For this to change.

I watch people
Walking along,
Nodding their heads
In time to some non-existent music,
Wires trailing from their ears,
It's something I will never do.

Next door
A television apparently blares,
The volume turned up full
But I hear nothing,
I just watch the pictures
Flickering through the window.

At night
Some distant music plays
But I hear nothing,
The only signs
Are the vibrations
Shaking my fingertips.

But four other senses remain
Guiding me,
Showing me
What life is really like,
Without taking things for granted,
I know I will never hear.

Annabel Blackmore (12)
St Egwin's CE Middle School, Evesham

'Bout My Generation

Grandad listened to the radio,
Dad had a black and white TV,
My generation can go on the World Wide Web.

My generation know about computers, E-mail, MSN and Bebo,
But we also know about cyber bullies and weirdoes.

My generation like lots of things,
Like football, dancing, rugby, cycling, music,
But we also don't like lots of other things,
Like exams, bullies, chores and schoolwork.

My generation are lucky to have iPod, Xbox,
Nintendo and PlayStations,
But we are not so lucky to have global warming,
Bird flu and terrorism.

Grandad worried about World War II,
Dad worried about the Cold War,
My generation worries about the War on Terror.

Ciarán Grant (13)
St Egwin's CE Middle School, Evesham

Rescue Me!

Just sitting there, all alone
No one to speak to, no one to listen
Wondering whether anyone cares
Never knowing what it feels like to be loved.

Feeling the tension of someone coming
And moving me away from the doorstep
Someone taking my blanket which I use as a duvet
Feeling so anxious that I am shaking to death.

I try to stand up, but all I do is stumble
No one wants to help, so I just keep myself to myself
Every night I sit praying and praying
Hoping one day someone will come and rescue me.

Jasmin Candler (12)
St Egwin's CE Middle School, Evesham

To Keep The World Running

What is the meaning of life?
I say to myself again and again.
It echoes through my mind,
As if I were in a church,
When the clock outside strikes three.

What is the meaning of life?
If some people live, but don't want to,
As they are lonely and have no one to talk to,
They are in need of help.

But my generation should,
Keep the world clean and buy pretty dresses,
Be nice to each other
And always lend a hand when someone is in need.

Then life would have a meaning and that meaning would be,
Keep the world running.

Lucy Webb (12)
St Egwin's CE Middle School, Evesham

Our Planet Earth!

I am sitting on the top of a hill,
Under the blue night sky,
The moon resting on the treetops, almost full,
In the distance all I see,
Above the spires of blue night church,
A blue and green glow,
Where the sun set just a few minutes ago,
The two bright points of light,
Them being Venus and Mars.

As I sit here on this hill,
I am struck by the vastness of this world,
Now I realise that this is the rebirth,
Of our *planet Earth!*

Gabi Crew (12)
St Egwin's CE Middle School, Evesham

Talkin' 'Bout My Generation

You know,
It's annoying,
When you're a kid,
Walking through a busy town,
With all these people,
Towering over you,
Like mountains over tiny villages.

You're walking
And you're holding delicate things,
And then,
Crash!
Your things lie in millions of pieces,
Like a sea of glass,
Crinkling with every touch.

These giants,
They just ignore you,
They bang into you,
Shove you,
No consideration for your well being if you fall,
Just walk away,
Don't even say sorry,
Like bats,
Or as deaf as one.

So,
You scoop up the remains of your things,
You wipe yourself clean
And you think,
No,
No more giants towering over me like meerkats on patrol,
Now it's my turn.

Lizzie Johnson (12)
St Egwin's CE Middle School, Evesham

The World's Problems

What is the world coming to?
Murders and drugs and alcohol,
Just some of the world's problems.

Cannabis, ecstasy, heroin,
Marijuana, cocaine and opium,
Just a few of the world's problems.

Red, white and rosé,
Roll-ups and tar,
Just a few of the world's problems.

Jonathon Hancox (12)
St Egwin's CE Middle School, Evesham

Sight

I sit at home by myself,
Unaware of anything around me,
People come to visit,
I hear them talking,
But I can't see them,
To me they are just a voice.

I go outside,
With only a dog to guide me,
I feel the breeze on my face,
I hear the wind blowing through the trees,
But I can't see them,
To me it's just a sound.

The world can see me,
But I can't see it,
To me it's just a voice.

Ross Paxton (12)
St Egwin's CE Middle School, Evesham

So Different, Yet So Similar

Many traditions, so different,
Many opinions, so different,
Many styles, so different,
Many generations, so different,

Many aspects, so similar,
Many childhoods, so similar,
Many views, so similar,
Many generations, so similar,

People can change,
Or stay the same,
But their generation,
Oh, their generation stays one way,

I've seen countless numbers of people,
From a range of generations,
They all seem to disagree with others' choices.
Just this morning I passed an elderly lady,
She looked so sweet,
Who could harm her?

Youths, gangs, mobs, whatever the name,
They stay the same.
They could harm her.
A group of youths smoking cigarettes
Approached her like a puff of smoke from a chimney,
She let out a scream using her last breath
And her bags fell to the ground with her frail body frame,

The difference between generations
May end up almost like war,
Guns, knives and drugs are misused every day,
Taking citizens' lives away.

Lucy Button (13)
St Egwin's CE Middle School, Evesham

Why?

Why?
I sit here and wonder,
Why is it me you're after?
The group of people
All shouting my name,
The click of the mobile.

Why?
The shadows cloud my mind,
Like fog slowly covering everything in sight,
I wonder, am I different?
My fear is always there.

Why?
Each morning at the school gates,
I see them waiting there,
Sniggering and pointing,
You were once my friend.

But one day,
I'll get my revenge,
I'm not the problem,
I didn't change to fit in.

Under all that greed,
You're shaking inside,
Once my friend,
Now just a forgotten memory,
Whisked away by the wind.

Why?
You will understand
You should never have left me.
Why?

Savannah Harris (12)
St Egwin's CE Middle School, Evesham

Ode To Insignificance

Looks I get from the people towering above
Like sunflowers reaching for the sky
I am an ant in a city wandering about,
Avoiding the huge soles of shoes
Just wanting to crush me
People smile and wave, being polite
But soon they leave to carry on with life
Nobody knows what it's like to be me
They don't even take the time to understand
Sympathetic looks are all I get
Do people see me as some sort of threat?
I don't mind my life as a small goldfish
In a massive great sea
I will always be like this
Don't be sorry for me
Just take the time to find out
What my life is actually all about.

Kayley McPherson (12)
St Egwin's CE Middle School, Evesham

My Generation Recipe

Take 100 different cultures,
Mix with 1,000 different ideas,
Stir well with 10,000 emails,
Shape and mould into 100,000 children,
Cook slowly in 1,000,000 different homes,
Leave to cool for a lifetime,
Store it in my generation's memory.

Ellys Bancroft (12)
St Egwin's CE Middle School, Evesham

Gone

Brittle, broken, dead.
A long silence lingers,
Nothing but cries and screams,
Everything has gone.

Hundreds of white bags pass,
I'm just waiting,
Just waiting.

Mothers, fathers gone,
Sisters, brothers gone.
Best friends,
Or just neighbours gone.

Not long now,
Slowly dying,
Starvation, thirst and disease.

My ribs show through,
I can't walk,
In so much pain,
It's hard to breathe.

A bright light,
A loud scream,
A warm hand.

Gone.

Juliet Biddle (12)
St Egwin's CE Middle School, Evesham

Through The Eyes Of A Bully

What are they thinking, why and how?
Do they find it amusing and laugh behind their backs?
It's unkind and unfriendly
Why can't they see?

Do they know what they are doing?
Are they upset or hurt?
So they take it out on others
But they must be making it worse.

Making people feel uncomfortable
Unsure and confused
We do not understand, only they do
The unfortunate ones.

Are they being hurt themselves
Taking it out on someone else?
Like passing on a message
Throughout a crowd.

When they look in the mirror
What do they see staring back at them?
Maybe a handsome young boy
But ugly inside.

Jessica Dallard (12)
St Egwin's CE Middle School, Evesham

Gone!

The world seems to be falling apart,
My generation,
Almost not there anymore,
The world is crumbling in front of me,
No way out,
Nowhere to go,
There's talk about politics,
Murders and how the government
Isn't doing enough to stop crime.
Why can't it stop
Before the world is completely gone?
Wars, guns and fighting,
People being killed every second,
Why can't it stop?
Children scared of leaving their homes,
Only because of our faults.
Lives being ruined every day
Because of rows and break-ups.
Why can't it stop?
There are many good things in life,
Like new life, love and forgiveness,
But with a flutter of a butterfly wing,
Everything can change!

Amy Beaumont (12)
St Egwin's CE Middle School, Evesham

The Pinhole Of Light

Complete darkness except a pinhole of light.
All fuzzy and bright.
The colours I see are only yellow and white,
As I can see no other.

I have a dog to help me along,
He's called Lucky
And he helps me all day and all night long.
He is a cappuccino colour so everyone says,
But I wouldn't know as I can't see him.
He is there for me all the time,
Especially when I am in need of a trustworthy friend.

I hear my peers surrounding me,
Screaming and shouting, having fun,
Messing about on the swings and slides.
The birds are tweeting and singing their song.
It would be great if I could go and join them.

I sit there and wonder what it would be like
To see colours of the rainbow,
The tall trees towering over me like giants,
The golden sand,
Which bakes your feet as you walk across it,
The flowers that surround me,
Dancing about in all different colours like pixies at a ball,
The dark blue sky that looks like an enormous sheet
With stars that sparkle and glitter.
It would be amazing.

Everything is going all fuzzy and blurry,
I can't see a thing, none of the wonders of the world,
It's just darkness, as if the light has been put out
Or like it is night all the time.
The pinhole of light has disappeared as if by magic,
I can't see, not any more.

I wonder what my generation looks like?

Kelly-Anne Archer (12)
St Egwin's CE Middle School, Evesham

Maybe Future

Never want to see my mother cry,
As I place a veil on my head,
See my father's eyes swell up,
As I walk down the aisle.

My hair would shine,
Like the sun,
My smile would dazzle,
It would be my special day.

Maybe not . . .

I would speak standard English,
Wear tight suits and pretty shoes,
My hair tightly in a bun,
Full make-up smothered across my face.

A briefcase in one hand,
Hot coffee in the other,
Spare change clinking in my pocket,
Money pouring out my ears.

Maybe not . . .

My feet would sink,
With a squelch,
Into the golden sand,
My hair wet and free.

My friends around me,
Laughing at my jokes,
My pretty, white cottage,
Stood in the distance.

Maybe not . . .

Going to parties,
Watching long films,
Fashionable clothes and nice hair,
Yes, I think I prefer this one,
                Being a teenager.

Ophelia Di Pasqua (13)
St Egwin's CE Middle School, Evesham

Misunderstood

Hoodies, druggies and mischievous chavs,
Are all types of our generation,
That is why we are so misunderstood,
As there is good among us, in our generation.

We get misunderstood as others are outnumbered,
By vandals and scandals and street corner huggers,
They want to cause a lot of distress,
While frightening old ladies and causing masses of mess.

Yes, the rest play on the computer,
But what harm is that causing?
We have no real responsibility as yet,
So surely a computer game is a good thing.

Benjamin Taylor (12)
St Egwin's CE Middle School, Evesham

Disabled

S eeing people walking
P eople playing games
A nd running around
R eality hits you, you think, then you know it will never happen
E verybody laughs, mutters and points

S cared, you leave, worried if they are following
O nly you don't turn back, so you don't know
M um and Dad ignore you as if you're someone else
E ven your best friend has abandoned you

T ell me why you don't love me anymore
I s it because I'm different?
M e and me alone is who they hate
E veryone has disowned me, I'm on my own now.

Amelia Trivett (12)
St Egwin's CE Middle School, Evesham

Wars

I am a happy person,
His mind is as empty as a pitch-black cave,
My breakfast is a bowl of lovely cereal,
His breakfast is dead rats,
My school is a very big school,
His school is an old and tatty school that he risks being killed
to get to,
My hobbies are football, rugby and golf,
His hobbies are sitting down like a tiny, tearful doormat,
My life is a paradise,
His life is a living nightmare.

Jack Skelton (11)
St Martin's Catholic School, Stoke Golding

The Victim

Playtime fills me with dread,
I have to be careful where I tread,
In the playground I stand by the gates,
As I don't have any mates,
That boy over there is a bully,
He does not understand me fully,
He fills me with dread and fear,
Please don't let him see my tears,
He picks on me and calls me names,
I just want to join in the games,
But I am alone,
I have to play on my own.

Adam Beeston (12)
St Martin's Catholic School, Stoke Golding

Burn

It was but three years ago,
When I lost my life,
To a ferocious fire
And died in it my wife.

So now I sit here with this bottle,
On this wretched bench,
Receiving looks of death from public,
Due to my foul stench.
I can't really help it,
I'm not spared a dime,
I'm just so sick of eating garbage,
Tired of chatting this rhyme.

I beg, I borrow and I steal,
Endure sleepless nights,
Thinking of my dearest,
Wishing she was nearest,
Wishing it was me.

Mortality can prove a challenge,
When it comes to eating,
Pick pennies all day long,
Looking and competing.

Property: not much of an issue,
A sleeping bag is all,
On you: your tweed jacket,
That you obtained in a brawl.

I beg, I borrow and I steal,
Endure sleepless nights,
Thinking of my dearest,
Wishing she was nearest,
Wishing it was me.

It is a funny thing, you know,
Killing your own wife,
By mistake of course,
You took a bloody life.

Love is the least of your worries,
No matter how you yearn,
When you live on the streets,
Rapidly you learn.

Evie Kness (13)
St Martin's Catholic School, Stoke Golding

But Why?

There he stood looking at the emptiness
That lay in front of him.
A single tear fell from his eye,
But why?
His fight for life was harder than expected,
Nobody was there to comfort him when he cried.
But why?
His skin was as rough as an elephant's body.
His eyes imagined things far from the truth.
But why?
Ten pence given a day for looking through things
That would stick in his mind forever.
But why?
The clothes he wore were as torn as a teddy
The dog had had for two years.
But why?
He felt like millions of gold daggers
Were stabbing into the already broken heart.
But why?
Why do these things happen to such kind, sweet-hearted people?
Because . . .
Nobody knows.

Sian Pretorius (12)
St Martin's Catholic School, Stoke Golding

There's Enough For Everyone

Children starve,
What a disgrace,
When we are here all full of grace.
Their eyes look empty,
Ours all bright,
They worry where they can sleep at night.
Lurking around for food to eat,
We have lovely things,
But theirs, from the street.
Our faces are smiles,
But theirs are blank.
Lonely, with no hope to play,
As we just stand there chatting all day.
They are in poverty,
Living in hope,
They're scared about dying,
I think we can help.

Becca Smith (12)
St Martin's Catholic School, Stoke Golding

The Bully

There I stand across the hall,
My face a blank grey page,
My eyes small sunken shadows.
Then he approaches me,
Violence his weapon,
Fear my weakness,
Loneliness my classmates,
I walk away,
But he follows.

Megan Skipper (12)
St Martin's Catholic School, Stoke Golding

Make A Difference!

Here we sit, healthy and fit,
While they are sick, we are having a kick.
Here they search the waste,
We only get a taste
Of the lives they live.

We are lucky, they are poor,
We have no purpose to live anymore.
They get sore,
As we pour more.

So come on, give us the tour!
Is there much in their life to live for?
People cry and stare, but are still unaware.
Is that what they want, for us to care?

Make a difference!

Alex Cottrill (12)
St Martin's Catholic School, Stoke Golding

How Selfish

Here they scavenge through the waste
And see us with a big smile on our face.
Their skin is dry, like a hot day in the desert,
And our skin, well that's very pleasant.

Looking into their eyes, a dark pool of blood,
One of their only friends is a pile of mud.
We see them on the TV crying and sad,
And all we do is feel bad
And eat more food and move on.

Tyler Jose Leon-Pardo (12)
St Martin's Catholic School, Stoke Golding

Different People

Me in my warm, safe house,
He in his cold, rough hut,
Walking for four hours to get water.
It takes me seconds.
My eyes are blue happiness marbles,
His are dark black holes.
Me and my life have food,
He is as hungry as a lion.
So desperate for money, they sell body parts.
We have bank accounts and jobs.
I have warm clothes,
He has cold rags.
This is my life and that is his.

Declan Rollings (12)
St Martin's Catholic School, Stoke Golding

Life On The Streets

My pockets are empty,
My feet are bare,
I have no money, only despair.

No clothes on my back to keep me warm,
Not even a coat to protect me
From the storm.

I scavenge through bins looking for something to eat,
You can just imagine
What it's like living on the street.

Ashley Moss (12)
St Martin's Catholic School, Stoke Golding

Different Lives

My eyes are balls of happiness
Their eyes are dull grey stones
My joy is to see family and friends
Theirs is just eating
Moving around the keyboard, my fingers scurry
Their fingers are scurrying around waste
To fill a sack up with plastic.

My job is to empty the dishwasher
I moan about it most of the time
But I would much rather do that
Than scavenge around in a dump.

Emily Harrison (13)
St Martin's Catholic School, Stoke Golding

Poverty

The dumps lie waiting for them to arrive
Then slowly up the road they come
They are slouching from all the work they have done
My skin is healthy and theirs is rough
These children are so strong and tough
Little tears trickle down their face
Whilst working at a very fast pace
These children need money that we can give
So please donate some to help them all live.

Elly Del Busso (12)
St Martin's Catholic School, Stoke Golding

My Poem

I'm thinking of what to wear tomorrow
They are thinking of what food to catch tomorrow
I'm thinking of hanging with my friends
They are thinking of what's around the bend
My skin is as smooth as a piece of silk
Their skin is as rough as a tree
My eyes are full of happiness
Their eyes are full of loneliness
They can go for days without food
If I don't get any food I get in a mood
So don't just sit there when those adverts come on the telly
Don't eat your jelly, give it some welly.

Molly Edwards (12)
St Martin's Catholic School, Stoke Golding

Alone!

My skin is smooth
Like a baby's bottom
Their skin is a rough
Crocodile's tail.

My eyes are filled with happiness and hope
Their eyes are empty and never to be filled
With joy and laughter.

My life is cool and relaxing
I can eat to my heart's content
Their stomachs are a barren desert waiting to be filled.

Kelly Kalsi (12)
St Martin's Catholic School, Stoke Golding

Jewels

Weak and slow she limps
Eyes red, feet ache
She hunts and digs for treasures of plastic
In the pile of horrors and pain.
Then plodding home slowly
She takes the bag of plastic jewels
Cradling them like a baby.
Her head is an empty cave
An empty cave of horror and painful poverty.
Next day the same routine
Hungry and tired
Mother and Father ashamed and sorry.
How did it come to this?

Siân Tansey (11)
St Martin's Catholic School, Stoke Golding

War

My ears are full of footsteps, guns and knives
The screaming of families when their children die
What's the meaning of life
When there are bullets and blood and people who cry?
Peace is our hope, though we are far from it
The army kidnap the youngsters
Never to return
Famished families flourish in the clouded murk
The children's lives are now hell
Eating the scraps of dead rats
They hold the gun in their bony fingers
Their minds are full of death.

Gregory Hill (11)
St Martin's Catholic School, Stoke Golding

What's The Meaning Of It?

Us, them . . .
Is there a difference?

Our eyes are like marbles of rich colours,
With hope and future dreams filling them to the brim!
Their eyes are like dungeons of danger and despair,
With hunger and sadness killing them inside.
As we scoff our faces with chocolate and sweets,
They are going hunting for hours and hours!
Me . . . hungry? *Never!*
I just go to the fridge and pick out something I fancy.
Them . . . hungry? *Always!*
They hunt for hours and hours,
Even then sometimes unsuccessful!
We children take school for granted,
They might sell their dearest possessions
Just to send their children to school.
We just take the school bus to get there . . .
They might have to walk miles and miles.
We prance around like daisies,
They sit around like melons.
We live a life of laughter and happiness,
They live a life of despair and sadness.
We just spend our money on things we don't really need . . .
Ever thought about the poorer people of the world?
They need you!
Fact: every three seconds
A tiny baby somewhere around the world . . .
Dies!

Jessica Tallis (12)
St Martin's Catholic School, Stoke Golding

For The Last Time

Staring softly,
Her crystal tears crumbling down her anxious face,
She tries to smile,
But her sobbing heart and famished stomach
Condemn her to tears . . .
Again!
Blinking for the last time, she stumbles
Into the pit of death and fades out of sight,
Smothered by the dark ignorance that eradicates her,
Like so many others,
From our world - the world she was never allowed to know.
Her eyes of stone whisper her thoughts.
Her lips - like the earth she lay upon - cracking and desperate;
Her stomach drained like the lake she used to play in.
However, she is no longer a human,
Merely prey for any passing vulture -
As her soul departs
Without expectation that any place could be better than this.
Yet in her place is another . . .

Staring softly,
His crystal tears crumbling down his anxious face,
He tries to smile,
But his sobbing heart and famished stomach
Condemn him to tears . . .
Again!
Blinking for the last time, he stumbles
Into the pit of death and fades out of sight . . .

Aisling Lynch-Kelly (12)
St Martin's Catholic School, Stoke Golding

Through The Eyes Of A Scavenger

Through the eyes of a scavenger,
There is hardly any light,
The meaning of happiness is unknown,
To those who scamper like rats,
Through the grimy dirt and pollution of a dump,
At last one bit of flimsy rock;
Clear, small but all the same it's something,
Light does not show to everyone.

Through the eyes of a poor orphan child,
There is hardly any light,
The meaning of happiness is unknown,
To those who have no family,
To care, to comfort or to love them,
And then when no fuel can be provided,
It always sinks deeply in that there truly is nobody,
Light does not show to everyone.

Light to some people does not show,
But when one shares light with another,
More than light can be seen!

Grace La,Piccirella (11)
St Martin's Catholic School, Stoke Golding

Hell And Heaven

In goal I am an eagle swooping his prey
He is a fully armed soldier
At school I am a troublemaker
He hopes one day he will go to school
My eyes are molten blue marbles
His eyes are flames of fear
I eat lovely chicken
He eats a skinny rat.

Michael Caffrey (11)
St Martin's Catholic School, Stoke Golding

Poetry Of War

Through the eyes of war he looks,
And then points on in horror,
Through the eyes of fun I look,
Watching that film at home.

Looking through the reticule,
Tensing his finger now,
Looking at the television screen,
I'm laughing here and how.

Thinking of his life so grim,
What future will become of him,
Thinking of my life so fun,
I know what I want to become.

The chicken is warming in the oven,
The peas are in the pot,
The rats are scurrying below the ground,
Their hands are in the sand.

Adam Pole (11)
St Martin's Catholic School, Stoke Golding

My Life And His!

Through his misty eyes, he cries,
As well as his pounding heart.
His weeping heart is now empty,
But the love is still there.
He misses them so deeply,
True,
You can't believe he is living
Such a rigid life!

My eyes are filled with guilt,
After seeing the life he lives.
My heart is choc-a-block.
I see my loving and caring family
Every day living their lives to the max!

Chloe McDougall (11)
St Martin's Catholic School, Stoke Golding

The Meaning Of Life

The meaning of life is peace and joy
But we are far from it with bloodshed and tears
This is not a fantasy
This is reality, however terrifying it is
As he strode empty, not knowing what he had done
He is a robot being controlled through emptiness
He is given a gun to be fired
But he is scared, just like everyone else
For the kidnappers come and go
Stealing kids and adults, men and boys
Full of love and joy
Killing kind kids is what they do
They are turning them into killing machines
Shooting everything in sight
Lead them into battle like a dog leading sheep
This is not life, this is death
Leaving families to grieve and rot in tears
This is not the meaning of life
This is death and pain.

Adam Waters (11)
St Martin's Catholic School, Stoke Golding

War Poem

A chair, a table on the floor
But no one lives here anymore.
As he lay there in a heap,
His lovely wife began to weep.
Her howling was a baby's cry, she howled
These words before she died:
'One day bright,
The next a fright,
My husband lies here on the floor,
As they killed him in front of the door.
And here I weep more and more,
All because of the stupid war.'

Naomi Cotton (13)
St Martin's Catholic School, Stoke Golding

The Fear Of War

My mind is a constantly ringing phone,
The darkness of the cupboard blinds my eyes,
The latch unlocks with an old steel click,
The light of the day swallows me up.

I step out the cupboard with the heartbeat of a racehorse,
The belt lifts up and grasps around her hands,
I step back into the darkness of the staircase,
And run upstairs and into my bed.

I pull the itchy covers over my head,
I hear someone come up the stairs,
I wake up and it was all a dream,
As the bombs fall over the silent city.

Ben Burgess (11)
St Martin's Catholic School, Stoke Golding

On The Streets

When you're lying on the streets,
Your only companions are the sheets.
When the sun is setting down,
You do hope you'll drown.
When you're begging for money,
You're wishing for a honey.
Hour by hour,
You're begging for a shower.
When you're kipping on stone,
You wish you were home.
When you're on the streets,
Be careful who you meet.
If you're happy in heat,
Don't live on the streets!

Ben Waters (13)
St Martin's Catholic School, Stoke Golding

Other Children Around The World

I have got lots,
He has got nothing.
I have got fun,
She has got work.

I go to school,
He goes to work.
I go on holidays,
She is in Hell.

I am unchallenged,
He has no choices.
I am happy,
She is sad.

I should be helping,
He should be praying.
I should be worrying,
She should be waiting.

My eyes are brown spears of glass,
His eyes are dust balls.
My eyes are bright and sharp,
Her eyes are seas of tears.

I see trees waving hello,
He sees trees lying down dead.
I see water clear as could be,
She sees water contaminated and deadly.

I stroll along the path,
He scurries like a rat.
I play most of the day,
She works for her life.

Tom Clarke (11)
St Martin's Catholic School, Stoke Golding

A World For The Future!

A world for the future is a world full of peace
A world where children do not have to work
But can play and learn all day.
A world for the future is a world where everyone cares
A world that is not just a place, but a friend as well.
A world for the future is a world not in poverty
A world where not just us, but everyone prospers and is at peace.
A world for the future is a world that grows in love
A world where everyone's helpful.
My world is all of this and more.
His world is none of this and could not get much worse.

Jasmine Smith (12)
St Martin's Catholic School, Stoke Golding

Forced To Fight

It was nine o'clock when the kidnappers came,
Taking all the children,
They were going to the army,
And wouldn't return,
They were put to torture,
They were whipped and beaten,
Until they were fearless empty shells,
They were sent to the front with nothing but a pistol.

Their enemy army was twice the size,
The men fled in terror,
Leaving the children to stand and fight,
Against machine guns and rifles,
Many fell, but none fled,
For fear of what awaited them,
Until the police found the kidnappers,
This happens monthly.

Scott Hicklin (12)
St Martin's Catholic School, Stoke Golding

My Poem

Through the eyes of celebrities,
Poor children have no fun,
Working day and night,
Quite a few hold a gun.

If this carries on,
The future for them is dim,
Looking through junk for plastic,
Staring at him.

For a full bag of plastic,
It is only 4p,
It takes a week to fill a bag,
If that's all they see.

The city is like a bone house,
With all the children working,
Working ten hours a day,
With all the 'nappers lurking.

Miles and miles of junk,
Searching for an item,
Which is called plastic,
And it must frighten.

My work is schoolwork,
His work is finding plastic in junk piles,
My school is a big and cosy school,
His school is a tiny, one-roomed, uncomfortable school.

Matthew Shorney (11)
St Martin's Catholic School, Stoke Golding

I Dream . . .

I've been there
To that place
The place of nightmares
Illness
Sorrow
Death
I'm not going back
I'll try to change it
It will change
It has to
Poverty tears at their rags
Their empty pea-sized stomachs
Scream for food
They won't go hungry
They won't be hurt
They won't die
Waking up in a comfy bed
Not working there
Happiness
That is my dream for them
Happiness
We'll make it better
We'll help
Their dreams and our dreams
Will become reality.

Charlotte Ferguson (12)
St Martin's Catholic School, Stoke Golding

Homelessness - Could You Cope?

Cold;
Alone with nobody to keep you company.
Trust; well that doesn't even exist in my situation.
You can't rely on anything.
Think you have your spot to sleep . . .
Wrong: you're forced to give it up most of the time by some thug;
Then they always end up taking something of yours.
It's not like I have a lot to take;
They always find something though.

Hungry?
Not really an option.
Money? You can buy something if you have enough -
If you have spent the week begging,
Or if you haven't spent it on coffee just to keep you awake.

Bumps, bruises?
Though I can't do anything if I hurt myself.
No money to go to get it fixed.

Friends . . .
Not many of them.
Like I said, trust nobody.
If they offer you money, take it.
Try to look like you are sticking with them.
Nobody ever approaches you if you are with other people.
You become more difficult to target.

Molly Lissaman (13)
St Martin's Catholic School, Stoke Golding

I Carry A Dream!

I lean against the uneven wall,
The rain batters down like serrated shards of glass.
My eyes leak a river - hatred streaming into my mind,
Sealing it with pure venom.
During school, on the bus, at home;
They can trace me from a mile away -
My skin is not like theirs.
Angry thuds approach me,
Bang!
Their firm fists lash out,
Their panther's claws tear my face.
I cower down; they back me into a corner.
A flash of good memories seep into my neglected mind,
Trying to hold onto them, before they fade away forever
- too late!
They abuse me with language of hate
And they kick my shins with the force of a hurricane.
Is this what I live for?
I ask myself this question every day of my life.
But *I* live for others, not myself.
I know I'm strong;
I draw my determination from those before me.
Martin Luther King had a dream,
A dream to fulfil before death,
A dream he passed on to others,
A dream that I carry on.

Alicia Myroslava Serednycka-Poole (12)
St Martin's Catholic School, Stoke Golding

The Effect Of War

A little boy living in Africa,
Living a normal life,
But his life was taking a turn for the worse.

War comes,
And his eyes become empty black discs.
Listening fearfully,
He hears guns and bombs

And at once,
His bravery disappears,
Hunger instead plagues his mind.

One night, as he sleeps,
He is kidnapped by the foreign army.
Waking, he sees his captors, and at once they
See him too.

Baffled by their foreign language,
The boy listens.
'Help!'
He manages to shout out.
'Help me!'

Hannah Musson (11)
St Martin's Catholic School, Stoke Golding

Football Poem

He runs up the pitch like a cheetah,
He weaves in and out of every player,
He is a really talented striker,
He's got the agility of a BMX biker.

The upcoming match is the Community Shield,
The main man plays in midfield,
He thinks it is going to be a catastrophe,
But surprisingly, they win the trophy!

Sam Reynolds (11)
St Martin's Catholic School, Stoke Golding

People At War

People at war, not their fault
A door opens, a glitter of hope
Family's in tears, of once their little boy
Hugging onto that small, small toy

One memory of that horrible day
It wasn't nice, I have to say
Screaming and shouting, scared stiff
What's going to happen with them next?

Not eaten for days or months
Don't care, but carry on with nothing to spare
Dirty water, waterfalls of mud
Trying to find some way to live

While dancing to our pop songs
They dance to an African beat
As I read my poem
I hope you understand
About how bad it must be
To live in a place like that.

Rebecca Bott (11)
St Martin's Catholic School, Stoke Golding

Full Of Hunger

My breakfast is cereal,
Their breakfast is often nothing.
My lunch is pizza,
Their lunch is rats.
My dinner is fish and chips,
Their dinner is food off the floor.
My mind is full of joy and fun,
Their mind is full of unhappiness, a blown-up battlefield.
My life is great,
Their life is a hard, hungry struggle.
My school is bright and cheerful,
Their school is cold and damp, if they go to school.

Nicholas Wright (12)
St Martin's Catholic School, Stoke Golding

It Kills Them!

Like a thousand knives their hunger pierces through their stomachs.
It hurts them,
It kills them.
Rolling over one another on the cold hard floor with no quilt.
It aches them,
It kills them.
The bruises and scars over their bodies make their teeth lock together.
It scares them,
It kills them.
Their bones shatter like windows,
Their hearts are as dry as sponges,
Their legs wobble as they hold their bodies up.
Children live with this every day,
Don't pity them,
Help them!

Brittany Hine (12)
St Martin's Catholic School, Stoke Golding

Poverty In The World

All this time in our wonderful world innocent people die,
All this disturbing poverty is sure to make you cry.
Normal people like you and me are rotting in disgusting slums,
But we do nothing, we just sit around like zombies,
This would be heaven for some.
AIDs and malaria are horrible diseases,
Both of these won't just give you coughs and sneezes.
As you can see, something needs to be done,
So by raising our voices,
We can persuade our leaders to give these people a lot
more choices.

Josh Diboll (11)
St Martin's Catholic School, Stoke Golding

People Drowning In War

As I watch the television,
I am seeing a vision,
Of the people drowning in war.

My eyes are full of happy thoughts,
Theirs are full of dark, rotten stones.

I play with my toy guns,
But theirs are real.
I jump up and go on the computer,
While they lie on the floor crying out for help.

The fights with my sister are just pretend,
But they fight for real.
I eat what I want and when I want,
They eat the little food that we offer and walk miles for it.

We learn to read and write,
Whilst they are taught to fight at war.
As I play in the garden happily,
They are scared that they will step on landmines.
I drink water that has been sanitised,
The water they drink is from dirty streams and wells.

My clothes are clean,
Theirs are all dirty,
Ours are fashionable,
Theirs are all torn.

We have two or more bedrooms in our house,
They have to stay in the straw huts.

The shoes we wear are comfortable,
However, they walk around barefoot.

I jump into the car to go round the corner,
But they have to walk miles to get water.

Now that makes me think all about the people
Elsewhere in the world,
And that makes me feel grateful
For what I have!

Siân Sippitt (11)
St Martin's Catholic School, Stoke Golding

What Is It?

Its black furry body gleams powerfully in the shimmering moonlight.
Its echoing call runs through the dark gloomy woods.
Its thick shaggy coat blows gently in the cold wind.
Its great powerful legs sprint softly on the dewy grass.
It hunts for new explorers who are tired after days of walking.
Its yellow stunning eyes look out sharply for prey.
Its energetic smooth body wrestles with other members of the group.
Its twitching black nose sniffs for evening meals.
As the burning bright ball falls, the animal is content.

Jack Lawton (11)
St Martin's Catholic School, Stoke Golding

What Have I Done?

What have I done?
My home is being destroyed!
My family is being hurt!
These two-legged creatures have scary things!
What have I done?
My baby is gone!
My home is gone!
What is happening?
What have I done?
Bang! Bang! goes the scary thing!
My mother is falling out the tree!
I scream and shout!
What have I done?
Why are they taking them away?
What do they want with us?
We've done nothing wrong!
What have I done?
They beat us with sticks!
A tear runs down my cheek,
Skies turn grey!
My life was peaceful and joyful,
What have they done?

Shayde-Holly Woolard-Killick (12)
St Martin's Catholic School, Stoke Golding

Abandoned

My tail is long and patched with fur,
I can hear other animals in rooms that purr,
I feel like I am trapped in a bundle of fire,
The heat is getting higher and higher.

Now this animal is black and white,
And I am harmless so I don't bite,
Chained to the walls and bars,
Bumping into everything like a bumping car.

I am small and smell like a hog,
So I guess by now, you know I'm a dog,
Chasing postmen and ladies delivering milk,
I used to have a tail that felt like silk.

Roaring loudly at the crowd,
Hearing voices that start off loud,
Creeping here and creeping there,
A happy frog hopping like a hare.

Now you know how we feel,
So sponsor an animal and we have a deal.

Michaela Needham (11)
St Martin's Catholic School, Stoke Golding

Abandoned

My tail is short and patched with fur,
I feel like I'm trapped in a bundle of fire,
Waiting for someone to care for me,
I sit and watch people walk by.
They look at me and carry on walking.
My parents didn't care for me properly,
In the end they chucked me out.
Now I'm left in one of these kennels,
So I'm going to sit and wait
Until I find someone who will care for me.

Romey-Mae Archer (11)
St Martin's Catholic School, Stoke Golding

The Meaning Of Life

The meaning of life can't be found under a rock,
Or buried under the sun's Earth.
The meaning of life takes time to find,
So be patient and life will find you.
Travelling through life, friends will come along,
Friends whom to trust and friends to care for.
This is all part of life's journey.
So what is the meaning of life?
The meaning of life is all things to all people,
Happiness to some, sorrow to others.
We travel down a road, littered with questions
And always we try to find answers.
Our personality usually leads us to the end result
And hopefully the right direction.
As time passes by, the circle of life changes.
No one knows what can happen,
No one can predict the future.
We try to give our life a good beginning,
To enable us to make good decisions for the future.
Our parents, as they lead us in life,
We learn their ways.
Hopefully, as we grow older, we will understand
What they have taught us and why.

Amy Butterworth (11)
St Martin's Catholic School, Stoke Golding

Lucky Us

We don't realise how lucky we really are
Some children sleep on hard floors
As cold as a winter's night.

No food or water to help them grow
Suffering from fatal illnesses.
Their only clothing is a dusty old rag.

They walk miles to school every day
Dying on the way.

Ollie Richards (12)
St Martin's Catholic School, Stoke Golding

Bully

'Time to get up'
Said my mum
Sucked my thumb
Thought about school

Pretending everything's OK
When my world is more of a dying desert
My friends . . . friend, she doesn't stick up for me
All of them think they're so cool

Just because I am not like the rest
Doesn't mean I can't be one of the best
They run around playing basketball
None of them thinks I'm cool

The main victim is life itself
Death is around every corner
You think there's not much you can do
When you see a beating in the schoolyard
It's tough.

Sam Cordingley (12)
St Martin's Catholic School, Stoke Golding

The Tiger

A vicious predator,
Like a stripy devil
He watches the forests of Siberia
Like a vulture
He spots the poachers
With their guns
He shoots like a bullet
To warn his family
The poachers approach their hideout
The tigers flee into the mountains
To warn the others of the danger they're in
The poachers hear the tigers' call
So they did it, they retreated.

Matt Knight (11)
St Martin's Catholic School, Stoke Golding

Poverty Poem

My stomach is full,
Her stomach is empty.
My eyes are pools of blue,
Her eyes are as brown as rocks.
My water comes from taps,
She fetches water from miles away.
My bed is soft,
Her bed is a mat.
I am woken in the morning,
She wakes at the crack of dawn.
I get an education,
She has to work.
I live in harmony,
She lives in poverty.

Help end poverty today
And give someone a life.

Harriet Keeton (12)
St Martin's Catholic School, Stoke Golding

Other Children

As we are doing what we are doing now
People are dying
Children are crying.
We have our health
Others may be ill
Until they lie still.

Many must seek out their food
We just buy it
Others supply it.
Some must sleep on a bed of hard mud
Ours is snug
As a bug in a rug.

Our lives would be heaven for some.

Jamie Thompson (12)
St Martin's Catholic School, Stoke Golding

Why Do They Have To Live In Poverty?

Sitting here eating my tea
My plate is piled high,
I'm well fed, that's not hard to see,
But some people aren't.
I ask myself why them, why not you or me?
Why do they have to live in poverty?

Going to bed on an empty belly,
No fruit, no wine, no sweets or jelly.
Everyone from the age of four,
Working from dawn till dusk and more.
No comfy bed to lie in and snore,
Instead they'll retreat to a dusty floor.
And it all comes back to this question,
Why them, why not you or me?

Georgina Short (12)
St Martin's Catholic School, Stoke Golding

My Favourite Animals

I used to have a rabbit
In his own special hutch
I now have two playful kittens
I love them very much
I feed them in the morning
Before I go to school
I cuddle and stroke them
So they will love me too
My favourite one is Tigs
Because she feels like silk
Diamond is the fat cat
Who likes to drink the milk
I hope you like my poem
About my favourite pets
Let's all hope
They never go to see the vets.

Matthew Gisby (12)
St Martin's Catholic School, Stoke Golding

Will Anybody Listen?

Flash! Bang! Wallop!
Flash! They appear from nowhere in a flash -
Bang! They hit you over the head before you know what's happening
Wallop! They wallop you in the stomach, so you bowl over
And it is easier to attack you yet more . . .

Smash! Gang! Lollop!
Smash! They punch you in the face -
Gang! There is a whole load of sniggering, sneering sinners,
You can't possibly get away -
Lollop! Finally they lollop away, grinning with satisfaction,
Leaving you crumpled on the ground, bleeding . . .

Gash! Hang! Who knows what else?
Gash! There is a long gash on your face, but you can't tell Mum why,
So what are you going to tell her?
Hang! You endure this every day, are you going to put up with it,
Or put a stop to it all and hang yourself?
People think it is a joke, but I do not.
I think it is torture, but what can I do about it?
I'm crying out, but nobody is listening!
Help!

Grace Woolmer (12)
St Martin's Catholic School, Stoke Golding

Poverty

My stomach is always empty but quickly filled,
Their stomachs are a rumbling cave of emptiness.
My eyes are two moons gleaming,
Their eyes are two glazed pools of oil.
In the morning when I wake up to have my breakfast,
I know that they are hunting to survive.
I have an unlimited supply of water,
They would walk the extra mile for a single drop.

Ashley Prime (12)
St Martin's Catholic School, Stoke Golding

Barren Wasteland

I look onward at the barren wasteland that I call home
Weak, thin bodies covered in rags lumber around
Children are wailing
No one comes for us
No one cares for us
I make my way towards a muddy pool
Scooping water out with my rough, dirty hands.

Like an ape, my younger brother bounds towards me
He always brings hope when all light is gone
His eyes are shining diamonds
He talks of Mother being ill
And drags me to our house to look.

Mother is on the bed
Her frail body hardly moving
I hear her breathe her final breath as she closes her eyes
Tears roll down my face
I am left in the darkness
Just me and my brother.

Please help me.

Patrick Brown (12)
St Martin's Catholic School, Stoke Golding

Worried!

I am a lion stalking its prey;
My skin is rough as rock, whipped and beaten.
My tears are a waterfall trickling down the mountainside.
Slowly sinking to the ground, I hear the shots fired!
As I walk round the horrifying dump,
The syringes roll around the ground strangely watching me.
Bags of bones lie crooked and bent in piles of unhappiness,
Soaked in mud.
I walk over sharpened glass and shrapnel,
Slicing my feet like razor-sharp blades busy at work.

Louis Simpson (11)
St Martin's Catholic School, Stoke Golding

Walking On

Her swollen stomach is like a bag of air.
It was either her or her baby sister who ate -
Although a couple of grains of rice is hardly a meal!
That's what I thought!
Her fate already decided, she stumbles on,
Her limp and thin legs powered only by air and desperation.
Her lost and lingering eyes scan across the empty desert:
The hard, cracking earth,
Ignoring those life-promising seeds that didn't grow -
Once again!
Sizzling in the daylight,
Like a succulent sausage tenderly cooking on a barbecue,
The sun beams down,
Crumpling any glances of hope - any life . . . any food.
She tries to shout -
Scream for her family,
Yet all that remains in her voice -
Which has gone astray like a lost, lonely dog -
Is a pathetic squeak.
Tears stain her beautiful beige skin -
The only source of water she's got
And now that has been devoured by the everlasting sun.
She walks on . . .
Hopeless . . .
Pitiless . . .
Lifeless.

Katharine Lynch-Kelly (12)
St Martin's Catholic School, Stoke Golding

Through The Eyes Of The New World

The new world is different,
Better but worse,
Richer but with more poverty.

There is the good,
There is the bad,
There is the dying.

They work, day by day
Dredging through the dirt,
Their bony and edged figures creep around.

Our stomachs full,
Shovelling in more,
Bursting out of our newly bought clothes.

We just take our food for granted,
They are scraping for it to live,
We should join together.

There is no life within them,
They work like programmed robots,
They work their day and die,
We love and play, and sleep.

The quickly ending love between them,
It keeps them thinking strong,
Without this small shard of love they would not be here.

We can help them,
We can stop it,
We can give them love.

Millie Vozza (12)
St Martin's Catholic School, Stoke Golding

My Life

My home is
everywhere.
My daily meals
consist
of anything or
nothing.
My knick-knacks
and baubles
are the clothes
I
wear.
My money
is
only what
others
give me.
I am a being.
I am human.
I am homeless.

If only people
could see
where I stand
and
help me
through
this all.
Will this loneliness
ever end?
Will I begin
a
new life?
Does
anyone
care?
Because
I
am here.
I
am
real.
I
cannot
be ignored.

I am a person.
I am alive
and . . .
I am homeless.

Matthew Bridgewater (14)
St Martin's Catholic School, Stoke Golding

The Same?

I stand thinking against the wall outside,
I'm fine, some aren't,
I'm well, some aren't,
I'm happy, some aren't.

Should life be like this?
People dying dreadful deaths,
Homeless, starving, thirsty,
I'm on the moon,
They're in the hard, rocky core of the Earth.

Dark, murky water to drink,
Pop, squash, juice and milk,
Tasteless scraps,
Sparkling Sunday dinner,
The same?

Some people have a hard life,
Some people have an easy life,
Together let's make it history,
Make poverty history.

Black, white, the same really,
Big, small, the same really,
Clever, daft, the same really,
All the same, all - human.
Yet not equal.

George Russell (12)
St Martin's Catholic School, Stoke Golding

The Lion

The air is cold, the floor is hard,
I am sick and tired.
Eyes stare at me,
Some fingers point,
How did I end up here?
Big metal bars trap me,
Scared and lonely am I.
Why, oh why can't I go home
Where no metal bars exist?
My mum and dad
Were killed for their fur by hunters.
I was left to fend for myself.
I played with other cubs
And taught myself to kill my prey.
When I was cold
I slept under trees.
When I was hot
I slept in the shade.
But then, one day,
I was caught.
My mane was big and bushy,
My claws were long and sharp.
I hated being handled,
Humans really scared me.
Now I am no longer scared,
But bored and very lonely.
You try being on your own for 2 years.

Chloe Holden (11)
St Martin's Catholic School, Stoke Golding

Homelessness

There I was,
Walking down the street.
9pm,
Quiet streets,
No sound,
No nothing . . .
Until the next corner.

It was then,
Then when I saw him,
Squashed up in a doorway,
Awake,
Reflection from the street lights glistening in his eyes.
Then there was the stench;
That
Horrible
Stench.

Did I feel sorry for him?
Should I feel sympathy?
Should I give him money?
Was it his fault he was there?
Should I look away with disgust?
Should I feel embarrassed to be here?

Many thoughts in my head.

Which one to listen to
Is the question.

David Wright (13)
St Martin's Catholic School, Stoke Golding

Just One Touch

My feet are numb, as blue as a teardrop . . . bare.
My feet feel warm, rosy like a cherry . . . protected.
My legs are rough and tired from walking miles and miles.
My legs are smooth and resting after a day out.
My stomach lies empty, crying for food.
My stomach is content, gorged with satisfaction.
My lungs are filled with dust and infection.
My lungs inhale the fresh air, feel clean and healthy.
My heart has been broken, watching the deaths of my family,
wondering when it will be my turn.
My heart full of joy and happiness, pleasure buzzing all around.
My throat is sore and aching from desperate thirst.
My throat is clear and resonant.
My mouth dry and lonely with no comfort.
My mouth filled with friends, company every day.
My nose drips with the flu.
My nose taking in every lovely aroma.
My eyes are tearstained, empty, lonely, scared.
My eyes, with perfect vision, contentment in each corner.
My soul is my only companion, yet damaged and hurt, battered
and bruised.
My soul is as happy as can be, free as a bird, light as a feather.
My spirits are raised to have received just one touch of kindness.
My spirits are raised to have given just one gesture of generosity.

Faith Dunne (12)
St Martin's Catholic School, Stoke Golding

Homelessness

Cold, alone, depressed.
No one to comfort you.
No one to listen to your troubles.
No one to whisper your secrets to.
No one at all.
Just you.
Cold, alone, depressed.
Lurking shadows and dark corners.
Furious wind whistling through your mop of hair,
Stinging your vacant eyes.
Your knuckles are sore, your knees are swollen,
Your heart is an empty treasure chest, hard and brittle.
Cold, alone, depressed.
Inside your head murmurs unwanted memories
That taunt your soul,
Memories of joy, memories of laughter,
Memories of love.
Tears begin to bleed from your eyes,
They bleed fast, but tender.
You wish the cool pavement would swallow you
Between its cracks.
Life doesn't seem worth living.
You know, you've brought this upon yourself.
You know there's nothing left, not even hope.
Cold, alone, depressed.

Charlotte Ayres (14)
St Martin's Catholic School, Stoke Golding

Homelessness

Alone - again,
Nothing to see,
Close my eyes,
Think where I'd like to be,
A house, a home,
Somewhere warm,
Not stuck in the cold till dawn.

Soaked to the bone,
On a cold winter's eve,
Passers-by hoping I'll leave,
Just a pound or two,
Not much one might say,
Still, gets me through the day.

I lie on a bench,
I don't make a sound,
Till someone awakes me with a frown,
Some drink,
Drown their sorrow,
But I'll save my pound,
Never know, might need it tomorrow!

Abbey Short (14)
St Martin's Catholic School, Stoke Golding

African Children

My eyes see nothing except good things
His eyes stare in shock and fear
My life is a theme park, filled with fun
His life is a funeral, filled with sorrow
At school I am joyous at seeing my friends
His heart's desire is to learn about our world
My dinner is a mixture of lovely foods
His dinner (if he's lucky) is one skinny rat
All in all, my heart and soul are filled with happiness
And his have been ripped with the horror of life.

Ned Vavasour (11)
St Martin's Catholic School, Stoke Golding

Homelessness

Life on the street is hard
When everything's on the cards,
When no one gives you a second glance
And your life is crushed to shards.

So you try your best to survive,
In a world where nothing's alive,
Where trees are the ones that stop and stare
And the cold hits you like knives.

The night is worse than the day,
And for warmth is all that you pray.
You're let down virtually every time,
You find somewhere to stay.

These streets are smothered with sorrow
And the life that you have is borrowed,
There's nothing to carry on fighting for,
Except for the hope of tomorrow.

Alex Wilson (13)
St Martin's Catholic School, Stoke Golding

Homelessness Poem

Sitting down on the cold wet floor
Everyone passes, nobody cares
Why should they care? I say to myself
I'm just homeless, it's my fault.
On my own, no company
It's a one-man show though nobody watches.
You might get six pence if you're lucky
But more often than not, you get nothing.
You dream of a home with a family
You reach for that dream but it never comes.
Nobody knows what it's like here
Except for me and the other millions
And now you.

Patrick Crich (14)
St Martin's Catholic School, Stoke Golding

Homelessness

As I sat there in the freezing wind,
I noticed something odd,
There was a little girl opposite,
Sitting on the doorstep looking skinny and frail,
Like the rain had drenched her little frame down to the bone,
Upsetting such a sight is to see,
But you wouldn't understand in your world full of glee.

Fire blazing in my eyes,
As I stare into the windows of happy homes,
I want to curl into a ball,
Let the pavement swallow me up,
But I cannot rot away - I must make a stand,
There's no one out there for me to say things will be okay and come and hold my hand.

You might think that living free amongst the streets sounds exciting and okay,
But you haven't seen what I have,
You haven't experienced tragic things go wrong,
The tears just don't stop running,
Flowing down my cheeks,
Save yourself from this, kids,
For there's no going back after this.

You'll never get over the smirking faces,
The pure satisfaction in their stance,
Pretending like you don't exist,
You don't mean anything now,
You never did - you're a waste of space.
A disappointment to society,
Now they'll never leave you alone and you'll never get any privacy.

Emily Cottrill (14)
St Martin's Catholic School, Stoke Golding

Poem

Settle down,
Settle down,
Against the rainy day,
Cuddled in a ripped blanket,
Just the same as yesterday.
Tears drip from my spiky eyelashes,
Entwined against the rain,
Let's imagine I'm at home again,
Or let's not,
Let's avoid that pain.

Lie down,
Lie down,
Against the concrete floor,
I have my dreams to look forward to,
But the nightmare of evermore,
I cannot bear to think,
Lying on this floor,
Till next year or the next,
Maybe even more?

Think on,
Think on,
Of my mother's expectations,
My sister proudly doing well,
My father's hard, solid punches . . .

I can remember my mum asking me,
'When you're older, what will you be?'
I replied,
Looking deep in thought,
Then smiled and said,
'I'm going to be an astronaut!'

Samie Kerr (13)
St Martin's Catholic School, Stoke Golding

Solitary, Homeless

I'll look towards the night sky
Here I am again
No one here beside me
No friends to hold my hand

I am starved
I am cold
This is the only life I hold
It wasn't always like this
I had a mum
I had a dad
But they're a mere memory in my head
I might as well be dead

Who would've thought I'd end up begging
Who are you to walk on by?
Comfort and warmth are unrecognisable feelings
Can't you see these tears that I cry?

Paula Dunne (14)
St Martin's Catholic School, Stoke Golding

What Happens Next?

The world goes by so fast
As I watch these stroppy snobs walk by
Nobody knows about me
Nobody cares about me
I'm just an invisible nobody
As I watch people going from A to B

Lying on this cold stone floor
Who knows what's in store for me next
Maybe I'll get a broken rib like last night
Or maybe I'll be approached by some stranger like the night before
But tonight I just hope I'll get one good sleep on this cold stone floor.

Joe Rollins (13)
St Martin's Catholic School, Stoke Golding

In The Eyes Of A Poor Boy

Awoken at five o'clock
No breakfast
No shower
No clean clothes.
A five mile walk to school
His mind - a determined warrior
His body - a weakened bone house.
At school he's beaten, bullied
And locked in a dark, damp dungeon.
Coming home - hungry, thirsty and tired
Getting none of them at all
But a field full of rubbish for him to clean.
Rats, diseases, everything dangerous in there.
Finally done, ten o'clock at night
All he gets for his efforts
Rats, dirty rats, but it's the only food he'll get.
Settling down for a rest - at last
Lying on a wooden floor
Covered in a blanket, thin as paper
But he's grateful for that.
That's how poor he is.

Alex Franklin (12)
St Martin's Catholic School, Stoke Golding

Me And Them

In the morning, my CD player wakes me up
In the morning, cries of hunger wake him up.
Money to me is no problem
Money to him is hard work all day just to get little pay.
Food is always my choice
Food to him is only ever rats and scraps.
Clothes are always in my wardrobe and drawers
Clothes for him are plagued with disease and are rags
Life for me is easy
For him there is no point to live.

Matthew Palk (13)
St Martin's Catholic School, Stoke Golding

Homelessness

Life ain't fun on the street
I'll tell you that for free
You never know who you'll meet
But nobody cares, it's just you and me.

It's hard and it's cold
And that's just the floor
The novelty will get old
Look, face it, you're poor.

You'll wake up needing the loo
And you'll do anything to survive
Try your hardest, but all you can do
Is wait for something good to arrive.

A life without fun, laughter or peace
No music, no friends, no TV
The daily struggle looks unlikely to cease
Something good will happen though, you see.

Won't it?

Nick Highton (14)
St Martin's Catholic School, Stoke Golding

Homelessness Poem

Cold, hard and cramped.
Those are the thoughts of myself trying to sleep on the streets.
How can they sleep? I think,
'When I'm out here suffering the harsh conditions?
I am alone in this world.

In the morning,
If I wake up,
I'll sit on a bench or beg for money . . .
Alone.
If I'm lucky I might get a pound or two
But I'm still alone.
How did I get here?

When the sun goes down,
So do my hopes of more money.
I'll walk around for a bit before finding a door.
Once I've found it,
It all starts again . . .

Liam O'Boyle (14)
St Martin's Catholic School, Stoke Golding

Homelessness

Homelessness - the worst thing in the world,
Hunger, thirst, hypothermia.
All the things we people go through every day,
Begging for money, anything, anyone.

Lying in doorways, fearing for our lives,
People starving, no one cares.
No one stops, no one cares,
It's me and my rucksack, no one else.

The beatings, my family,
The people who are supposed to care,
But do they?
I think not.

Homelessness is like being a little fish,
Scared of being eaten, scared for your life.
Homelessness is the sun,
Round and round you go.

People just stand and stare.
People just do not care.
They could help - a penny or a bit more,
But no one stops, no one cares.

Homelessness could be something more,
A bit of help is all we need.
A bit of love could help a lot,
No, everyone stares - no one cares.

Ryan Ward (13)
St Martin's Catholic School, Stoke Golding

Dying In Poverty

Five till three, five till three,
Four years old,
But certain death awaits,
HIV lurks around corners,
Ready to capture,
Nowhere to hide,
This lifestyle, for a bag of plastic.

Screaming, shouting,
Lying still, no talking,
Thinner than paper,
A smile lights his face,
For what?
Just to be on our planet?
Not to die - not now.

Just before death
Staring
At the blood-ridden sky
'Look after her'
With a gasping
Last breath
His soul leaves his body
Never to return.

It's happening all around us,
Every minute or two,
It could have been prevented
And it could be you.

Charlie Smith (12)
St Martin's Catholic School, Stoke Golding

Life

She's only small, she doesn't know,
A baby, harmless, cute and sweet,
All innocent, she's an angel sleeping,
She's only small, she doesn't know.
Her brother, only small as well,
Kidnapped in the dark of night,
Now fighting, frightened for dear life,
He's dead, that doesn't mean anything though,
There are plenty more young children to fight,
He's nothing more than the cracked ground he's lying on.
She's only small, she doesn't know.
Her mother, died of hunger too,
Her body so limp she could barely move,
Her eyes displayed the emptiness and hatred she was feeling,
Her skin had formed around her ribs,
Her hunger was eating away at her soul,
She's lying, lonely on the cold ground,
She's only small, she doesn't know.
Her father held captive, to say her whereabouts,
Fighting away the cause of death,
He wouldn't tell, he wouldn't give in,
He knew where she was, but didn't tell,
Instead shot dead right there, right then,
No more Daddy, no more Mummy, no more love.
She's only small, she doesn't know,
Of the dangers awaiting her now protection has been and gone,
The hunger, the death, the cold, the violence,
She didn't know she could last that long.
She died a few weeks later, knowing nothing of her life at all,
She was only small, she didn't know her life wasn't worth living.

Laila Watchorn (12)
St Martin's Catholic School, Stoke Golding

Homelessness

Cold,
Alone,
Helpless,
Lying there in my doorway,
Tossing,
Turning,
Unable to sleep.
The cold nights,
The rain,
The empty feeling in my stomach,
That all torture me every day,
They never go away.
My only company is the silent whisper of the wind
That creeps around me, following me everywhere.
I watch the passers-by,
Watch them avoid me,
And give me dirty looks.
It's his fault, his fault I'm out here,
Living on the streets of London,
The one living with my mother,
The one who enjoyed hating me,
Abusing me,
The one who nearly killed me,
It's his fault, not mine.
The sun has risen,
Another day on the street begins.
No money,
No food,
No sympathy.
But that's homelessness for you . . . that's my life.

Florence King (13)
St Martin's Catholic School, Stoke Golding

My World At War

I live in a world at war
I cannot read or write
But I know how to hold a gun.

I live in a world of war
I don't live in a house
I live in a box with a blanket to keep me warm at night.

I live in a world at war
I have no clean water to drink
I eat the scraps of the village to stay alive.

When the dust settles
When the smoke clears
I'll be able to see the better
What sort of world I live in.

Scott Cumbley (11)
St Martin's Catholic School, Stoke Golding

Homelessness

As I walk down the street
I see so many of them
Sitting, with barely any meat
The cold seems to wrap around them
On the cold concrete steps
Some are fortunate enough to have a sleeping bag
Some have nothing
Most of them begging for a fag
As it gets rid of some of the pain
And seems to shelter them from the rain
Alone, cold and poor
Homelessness.

Will Turton (13)
St Martin's Catholic School, Stoke Golding

Sitting

Homeless is shades of grey,
Loafing on the kerb.
Danger lurks in every eye,
Suspicion read on each face,
Apathy skulks in any alley,
Cessation of animation.

Disillusion is black,
Inclement and passive,
Despondent and sinking,
No ray of light.
Fatigue and torpor,
As still as a corpse in the dead of night.

Despair is a leaky blue,
Draining friendships away.
Weariness is a burden,
Languid and laden.
Bonding is limited,
Fellowship rare.
Being, is a trial,
So, beware!

Georgi Hall (13)
St Martin's Catholic School, Stoke Golding

Talkin' 'Bout My Generation

In thirty years' time, what will I be?
Will it matter much if I fail GCSE?
Will I get my dream job,
Or will I have to rob?
Youths seem to think you 'gotta be cool',
It doesn't matter if you don't do well in school.
Although it's the thing to smoke with the blokes,
In thirty years' time, what will happen to those folks?
So now I ask myself,
Is it worth being cool?

Esther Dowle (12)
St Mary's RC High School, Hereford

Gone

Rules, rules, rules
At home and school
There are so many, I get confused
They contradict themselves
Over right and wrong
And in a world of whirlwind
Of black and white
I find myself
Gone

Bullies, bullies, bullies
Everywhere
They mock my clothes
And pull my hair
It seems no one else will listen
It seems no one else cares
So I cry and
Wish I was someone else
Because I hate me
I'm all wrong
And in a flood of tears
I find myself
Gone

War, war, war
Misery and pain
There is so much
I'm going insane
A lethal struggle for power
Who's right? Who's wrong?
And in a storm of guns and blood
I find myself
Gone

Money, money, money
Some don't have it
It isn't fair
I starve and thirst
I get sick and die
I don't even have enough
Energy to cry
And in a plague of poverty
That no one deserves
I find myself
Gone

Friends, friends, friends
Laughter and smiles
They give you a hug
A shoulder to cry on
Some words of advice
And are always there
Through anything and everything
So when something goes wrong
I find myself
Gone
To my friends

They'll take away the pain, the strife
And are undoubtedly
One of the best things in life.

Ciara Davies (13)
St Mary's RC High School, Hereford

Talkin' 'Bout My Generation

When I was born,
There wasn't as much pollution,
Though people were torn,
Between right and wrong.

Most people said, 'Stop polluting, it's wrong!'
Though others just sat back and watched,
'Don't bother, it'll take too long,
It's not our problem, we'll be dead not long!'

Though my generation cried out!
They sat back and watched,
Though my generation, we shout!
They sat back and watched.

As I grew up,
More things were happening,
We were as innocent as new pups,
Things started to go wrong.

Now I'm older and Earth is too hot,
Gases go up, not out!
They are stuck there, like a babe in a cot,
Earth really needs gases to stop!

Though my generation cried out!
They sat back and watched,
Though my generation, we shout!
They sat back and watched.

When I am all grown up,
I will regret sitting back, to watch,
When Earth fills like a cup,
Full of gases, dangerous and more!

When I am old, my children will say;
'Why did you sit back to watch?'
When we make them all pay,
Why did we sit back and watch?

Now my generation cry out!
We will *not* sit back and watch!
Now my generation, we shout!
We don't have to sit back and watch!

Sometimes it falls on a generation to be great,
You can be that great generation,
Let your greatness blossom.

Charlotte Bray (12)
St Mary's RC High School, Hereford

Talking 'Bout My Generation

My generation are poisoning this life
Children dying in pain, in grief and in strife.
What are we making this world become?
Lifeless bodies cradled by sobbing mums

The wars and pain are ripping us apart
Driving like a knife into our hearts
Men sent off to their imminent deaths
The extremist bombers stealing their last breaths

Yet even bombs kill the innocent back home
The trains and buses destroyed and inwardly blown
Those returning from work and school
Crippled and killed in explosions so cruel

Racial hate fuels these homeward wars
Trying to stop the white ruling laws
It's taking religion and race to the extreme
Teenagers strapping bombs to their chests to obtain a dream

The rulers and politicians engulf us in lies
Whilst every day another brave soldier dies
The dictator's game destroys this world
As moneymakers hide behind the flag they unfurl.

Michael Griffin (12)
St Mary's RC High School, Hereford

My Generation

If I could think of one thing to say about my generation,
It would be . . .

That my generation is a great generation,
With technology, good music and more!
And my generation has plans for this nation,
Which will rock this world through to the core!

But my generation can be a bad generation,
Cos guns and drugs have found their way in.
My generation doesn't fit in to this nation,
Because it's rotten and filled with sin.

My generation is a thoughtful generation,
With ideas to make the world great.
My generation has ideas to change the nation,
Like to make peace and throw out the hate.

My generation is a smart generation,
Which will learn all the knowledge there is.
My generation will grow this nation,
With God as the prime witness.

My generation is a great generation,
With computers and planes which can fly like doves.
My generation is growing up in this nation
And hopes to share its love.

Casey-Anne Millin (13)
St Mary's RC High School, Hereford

Monster Daddy

'When did the love go?' I cry,
Daddy's eyes themselves reply,
Angry, empty, sad, why?
He is my monster daddy.

There are wars in this world, I know,
Perhaps I should care, and show,
I call this place home, this low,
He is my monster daddy.

They tell me to call 'Childline',
They think it will all be fine,
But I'm even scared to dine,
With my monster daddy.

And now I hide in my room
And I look into the gloom,
As he roars, crashes and booms,
Is this monster my daddy?

And now, I wait for the day,
When he will walk in and say,
'I love you, my darling Jay,'
Until then, he's monster daddy.

Henry Cosh (13)
St Mary's RC High School, Hereford

My Awful/Great Generation

Terrorists are everywhere
Death and turmoil cling to the air
Inherited from my parents' generation
As we lose our fading nations

Global warming, look at what it's made
As the ozone layer begins to fade
Produced by breathing, cars and burning
But still, my generation isn't learning

Forests and jungles are cut away
Just to make one motorway
Only to save cars ten minutes to drive
Making carbon dioxide grow and thrive

In the east there strikes war
Like nothing else that has happened before
Corpses everywhere in sight
Where nearby soldiers continue to fight

Crime rate of the world has grown
Higher than anyone has known
Murder, theft and driving bans
As villainous crooks cook up their plans

Would you like to be in my shoes?
Thought not
But
There are a few things which are good.

Technology has grown higher than ever before
This time of court, politics and law
Song and music flood through this age
Making this a happy place.

Daniel Heathcote (12)
St Mary's RC High School, Hereford

Global Warming

The world is all wrong.

As the lone polar bear prowls through the ice,
Hungrily hunting for some much needed food,
No one even cares.

While the bear cubs excitedly play their friendly game,
While the powdery snow flies in the air,
No one even cares.

The icy water slowly trickles down the melting ice cap,
Into a steadily growing pool of melted ice,
But no one even cares.

Nothing but seemingly everlasting sea in the distance,
The boiling iceberg shrinks every day,
But no one even cares.

Though all these things are here right now,
In what seems like a heartbeat, so soon, they'll be gone,
But no one even cares.

Carelessly leaving the electrics on,
Polluting our beautiful world,
These are things that show that no one even cares.

'We're all doing our bit,' you say,
But there's no difference at all, not at all,
This just goes to show that no one even cares.

When you think it's the end of the world, but you're just overreacting,
Remember that polar bear, white as snow, all skin and bones.
Why don't people even care?

The world is all wrong.

Victoria Roskams (12)
St Mary's RC High School, Hereford

Misery

Down in the dark of the dank London slums,
Sit figures of misery who no longer have mums.
Hungry, cold, tired, lonely and bare,
Staring at the world with a dull, listless stare.
Hunger, thirst, loneliness and dying,
Exhaustion, cold, misery and crying.

But there you are, sitting in front of TV,
Full of relief, thinking, *I'm glad it's not me.*

Misery hangs in the air with the fog,
Over children watching wistfully into the smog.
Thin from starvation, bones sticking out,
This is misery, of course, there is no doubt.
Hunger, thirst, loneliness and dying,
Exhaustion, cold, misery and crying.

While they sit in misery, all lonely and scared,
You sit with a book in a comfy armchair.

Dogs and cats, yowling pitifully for love,
Wishing for wings, to fly away, like a dove.
Fur falling out, just skin and bone,
Unnoticed, unwanted, like slabs of cold stone.
Hunger, thirst, loneliness and dying,
Exhaustion, cold, misery and crying.

Absent-mindedly pushing the cat from your lap,
Taken for granted, as it goes for a nap.

Dreams and wishes of the children are great,
To live in a house with a garden and gate.
To eat good meals and lie in a bed,
Forget all the past and rest dull, aching heads.
Hunger, thirst, loneliness and dying,
Exhaustion, cold, misery and crying.

Carelessly leaving the tap on; *drip, drip,*
While children in misery would give lots for a sip.

But that's all they are; fantasies and wishes,
As likely to happen as ants eating fishes.
What are we doing to make misery die?

'We're helping', the government says. That's a lie.
Hunger, thirst, loneliness and dying,
Exhaustion, cold, misery and crying.

A fiver a month? No difference it'll make,
It'll be years before change, or even too late.

Forgotten about, left to wither away;
Death's welcomed like sleep after a long, hard day.
Misery has stolen her life, now his,
Down in the London slums; that's where misery is.
Hunger, thirst, loneliness and dying,
Exhaustion, cold, misery and crying.

Full of guilt and regret in your wake,
The time to help came and went, and now it's too late.

Alexandra Smith (13)
St Mary's RC High School, Hereford

My Generation

Pollution and poverty,
What's that all about?
What your generation
Left us to sort out.
Blood spilling,
We're killing,
Surrounded by wars,
Each of us fighting for our own earthly cause.
Nelson Mandela, a great man and good,
He had some sense like most of us should.
You can be that great generation,
Let your greatness blossom,
Each and every one of us;
Down to the smallest possum.
The Third World countries are all in debt,
Because of all the money that we kept,
Starving little children living on the street,
Please won't you give them something scrummy to eat?

Sophie Bray (12)
St Mary's RC High School, Hereford

The Lonely Giant

He stands alone,
Unmoving, so quiet,
Inside he weeps like
A small child left alone,
No one to share his pain,
So lonely,
His companions have left,
Swept away like a feather in the wind,
Snatched by the hand of Man,
He stands crying,
He's seen things,
That no one should see,
His friends brutally cut cleanly at the base,
They were taken with no cause,
No explanation,
Where he stood was a forest,
It was great and tall,
Strong in its unity,
All that was here and it was real,
Now it's all but a ghost,
A thing of the past,
Here he stands caged in like an animal,
Constricted and cramped,
Longing for space to grow freely.

They come often,
To hack at him and amputate his limbs,
He no longer feels the pain,
For now he too is just a shadow of his former self,
He knows one day they will come
And do to him what they did to his friends,
He longs for that day,
A day he could be free,
Grow as he wished,
Be with his friends,

But today's not that day,
For now he is alone, a shadow in the dark,
He will wait,
Longing,
Hoping,
Wishing,
For them to come,
For him to be free,
In the silence,
There was that noise
Grrrrrrrrr,
That day has come.

Peter Dixon (13)
St Mary's RC High School, Hereford

Talkin' 'Bout My Generation

Polar caps melting away,
Land drying, becoming desert day by day.
Is this the type of world my generation will have to live in,
With hurricanes, earthquakes and tsunamis happening every day?
Is it our fault, are we to blame?
With our cities growing and forests burning every single day.
Cars and planes, rockets and trains.
I think that we *are* to blame.

What can we do? How can we stop it?
By building better cars or having less, which one is the best?
How can each person help to stop the planet from continuing to melt?
Because without a doubt our planet is changing throughout.

Walking not driving,
Planting trees,
Saving water,
If you please,
All these things they can help
And maybe our world won't continue to melt.

Tom Fawcett (13)
St Mary's RC High School, Hereford

Why?

Lives being thrown away,
Like rubbish into a bin,
Wasting time in front of the TV,
Time doesn't stop for us.

People cover up their feelings,
They put on a mask and pretend nothing's wrong,
Pushing feelings to the back of their mind, trying to forget,
Only time heals problems,
Not forgetting.

Smiles seem to be a sin,
If you want to fit in.
To be accepted, the world makes you believe,
You have to be picture perfect in every way.
Different is wrong
And gets ignored.
But why?

You make friends and break friends,
But they're always there.
Friends are like the sun,
Warm and happy.

Music is an expression,
It makes you feel happy
And can make you feel sad.
You get picked on for not liking the same sort.
But why?

So much anger.
So much hate.
It turns into bullying,
But why?
People get embarrassed and upset.
One person can do a lot of damage.

Yesterday's history,
Tomorrow's a mystery
And it can easily be changed.

Mia Hoddell (12)
St Mary's RC High School, Hereford

This Generation

In this generation
Of violence and pain
In this generation
Of grey skies and rain
In this generation
Of battles and fights
In this generation
Of hunger and plight
In this generation
Of heartbreak and sorrow
In this generation
Of a bleak tomorrow

In this generation
Of success and new light
In this generation
Of love and delight
In this generation
Of freedom and pleasures
In this generation
Of discovering treasures
In this generation
Of smiles and fun
In this generation
Of blue skies and sun

In this generation
Of laughter and tears
In this generation
Of all hopes and all fears.

Katherine Wibmer (12)
St Mary's RC High School, Hereford

Bare

We hear on the radio of the bird flu and gun crime,
But never once pause to think *what if it's our time?*
For the people, we don't know and the famine we haven't seen,
But if you look closer, that's where we've always been.

We hear, but we don't listen, we look but we don't see,
We are put into a dream, where we'll always 'be'.
The insights we have in newly founded things,
Covers up the reality that life always brings.

Look past the garden hedge and down to the street,
The litter-strewn paths and smashed windows aren't so neat.
See the last remaining swing screech its plaintive cry
And see the once deep blue, polluted sky.

As children, my parents would climb trees of pine,
Only garish towers climb and darken the skyline.
Down the high street you see division throughout,
Gun crime is 'the trend' but who cares how the victim felt.

The news always brings a new hideous story to tell,
But the papers only care how many copies they sell.
Children's views are easily corrupted by television,
But they can't be told not to separate with racism.

This is how today looks if you open your eyes,
If you see while looking, you'll get a surprise.
Behind the quaint houses and the merry May fair,
There is the whole natural world, totally stripped bare.

Elizabeth Young (12)
St Mary's RC High School, Hereford

Talkin' 'Bout My Generation

My generation has come a long way
From the latest fashions
To the weather today

My generation has its ups and downs
There are so many stresses
It turns smiles into frowns

My generation has poverty and AIDs
Be it first or Third World
It's sad when lives fade

My generation has no place to fit
Are you in with the in crowd?
You can miss or can hit

My generation grows up too quick
With our skirts too short
And our clothes too hip

My generation is too fat or too thin
Size zero or McDonald's
We don't know where to begin

My generation cares about tomorrow
Choices we make now
Could save us from sorrow

My generation is where we are now
It's our time today
We'll show the world how.

Emily Twigg (12)
St Mary's RC High School, Hereford

The World

The world is a plughole, sucking everyone into it.
We're now in too deep . . .
        The world has become a heap!

Just as we thought we could get no deeper,
Things began to change!
        For better or for worse?

The world is too dangerous, like those fighting in the war!
They have made no change to the law . . .
        What are they doing this for?

The world was once a colourful kite, bouncing with praises,
But now it has only found itself
        Lying in a tangled knot.

The Earth we live on is a hypnotiser . . .
        But we are none the wiser!

We are the firecrackers, waiting to burst,
        But it seems we are cursed.

God is the glue . . .
        Holding humans from the power of extinction!

Shannon Bakan (12)
St Mary's RC High School, Hereford

My Hobby, Football

Football is my game
Football is my life
When you win the game
You feel you have the fame
Through rainy days we'll work together
We'll never back down
We'll fight forever.

Scott Dutton (11)
Stoke Park School, Coventry

Talkin' 'Bout My Generation

G irls start spitting in the street
E vil eyes from whoever we meet
N ever good manners from children these days
E veryone is horrible in many ways
R ubbish and litter all over the floor
A horrible world, no one cares anymore
T errible! What is this world coming to?
I n horrible gangs or a stupid crew
O nly sadness is happening now
N ow I wonder how it happened? Oh how? Oh how?

Faye Stringer (11)
Stoke Park School, Coventry

My Hobbies

Dancing is my world
Dancing is my passion
Tap, jazz, any old thing
Get on your feet and dance with me
Bounce, bounce, bounce with me
Front drop, back drop, seat drop, knee drop
Any old drop
Just drop with me.

Amy Tranter (11)
Stoke Park School, Coventry

My Life

M P3 players are really handy
Y ounger generations are made happy

L istening to music day and night
I n homes, clubs and school at times
F ridays are my favourite day
E nd of school and time to play.

Thomas Barnwell-Edinboro (11)
Stoke Park School, Coventry

Talking About My Generation

T he future is bright in his eyes
H e thinks he can make it better
E lectric, flying cars and invisible glass homes

F eeling happy and optimistic, he wants the present to go
U nder his pillow, his brain dreamed dreams of the future world
T he world today is boring he says
U ncomfortable and unfriendly surroundings
R uffians will be no more in his future, it will be a calm and
peaceful place
E jecting the present when he grows up, he will start the world
of his dreams.

Joram Mary Joseph (11)
Stoke Park School, Coventry

Keep Me Safe

Roses are red, violets are blue,
Keep me safe and I'll keep them too.
Keep me clean, from rubbish and stuff,
Stop cutting my trees or I'll get in a huff!
My rivers aren't clean, it stops them from flowing,
So keep them blue or they will be going.
Think about the people, all hungry and sad,
They would be happy if you weren't so bad!
You could save some energy or have a quick shower,
That way, I will be gaining more power.
So keep me round, all green and blue,
Or I'll be no more and neither will you.

Danniella Evans (11)
Stoke Park School, Coventry

Talkin' 'Bout My Generation

M y family is the best family in the whole world
Y ou have got to have a family like mine to survive

F or getting shouted out once in a while doesn't matter
Because all of the loving and caring they give me
Makes up for it and even more
A lso taking me out for tea
M y family is the best in the world.
Get one like mine and you'll be extremely happy, just like me
I s your family as good as mine?
I really don't think so because mine's fine and even better!
L ots of presents and cards, also goodies and treats,
It's the best family by far
Y ippee, go me! Yippee, go me!

Lucy Herdman (11)
Stoke Park School, Coventry

Talkin' 'Bout My Generation

Through the eyes of time, God sees my generation,
But I'm not sure if He is happy with our grubby faces and dirty knees.
I wish He could rethink this generation, please.

I wonder how my generation will shape the future?
I wish I could control it.
If this world becomes a place of football players and hairdressers,
I would have a fit!

So through God's eyes in time,
Maybe He sees that humans will soon not be in their prime.

Samuel Barratt (11)
Stoke Park School, Coventry

The Ice Wolf

The ice is a wily wolf,
Waiting, waiting.
He lets out a piercing howl that cuts the air
Like a knife, calling his pack to him, to hunt for him.
His paws pound across the icy lake,
Doggedly pursuing his petrified prey,
Hunting, hunting.
Across his powerful, sleek body, veins stand out
Like knotted ropes against his shining fur.
His legs act like pistons, his battle-scarred paws
Barely touching the ice across the frozen lake
And beneath the ice, fathomless depths long to open up
To drag him down,
Down, down to his death.
The ice suddenly cracks under his muscular weight,
He speeds up, willing himself to be lighter, he fails.
He and his formidable pack feel themselves
Gripped in cold's icy, vice-like grip
And it pulls them, down, down, down . . .

Alfie Sheridan (11)
The Bishop of Hereford's Bluecoat School, Tupsley

The Stone Turtle

The sandy rock is a baby turtle,
Waves crash over it as it tries to crawl to the sea.
It takes its first few steps
As did you and me.

Another wave crashes:
It hides in its stone shell,
Which slides down the sandy slope
And touches the sea.
The sea touches back
With a great *smack!*
Of a wave over the turtle's back.

A few more steps and it will be there.
Another wave crashes
And there it goes,
Home again, home again into the sea.
It lies on the seabed,
The stone turtle is free.

Georgia Howe (11)
The Bishop of Hereford's Bluecoat School, Tupsley

The Driftwood, A Lion

The driftwood is a lion,
Roaring down at the sea,
Its eyes looking straight through me.
Its mane flying in the wind.
He's big, bigger than me.
Hour after hour he stands upon that hill,
Looking over his kingdom,
His head looking over the edge.
Then suddenly he topples,
He hits a ledge,
He falls again,
Falling, falling towards the sea.
Then *splash* -
Now he's sinking,
The cold, cruel, blue monster,
Dragging him down, down,
Into an endless sleep,
Never to resurface.

Sian Vale (11)
The Bishop of Hereford's Bluecoat School, Tupsley

The Stormy Stage

The tears of rain fall down from the sky
When something sad happens on the cloud stage.

The hiss of wind that releases red petals
As the bad guy stalks on.

The dazzling smiles of all the suns
When two lovers have a happy ending.

The blizzard of flowers thrown onto the cloud stage
At the end-of-year show, getting ready for the encore.

Emily Earp
The Bishop of Hereford's Bluecoat School, Tupsley

The Octopus

The driftwood is an abandoned octopus washed up
On the shore of Bounty Bay.
He lies there dying
Slowly, slowly waiting for the tide to come in.
His eyes scan the beach for any unsuspected movement,
As the cooling waves wash over his body,
His tentacles twitching on the sand.
The sun slowly dries him up,
He howls, asking for help,
No one hears him, no one sees him,
He is all on his own.
He lets out a groan and slowly, silently, softly,
Rests in peace.

Roisin Massam-Vallely (11)
The Bishop of Hereford's Bluecoat School, Tupsley

The Bush

The bush is a hedgehog,
With spikes sharp and long.
These protect his soft, smooth flesh,
While he gets his rest.

For as you know, a hedgehog hunts,
Silently at night.
They shuffle very quietly,
And run away at light.

During the day he sleeps so still
And doesn't move a muscle,
He lies so still, so still he lies,
On the top of a hill.

Finally it turns to night
And suddenly he moves;
And as his small feet paw the ground,
He lifts his head - the earthy mound.

Bethany Welford (11)
The Bishop of Hereford's Bluecoat School, Tupsley

A Rugby Match

As the two armies line up,
The commanding officers shout commands from HQ,
Whilst the warriors chant their battlecries.
Dust from the battle zone drifts up into the air.
Let the battle commence.

The peace seeker sounds his horn,
But the warriors attack anyway.
Their armour clamped in their mouths,
They clobber each other,
Each army is trying to catch the sacred egg,
Which has flown into the air.

The front line goes over the top first,
Because they are bigger
And the cavalry hang back, ready to charge later,
Whilst trying to keep out the breakaway enemy.
The battle-scarred machine gunners mow down
The first platoon and then the second.

One of the cavalry blasts through the third platoon
In the oozing mud,
He has metres to go . . .
Feet . . .
Centimetres . . .
He dives down in occupied territory behind enemy lines
With the sacred egg clasped tightly in his hands.
The war is won!

Henry Wilson
The Bishop of Hereford's Bluecoat School, Tupsley

The Mouse And The Snake

A giant snake,
Curled around its prey.
A helpless mouse,
Awaiting its end.
The small and the helpless,
Against the mighty and fearless.
The snake is alive,
It slithers through the grass.
The mouse, it lives!
But not for long.

Now, the mouse and the snake,
Are very good friends.
But for now, they fight,
Until it ends.

But, don't think of death and dark,
Think of light, and hope!
For the mouse and the snake,
Are only having a lark!

Now, if you are worried,
I will tell you the truth.
For the snake is a branch,
And the mouse is a seed.
And so, they will playfight,
Until the wind dies.

Conor Barry (11)
The Bishop of Hereford's Bluecoat School, Tupsley

Driftwood

The driftwood is a giant shoe
Great and white
She lies there on the beach all day long
With the clashing waves rolling over her
Minute after minute she stays there all alone

And when the night wind roars
And the moon shines down upon her
Shaking and cold she lies there still
Till dawn approaches she will be cold
Then when she awakes, she will do the same until . . .

Continuing on her trail she gets moved on to another place
There she then will lie until the next time she will move.

Becky Dodd-Cox
The Bishop of Hereford's Bluecoat School, Tupsley

Treasure Hunt

The family next door are a pack of hyenas,
Laughing and howling all day long.
Ears, pricked for prey,
Listening for opportunities,
Hunting in my garden.

The family next door tear up their food,
Savaging it and swallowing it whole.
Teeth, black with decay,
As sharp as razors,
Drawing blood instantly.

The family next door runs on all fours,
Chasing, hounding, their terrified prey.
Like Olympic athletes hunting a gold medal,
Slowing only to claim their reward,
Feasting on their glorious treasure.

Noah Callaghan
The Bishop of Hereford's Bluecoat School, Tupsley

White Horse

The sea is a white horse racing forward, charging to the sand,
Reaching out for land.
The mane is the top wave swishing side to side, left and right.
The tail lapping onto the shore before the tide.
Thundering hooves chasing, chasing, chasing.

The white horse gallops through the field in a herd,
Jumping the rocks as they go along.
Then suddenly they stop; they swish their tails,
Nod their heads for the last time and begin to graze.

Ella Wilmot (11)
The Bishop of Hereford's Bluecoat School, Tupsley

The Mermaid's Hair

The seaweed is a mermaid's hair,
Racing through the sea,
Trying to find the right head,
For its shampoo tea,
Waiting, waiting, waiting,
Washed up on the beach all day,
Waiting to be found,
A citizen from Cardiff Bay,
Throws it into the sea without a sound,
Drowning, drowning, drowning,

As the wicked waves wildly clap with a clatter,
Something flies into the air,
With an enormous shatter,
People are left in despair,
Wondering, wondering, wondering,
All alone beneath the deep,
So lonely with no friend,
Not being able to get sleep,
Wondering, *is it the end?*
Lonely, lonely, lonely.

Grace Alexander (11)
The Bishop of Hereford's Bluecoat School, Tupsley

Driftwood

The driftwood is an old, battered seal,
Rolling in the sand,
Tired and weary he cries,
As he stares deeply into my eyes.

The cruel, crashing waves have almost worn his flippers out.
His slippery skin is rugged and torn,
His eyes are empty and hollow,
Beaten out by the storm.

When the waves wash over the shore,
He is pleading, he just can't take anymore.
His dream to dip and dive in a beautiful sapphire lagoon,
Is ending as his heart grows slower, slower, slower.

The storm is drifting away,
The warmth of the sun is drawing nearer,
He tries to waddle towards the calming, clearer water.

His fragile whiskers gently flicker
Around his motionless head,
Exhausted, he falls
Into a never-ending sleep on the golden, sandy bed.

Maddie Pickering (11)
The Bishop of Hereford's Bluecoat School, Tupsley

The Night Sky

When I look up to the night's sky I see
A cape fit for a queen and encrusted with diamonds,
Or the Devil dressed in black,
Staring at me with 1,000,000 eyes.
The perfect painting hung up to dry,
Or the whirlpool of the night
Lashing out to try and catch me.
The sky is:
The protector that kills sin and worry with his lightning
And a voice to scare away evil,
Or a monster that sends down deadly sneers of light
And great roars of madness.
The safest haven that protects our lost loved ones,
Or a deadly war fought by those who have left us.
I see the sky as:
A child's bedroom lit only by one mighty torch,
Or a pathway lit with a white flame
To show the way for witches and all things evil!

The sky can be many things.

Ella Belfield
The Bishop of Hereford's Bluecoat School, Tupsley

The Treetop

The treetop is a hunting eagle.

Suspended in mid-air
Scaring off the mountain hare.

Flapping its giant wings
Shaking off all loose things,

Making its nest out of dead twigs and leaves
Towering over other trees,

On a windy night
It shows its might
It screams and leans.

But on a calm summer's day
You can hear the happy;
'Chirp, chirp, chirp, chirp'.

It gently sways in the breeze
Whistling with the other trees,

As the gales come around
The great eagle swoops to the ground.

James Wright (11)
The Bishop of Hereford's Bluecoat School, Tupsley

The Mermaid

The driftwood is a cunning mermaid,
Swimming to the surface.
Her hair floating on the water,
Like seaweed drifting along.
Lying on the beach all day,
Watching someone bathe.
As her eyes sparkled in the sun,
They stare at people having fun.

As night drew in,
The sun grew dim.
Everybody left,
So the mermaid slept.
A new day dawned,
The mermaid yawned.
As she smiled,
The sea grew wild.
She swam further and further up the beach,
As her tail flapped in the water,
She lay sleeping, sleeping, sleeping.

Ella Pace (11)
The Bishop of Hereford's Bluecoat School, Tupsley

The Crab

The driftwood is a crab,
His claws are splintered, dusty and drab.
He stands and shivers on the sandy shore,
Clapping his cragged and jagged old claws.
His spindly legs stretch out like fishing rods reaching for fish.

He shivers and shivers and shivers again,
As the ocean spray showers his barnacled back.
As the isolation increases he begins to feel more and more alone
On this dismal and gloomy old beach.

Into the depths he is swept, swallowed by the waves once more.
His arms are crooked, his shell is cracked.
The waves are forever wearing away his fingers and toes.
Will he survive these awful conditions?
Nobody knows!

Marcus Betts (11)
The Bishop of Hereford's Bluecoat School, Tupsley

The Wind

The wind is a galloping horse twisting and turning
In and out of its stud of mares,
And as the waves lap the shore he gallops to Heaven
Then back to Earth's door, in freedom.
But in the middle of the night his whinnying call echoes
Around the world, in freedom,
As he rears and runs along the plains
Darting then stopping at an excellent speed
Cantering freely with the wind in his mane,
Tossing and turning, with freedom, freedom, freedom,
Days and years pass before him but does not affect his time
For he is free to do his will now,
To jump and run in freedom,
To gallop the world's pathways in freedom,
As he is a wild stallion, the stallion of freedom.

Lyndi Thomas (11)
The Bishop of Hereford's Bluecoat School, Tupsley

Metaphor Poem

My home is like a safe harbour blocking out the raging sea.
My bedroom is like a gentle rocking boat on the sea in the middle of the summer.
My brother's bedroom is like a big steamboat struggling.

The door of my house is like a sea defence wall blocking out the sea.
The kitchen is the entrance to the busy harbour with all the boats going in and out.
The sitting room is like the buoys, so the boats can relax without floating off.

The spare room is the empty buoys waiting to be used.
My mum and dad's bedroom is the patrol boats keeping everything in order.
The hallway is like the lanes between the boats leading out to the sea.

Hannah Prestwich (12)
The Bishop of Hereford's Bluecoat School, Tupsley

The Ice Is A Dolphin

The ice is a leaping dolphin,
Jumping from the water,
Its sharp tail flicks and shakes,
As it shoots back into the depths.

When it moves through the water,
Its flexible body darts,
Forwards and backwards, side to side,
Its motion is swift and speedy.

It glides out of the water,
To softly take a breath,
Then dives back in the water,
Not feeling the bitter chill.

It chatters to other dolphins,
Underneath the sea,
Calls of danger, calls of happiness,
As it makes its journey onwards.

Flora Lewis (11)
The Bishop of Hereford's Bluecoat School, Tupsley

Why Must There Be Classes In The Moneymaking World?

Fifty pounds is a lot to the poor,
But a cheap bottle of wine for those who have more.

Living on streets in a cardboard box,
They're lucky if they can afford some socks.

Never-ending death or pain,
Drinking water from a drain.

Fresh water from every tap,
To buying a designer cap.

Having enough money to spend,
But not enough to lend.

Never taking anything for granted,
Every moneymaking scheme planted.

Ellise Leamy, Laura Pitaway & Charlotte Powell (12)
Waseley Hills High School, Rubery

Through The Eyes Of The Homeless

I have nowhere to live
I have nowhere to go
I am out here on the streets
Waiting for dough
The night comes, I feel insecure
I wish someone loved me for sure
I need to use some aftershave
But then again, I need a shave
Everyone trying not to cross my path
Only because I need a bath
I sit in this doorway yawning
Waiting for the morning
It's time to get up
To catch the morning rush.

Steven Biles (13)
Waseley Hills High School, Rubery

Through The Eyes Of The Homeless

Every doorway, every street
Is a home for the homeless to warm their feet.

Everyone just points and stares
I just give them a dirty glare.

I beg for money every day
And most of the time they do not pay.

I like to think I've got friends
But none of them lives round the bend.

I like to think that I'm people I know
But all I am is a stupid hobo.

I live outside a corner shop
And watch the kids who like to hop.

Luke Green (13)
Waseley Hills High School, Rubery

Bubblewrap The World!

If we could change some things,
About the world today,
It would be the wars in Iraq
And the starving poverty.
So if the rich and famous,
Could spare a little cash,
Towards HIV, AIDs and cancer,
To help bubblewrap the world.

They waste their money so foolishly,
They don't know what they're doing,
The cure could be right in front of them,
But they are too blind to see,
Life's just not fair for the patients,
Who are fighting till they fall,
Give a little patience,
To help bubblewrap the world!

Laura Harrison & Marie Dipple (12)
Waseley Hills High School, Rubery

Remember Me

Remember me,
Remember me for being there when you needed me,
Remember me for being a rock star,
Remember me for starting a new age of music,
Remember me for saving you in the war,
Remember me for inventing the weapon that doesn't kill,
Remember me.

Forget me for leaving you alone in the street,
Forget me for being booed off stage,
Forget me for copying other people's music,
Forget me for leaving you on the battlefield,
Forget me for killing millions with my invention,
Forget me.

I wanted to be a good friend,
I wanted to be a rock star,
I wanted my own music,
I wanted to be a good soldier,
I wanted to be famous,
But I waited,
Life is a gem, your gem,
Spend it how and when you want to,
Don't wait
And please,
Remember me.

Sean Dunn (13)
Waseley Hills High School, Rubery

Victim Of A Bully

I felt so sad today,
Oh why would the bully not go away?
Was it me, the way I looked
Or was it the way I dressed
And thought about the past?
Oh why would this never last?

I am so clever,
She is so silly,
That's why she made me
A victim of a bully.

She thinks she's 'it',
Stomping around,
She thinks she's so big,
But she looks like a clown.

Now I start to understand,
Why she has to pull me down,
It's just that she wants to feel proud.

To all the bullies out there,
This one's for you,
I know what you're going through
And feel so sorry for you,
You can't feel respect for yourself
If you can do that to me,
But it's OK, you're the bully, not me!

Brittany Colley (12)
Waseley Hills High School, Rubery

Why?

Why do people turn bad in the world?
Why doesn't everyone have a good heart?
Why doesn't everyone do good in life?
Why don't we all die happily?
Why?

Why do we have starving children in Africa?
It's just something that nobody knows.
Why don't they have a water supply
Or why don't they have a meal every day?
Why don't we all die happily?
Why?

Why don't people live to see the world?
Amazing places like Egypt.
Why do innocent people die like that?
Why do people get illnesses like cancer?
Why can't we all die happily?
Why?

Aaron McGowan (12)
Waseley Hills High School, Rubery

Homeless

H omeless
O utside in all weathers
M oving from place to place
E verlasting worry of things ahead
L iked by nobody
E verlasting struggle
S eeing the world go by
S o lonely, so sad, so alone.

Raine Parker (12)
Waseley Hills High School, Rubery

What Annoys Me?

What annoys me the most
Is a thing you get in the post,
A letter saying you have so long to live,
With no one willing just to give,
To give people a little light,
And help them get a good fight,
In a battle of a lifetime,
The battle of a lifetime is cancer.

It annoys me that,
The people who are dying,
Are left alone while they're crying,
And the people who are drunk,
And act like a punk,
Get treatment for their stupidity.

It is just so unfair,
That no one seems to even care,
About the deserving people in pain,
And others leaving their life in the drain,
How can someone be so heartless?

Hannah Eustace (13)
Waseley Hills High School, Rubery

Homeless

I sit on the street
With nothing to eat
I walk around, the pain hitting me
Yet no one seems to help me
I beg for money, hoping I'll eat
But I won't because I have nothing . . .
Nothing.

Ben Warren (12)
Waseley Hills High School, Rubery

The Dog

One day we went to the park
They tied me up and went to play
I saw them playing and having fun
I sat there tied to the post
I had been left there all day
Nobody came back for me
They had left me and were never going to come back
I loved my owners so much
I thought they loved me back
I was sitting there all night
In the shivering cold
I was really sad
I went to sleep attached to the post by my lead
Then in the morning
I was woken up by something strange
People were cuddling me and wrapping me up warm
I looked at them, I thought it was my owners
But no, I was so disappointed, but happy as well
I was hoping that they were going to take me home
They picked me up and put me in the car
Then we got to a little house on the corner of the road
I got put into a basket by a warm fire
They gave me some food
They looked after me better than my old owners.

Elle Horton (12)
Waseley Hills High School, Rubery

My Great Adventure

Life is but a dream to me
I travel alone, just me, me, me
Just me, my rope and my little dog
Together we fight a mummy or two
Fall in traps, lose a shoe

We went to Egypt to visit one day
I got lost in a cave
The floor just gave way
I thought it was funny at first
Just walking through the tomb all alone!

As I walked through the tomb
I closed my eyes and thought of home
Cobwebs, spiders all around
My knees were weakening
I fell to the ground.

I managed to escape that day
Out the tomb and on my way
It was a great adventure I must admit
But I was frightened just a bit!

But now I'm stuck back here again
In my office with my pen
Thinking of the world out there
Egypt, Spain, Africa, Asia, do I dare?

Charlotte Robinson (12)
Waseley Hills High School, Rubery

Through The Eyes Of The Homeless

I try, I try, I really do,
But all I get back is a pile of poo!
The words they say are not very nice,
But all I want is a bowl of rice.

They do not care how we feel,
They just think that we're not real,
I have no money or a job,
It's not my fault that I'm a slob.

The things I do are so embarrassing,
When people I know are just so ravishing,
They all go past with that dirty look,
It makes me feel that I'm the crook.

I sleep at night and in the street,
When all this time I have cold feet,
I want some tea in a big mug,
And my mom to kiss and hug.

Jordan Jones (13)
Waseley Hills High School, Rubery

Homeless

I sit here in the freezing cold rain
In this bloody doorway
Sparking up a fag and taking a drag
Sipping a bottle of Pusser's rum
As hunger rushes through my body
I suddenly feel a touch of frost on my back
As I turn there is a strange looking man
Like he's going to knock seven shades out of me
'Move, you lump of dirt, out of my doorway'
As I move in fear.

Toby Hardwick (13)
Waseley Hills High School, Rubery

English, Oh English

English, oh English, what a bore,
Who cares about some stupid metaphor?
Similes, metaphors, they're all the same,
If I don't know them, then who's to blame?

What was that, was it a comet?
Oh damn, it was just the bore of a sonnet.
My lessons are over, free from alliteration,
So I'm going to play netball, away from concentration.

But wait, I've just remembered I've got a detention,
Next time in English I'll have to pay attention.
I had to write about a load of nonsense,
Gurgeley spitya, laughing lipple constence.

Mr Hall told me to look up onomatopoeia,
So I leant forward, falling on my rear.
At last it was over, I was saved by the bell,
But now I've got German, I'd rather go to Hell.

Ruth Cornford (13)
Waseley Hills High School, Rubery

Dream Crusher

Dream crusher
Life rusher
Cancer patients in the dark
While idiots get a great new start
Chemo makes you tired and weak
Some people think that you're a freak
Drunks and druggies get help for free
But not for poor people like him and me
I could die today, will you remember me?
How I sat my kids on my knee
As I fade away
Tell them that I love them
I love them every day.

Chloe Eustace (13)
Waseley Hills High School, Rubery

The Universse

U niverse is where we all live. There are many galaxies and stars in the universe. We are
N ot alone in the universe. There are many solar systems
I n the Milky Way. The Milky Way is travelling towards the
V irgo super cluster alone with its neighbour, Andromeda.
E very part of the universe is different. Spiralling nebulae millions of miles across create stars.
R ed giants dominate parts of the universe. Supernovas are the largest of the stars. We live in the
S olar system with our sun helping us thrive on our home planet
E arth.

Thomas Hill (12)
Waseley Hills High School, Rubery

The Lonely Dog

I thought my owners loved me,
All the treats and love they gave me,
For a while they had been acting strange,
Then one night we went out for a walk.
It was the middle of winter and cold and windy,
We walked down the road towards the park.
He tied me to the gate,
Then he walked away and left me.
At first I thought he would come and get me,
I was there for hours howling and barking.
Then eventually a smart-looking woman came to get me,
She gave me dinner, treats and love and took me to a place.
There were loads of dogs there and they treated me really well,
They took me for long walks and played with me every day.
I stayed there for ages and then a family came to get me,
They took me home with them.
Now I have been there for ages and they are my new family.

Jade Evans (12)
Waseley Hills High School, Rubery

You Don't Know What You've Got Until It's Gone

I am there in the summer on the boiling hot days
I am there in the winter on the freezing cold days
You walk on me, spit on me, throw your rubbish on me
Let your dogs run on me
I save you from getting run over
I guide you on your way to work, school
Wherever you're going, I am there
No one cares about me, you take me for granted
If I wasn't there you'd miss me
I guess you don't know what you've got until its gone
Maybe you should think about someone else other than yourself
From time to time, including me, the pavement!

Mica Millward (13)
Waseley Hills High School, Rubery

My Tilly Tu Tu

My Tilly Tu Tu, my Tilly Tu Tu.
Morning arrives, jumps on my bed,
Nuzzles my face, it's time to get fed.
Lies on her back,
What about that.
Rolls in fun,
Now tickle my tum.
Sits in the window, stares into space,
When will Hannah return from that place?
Sleeps in the armchair without a care,
But pick her up if you dare.
Walks about the house, so proud and content,
With her head in the air, as if it's meant.
Eats spiders and flies, too slow to get away.
Always my friend to love and to play.
My Tilly Tu Tu, my Tilly Tu Tu.

Hannah Mantle (13)
Waseley Hills High School, Rubery

Big Bad Bully

Every day I dread going to school
There is a boy who makes me feel a fool
He thinks he's big, all hard and clever
But when I sit there I think, *yeah, whatever*
Every day he asks for my money
But I really don't find this funny
I ate my lunch as fast as I could
He was jealous, so he pushed me in the mud
I ran away all lonely and sad
Then I thought, *that big bad bully drives me mad*
I realised he really couldn't beat me
The very next day I will make him see
In period 1 he asked for my money
I said, 'You're joking ain't ya, stop being funny!'
Then a few days on
He made me number one.

Jill Sanders (12)
Waseley Hills High School, Rubery

My Best Friend

She is my nurse
She is my taxi driver
She's my security
And my nail painter.

She is my hairdresser
And my washer upper
She is the person who loves me
No matter what.

She is my role model
She is my homework moaner
She is my teacher
And my clothes buyer.

She is my best friend
And I call this person Mom.

Lucinda Hammond (12)
Waseley Hills High School, Rubery

In My Paws

There I sit, whimpering beneath his feet
As my heartless trainer taunts me with the meat
Every night I go to sleep terrified of him
He starves me till I'm skin and bone and gives me broken limbs!
I'm woken up at midnight as he tumbles through the door
A bottle of whiskey in his hand, he's never sober anymore
As I hear him climb the stairs, I start to tremble with fear
His footsteps getting slightly louder
I hope he doesn't find me here.
I lie in the shadows worrying whether this madness will ever wear out
Then he approaches the doorway and I think he's sniffed me out!
I know what I've got in store tonight
He'll perform the whole routine of beating, teasing, screaming
and shouting.
This stuff's more than mean
I think about what's in line for tomorrow
A day of impossible chores
Just think about what this would be like for you
Just put yourself in my paws!

Charlie Jaffa (12)
Waseley Hills High School, Rubery

Through A Cat's Eyes

C reeping towards mice and rats
A ctive at night
T ail's waggling, waiting to pounce
S leeping through daylight

E yes gleaming in total darkness
Y ummy fish swimming in the pond
E verything to play with
S itting on fences dreaming all day.

Laura Bennett (13)
Waseley Hills High School, Rubery

Through The Eyes Of A Blind Man

Nothing can be seen, it's all black
I have all senses except one that I lack
The one I lack is sight
It is all black, there is no light

The hardest thing of all
Is that everyone thinks I'm not cool
I use my ears to guide me around
If I wander off, I'll never be found

My guide dog stays by my side all day
He is very nice, he has no pay
My cane has served me very well
It has helped me around, I have never fell

All I can hear are people around me
I recognise their voices but I can't see
The sound of cars zooming past
As I walk, I don't go fast

Oh, how many times I wish I could see
If that's how God made me, it is to be
Our intellectual skills are as good
As the people who are able to see

The happiness of us blind in life
I have a great family and a great wife
We are as ordinary as those with sight
Even though we see no light.

Matthew Maneffa (12)
Waseley Hills High School, Rubery

I'm Sick Of It!

I'm sick of it!
Us animals being dumped
We're on the streets
On our own, hungry
Oh, I wish I was indoors.

I'm sick of it!
I'm bred to fight
Then I get rescued by the RSPCA
Oh, I can't go home
But I'm safe and happy now
I get sponsors and visitors
Here comes one now
I hate being a dog.

I'm sick of it!
I want to go home again
Me and the cats, at home again
I don't want to be with this man
He kicks my tummy
I hate being a cat.

I'm sick of it!
Being dragged around the beach
I'm a cheap funfair ride that's what many people think
It's not fair on me and it's bad for my back
All I need is a good home to help me get back on track
I hate being a donkey.

Helen Webster (12)
Waseley Hills High School, Rubery

Scouting

Scouting is so fun and great
Founded by Baden Powell
Watching over his largest troop
With the fleur de lys in its little loop

He trained me up until I was ready
To go on camp on one little island
It's Brownsea Island, it's special now
As one big stone stands to alert,
Guarding his big worldwide family of scouts, which he created in 1907

I wonder if he could see us now
Way up there with us making things as he once did
Doing crafts and making dampers and helping others as he told us
So there are a few words
I wanna say, it's that
If he didn't live then I
Wouldn't be here obeying
His laws and my promise

So happy birthday scouting.

William Bowen (12)
Waseley Hills High School, Rubery

This Is What It's Like . . .

This is what it's like being a boat
The everlasting struggle to stay afloat
I hate being in locks
I'd rather be in the docks
This is what it's like being a boat

I hate the winter
The river rises
And I struggle against the current
This is what it's like being a boat

In the winter my owners don't come
Other boats flee
To the marina or basin
This is what it's like being a boat

In the summer
My owners arrive in their Hummer
We go off down the river
For a spot of dinner.

Matt Bisp (13)
Waseley Hills High School, Rubery

Animal Farm

Old Major who everyone admires,
Wants the farm led away from liars.

Snowball and Napoleon are pre-eminent,
Snowball so intelligent,
Gets abolished by Jessie's puppies.

Muriel the wise, tries to advise,
But near the end she unfortunately dies.

Squealer the sly and mean,
Helped Napoleon sell his dream.

Boxer, the shire horse, so dependable and kind,
Works harder to support the system so full of lies - the workers cannot find.

Napoleon is overcome with power,
By his dictatorship and violence,
Over the others he hopes to tower.

People of Russia, China, Zimbabwe, Burma,
All have their voices hushed
When they speak of their leader's tyranny.
We need to help the people escape from
Hunger, disease and repression
To help their lives have a happier ending.

Stephanie Willan (13)
Waseley Hills High School, Rubery

The Lad From London

There was a lad from London
He loved to drink and eat
But then he began to realise
His talent within his feet

He trialled at a local team
His boots were sparkling gold
He had been watching all the videos
The legends new and old

His manager played him in all positions
But he knew he was best as a winger
He started to run past quality defenders
He could win games with his little finger

But then in late October
He was caught with a vicious kick
His teammates saw his leg was broken
The sight made them feel so sick

It had come to the end of the season
He was still to fully recover
A pretty girl had been staring sympathetically
He had a secret lover.

Mitchell Booth (13)
Waseley Hills High School, Rubery

See Me, Hear Me, Please Can You May?

I'm stuck in a world of coldness and pain,
I do things no one sees with nothing to gain.
Why are those people so much better?
Only way I get noticed is in a letter.
No one even sees me when I go past,
When will they notice me at last?
I try to make them see me, I do everything, I even do a card,
Why to me is life so hard?
People not seeing me is like being pushed to the floor,
My world is so poor.
My life's getting so old
And everything is turning cold.
How do I sum up my life, what do I say?
See me, hear me, please can you may
I try and I try,
But inside I just fry,
I write my life in a piece of text,
What do I do next?
They have nothing to lose, only something to gain,
So why do I sit in pain?

Connie Basnett (13)
Waseley Hills High School, Rubery

Do You Know What You Put Me Through?

Nobody knows the tears I've cried,
Maybe if it was dramatic, maybe if I died.
Nobody knows the pain I've felt,
All the insults and punches they pelt.
Nobody knows me, no one at all,
As I keep them all out by building my wall.
But bullies provoke, so they all carry on,
I want some help, but there is no one.

'Enough is enough' as my mom scanned the note,
Glanced over her shoulder and saw my red throat.
With one clean slash from the kitchen knife,
It was stolen from me, my precious life.
'Look what they've done, done to her now.'
'What they call fun, but I want to know how.'

So I leave some advice for you to take in,
So you never live regret, sorrow or sin.
Bullies aren't funny, clever or kind,
So be who you are and bear this in mind.

Heather Rogers (13)
Waseley Hills High School, Rubery

To Change The World

Kids have to put up with a hell of a lot,
Of the stupid ones who don't want a life,
Of school uniforms that make you itch,
And all sorts of trouble and strife.

And another thing, money,
While Beckham is out making truck loads
Of cash that he could put to better use,
Starvation is plaguing us like toads.

Have you got a fiver?
Would you give it to a starving dog
Or a starving child?
I know what I'd do.

In the UK we value dogs more than kids,
Scary isn't it?
Stupid?
Just a bit.

What would you do to change the world?
I'll leave you to decide.

Hannah Clarke (12)
Waseley Hills High School, Rubery

Who's To Blame?

In this world there's so much pain,
But who exactly is to blame?
Some with so much, some without any,
And those with it all don't give a penny.
Would it hurt to give a bit
With what you get for wearing a football kit?

Even the animals, it's not fair,
Lots of them don't get enough care.
Their habitats are disappearing,
When others just care about what they're singing.
Why should they get so much more than doctors and nurses?
Some of them don't have anything in their purses.

I think that it's just not fair, that hardly anyone seems to care,
About anything other than their clothes and their hair.
In this world there's so much pain,
But who exactly is to blame?

Louisa McKinley (12)
Waseley Hills High School, Rubery

Africa

My sister is dying,
My mama is dead,
We use a dustbin for a bed.
Living off scraps
And sleeping in rags,
Under our eyes sit big black bags.

It's late at night,
And Maya is crying,
I whisper to her, but I know she's dying.
We've had nothing to eat,
For a fifth night in a row,
For the weather is too hot
For our crops to grow.

It's really early, 5am,
And I'm off to work, at only ten.
Never will I see school again.
I'm earning pennies,
But it gets us some bread,
Without the money,
We'd both be dead.

When I get home, Maya is bad,
Looking at her is making me sad.
When, when, when will I be glad?
She closes her eyes,
And I know she's dead,
I place a rag over her head.

She's buried next to Mama,
Under the tree,
I can't believe it,
Maya's left me.
So, I'm still here,
One month on,
I have nothing now,
My family is gone.
For how long will I be the only one?

Alice Coley (12)
Waseley Hills High School, Rubery

TWMC

T he world must change
H owever some things must be left
E ven all the people and, unfortunately, the schools

W e should all work together
O r at least most of us should
R ight
L eft
D on't hide, change will happen

M e, you, everyone
U ndoubtedly
S hould all work together
T o change the world for good

C ome now to help us
H ang on to our words
A bbreviate our sayings
N oah's done it once
G et in and help us again
E very single person.

Jamie Jones (12)
Waseley Hills High School, Rubery

A Cat's Life

A lways relaxed

C alm
A ttacking mice occasionally
T aking it easy
S ilently creeping

L ying around the house
I dle
F erocious in a fight
E ndlessly sleeping.

Ailsa Loane (12)
Waseley Hills High School, Rubery

Dreams

I dream of getting out of my cage,
To run around in the wild with my friends.
But this is just an ordinary dream,
They make me dance in the early dawn.
They hit me when I go wrong,
I stay in my cage tied up for the whole day.
They take me out at night,
I follow them with fright.
I wish I could go back home
To my family,
I wish I could snuggle up next to my mum.
I dream that one day I will wake up
Next to my friends.
I keep memories to help me survive.
I wish I had some food,
But they starve me.
They give me rotten meat,
I feel sick at the thought of eating.
I push back the pain
And dance like they tell me.
Sometimes I feel I should die
And end it all.

Tanya Shahnawaz (13)
Woodfield Middle School, Redditch

My Dream

I woke up this morning again
As usual there were loads of people round me
I was in the cage and they were staring at me
I felt so weird
I wanted them to go away
But no! they have to stand there all the time
I don't understand . . .
A while ago I was with my mom and brothers
Now, I just have to sit here
I'm not having fun at all
They don't even feed me properly
I want to be with my family again!
I had a dream last night . . .
I was with them and they were running around
We started chasing each other
Like we used to - quite a lot
Then I woke up
Well, I wouldn't if not for all those children
Why do they have to be so loud?
This is just tiring . . .
Am I so bad?
I want to go back.

Weronika Hanczewska (12)
Woodfield Middle School, Redditch

The Chicken

I wish I could run around as a free-range chicken
I wish I could be snuggled up nice and warm in a chicken hut
Well I'm not
I'm cramped, cold and hungry
I wish I could keep my eggs warm
And see them grow to little chicks
Well, they take them away
Feed them to you lot
What have I done to you?
If you kill me
How will my dreams come true?

Amie Coles (12)
Woodfield Middle School, Redditch

Dreams

I dream, I dream of wonderful things
Elephants dancing and pigs with wings.
I dream, I dream of all the money then
I think of all the kids with no food in their tummies.
I dream, I dream that they're alright
All through the day and all through the night.

Toni Maoudis (12)
Woodfield Middle School, Redditch

Dream

I dream, I dream of sparkling things,
I look up at night and see fairy wings,
I dream about a fairy tale all of the time,
I wish I could live one, it would be so fine.
Another night comes, I tuck up tight,
And wish tomorrow would be another surprise.

Brooke Taylor (12)
Woodfield Middle School, Redditch

Dreams!

I dream of birds flying in the sky
Flapping their wings fast as they go by.
I dream of a butterfly being all different colours
And shining in the sky.
I dream of winning the lottery
And getting a big, big house.
I dream of having a St Bernard.
I dream, I dream, I dream.
I dream of being a national netball player shooting hoops.
I dream of being in a fantasy of my own.
I dream, I dream, I dream.
I dream of being an artist.
I dream of being a diva star.
I dream, I dream, I dream.
I wish I wouldn't fill my head
With all these beautiful dreams.

Elisha Prosser (13)
Woodfield Middle School, Redditch

My Dream

Here I am sat in a cage,
As cramped as cramped can be.
Where on Earth is my dream?
Why can't it come true?
I am here all day through.
My dream is to have luscious green grass to chew
And fresh water to drink.
I wish that I never had to see bars of a cage again
And had open-space fields with trees for shelter too.
Why aren't I free?
What did I do to you?
I know my dream will never come true!

Shannon Skett (12)
Woodfield Middle School, Redditch

Young Writers Information

We hope you have enjoyed reading this book - and that you will continue to enjoy it in the coming years.

If you like reading and writing poetry drop us a line, or give us a call, and we'll send you a free information pack.

Alternatively if you would like to order further copies of this book or any of our other titles, then please give us a call or log onto our website at www.youngwriters.co.uk

Young Writers Information
Remus House
Coltsfoot Drive
Peterborough
PE2 9JX

(01733) 890066

The Conduct of Meetings

by
T. P. E. Curry, Q.C., M.A. of Middle Temple and Lincoln's Inn
J. Richard Sykes, M.A. of Lincoln's Inn; Barrister at Law
and
Philip L. Heslop, B.A. LL.B. of Lincoln's Inn; Barrister at Law

Twenty-First Edition
1975
Published by
Jordan & Sons Limited

First Edition – 1910

Twenty-First Edition – 1975

ISBN 0 85308 083 0 Cased Edition

ISBN 0 85308 037 2 Limp Edition

Published by
Jordan & Sons Limited,
Pembroke Road,
Bristol BS8 3BH.

Printed and bound in Great Britain by
Butler & Tanner Limited
Frome and London

Preface to the Twenty-First Edition

The editors had been expecting some statutory changes to company law: but these have not yet come and accordingly the book has been revised once again and brought up to date in the light of decisions since the last edition.

In addition, there has been substantial re-writing of the parts relating to proxies and to the duties of chairman of company meetings: these matters have, in recent years, attained a greater importance in the changing attitudes and procedures. With the increasing vigilance of the City Panel, it is hoped that the changes included will be helpful to those who have to take decisions quickly.

T.P.E.C.

J.R.S.

Lincoln's Inn April 1975

Acknowledgement

The publishers gratefully acknowledge the editorial assistance received from both Professor Gordon J. Borrie and Mr. A. Harding Boulton in the production of this book.

Table of Contents

Table of Cases

Table of Cases

PART ONE

Meetings: General Principles

CHAPTER 1

Meetings

Meetings with which this book is concerned are of two main types: first, what are called public meetings, being meetings convened by individuals or bodies and to which there is an open invitation extended to any member of the public: secondly, meetings of bodies of which the members are limited and known.

Meetings of both categories are governed to some extent by the general law. In addition, meetings of the second category normally are governed by bye laws or regulations relating to the convening and conduct of the meetings and ancillary matters: these bye-laws or regulations may be statutory (*e.g.* for meetings of local authorities) or they may exist by agreement between the members of the corporation or association concerned (such, for example, are the relevant articles of association of a company incorporated under the Companies Acts). For public meetings, on the other hand, there will not be any such bye-laws or regulations. To a limited extent there may be regulations imposed by government or local authorities which impose restrictions or obligations, but that is all.

This book is concerned principally with meetings of the second category. The commonest type of such bodies is the company incorporated under the Companies Acts: in addition there are companies incorporated under particular Acts, companies incorporated by Charter, local authorities, clubs, trade associations, trade unions, unit trusts, industrial and provident societies, friendly societies, building societies, sporting associations, political associations, *ad hoc* committees set up for particular purposes, local amenity committees, and numerous other bodies.

The principles relating to meetings apply to meetings of all such bodies. Actual detailed provisions will vary in every case, as needs vary: for example, the needs of the Amateur Athletic Association are different from the needs of a local cricket club, or a local Anti-litter Society, and these in turn are different from those of a large public company with several thousand shareholders. There are differences between meetings of the governing body of an association (*e.g.* the directors of a company or the executive committee of a political association) and meetings of the members. But the principles are the same for all such meetings.

This book therefore deals first with meetings in general: and where convenient mentions particular requirements for certain types of bodies. It then contains separate sections dealing with Public Meetings (Part II), Meetings of Companies Incorporated under the Companies Acts (Part III) and Meetings of Local Authorities (Part IV). These separate parts must all be read in the light of, and subject to, the general principles in Part I.

The matters to be considered in relation to meetings can conveniently be broken up into separate headings:

(1) who may attend, and how are meetings convened?
(2) what constitutes a valid meeting and what business may be dealt with?
(3) how is the meeting conducted?
(4) how are decisions recorded?

The succeeding chapters of this Part I answer these questions in general terms. These general terms apply to all bodies except in so far as statute or their own regulations make modifications.

CHAPTER 2

The Convening of Meetings: Notices and Agenda

Before a meeting can be duly constituted it must have been duly convened. The body concerned will usually have regulations providing for this. These will state who may call meetings, who is to be entitled to receive notice, how notice is to be given, and the information to be contained in the notice.

In the case of a company incorporated under the Companies Acts most of the provisions as to meetings are to be found in the company's Articles of Association or in the Act. These are dealt with in Part III. Similarly, in the case of local authorities there are various rules contained in statutes which govern the holding of meetings, and these are dealt with in Part IV. Other bodies may be subject to their own rules as to meetings.

There is, however, a number of general principles applicable to most meetings of bodies of this kind. It should be borne in mind that the principles stated in this Part will apply only where the relevant rules governing the meeting in question do not otherwise provide. The application of these principles is further considered in Chapter 14.

So that a meeting may be validly convened, proper notice must be given to *each member entitled to notice* in strict accordance with the standing orders or rules of the body, organisation, or society affected, and such notice must be issued by the proper officer, person, or authority. Where the rules do not specify how much notice must be given, a reasonable notice must be given which will give those whose duty or right it is to attend the opportunity to do so. If a practice grows up of giving a certain length of notice, this will be held to be reasonable in the absence of any particular circumstance to negative such a conclusion.

The requirement for notice does not arise in some cases. Certain bodies, for instance, hold their meetings on specified days or dates and at specified times and places. Committees of local councils usually fix their meetings for the year shortly after the annual elections: many companies have board meetings fixed in advance. In some cases the practice grows up of sending out no notice, or only giving notice at the beginning of each year or session of meetings which will be held in that period. Such a practice is valid, unless, of course, it contravenes specific requirements of the regulations of the body concerned.

(1) *Notice must* (*in the absence of provisions to the contrary*) *be given to every person entitled to attend.*—The omission to summon one member to a corporate meeting avoids the acts of that meeting.[1]

In *Dobson v. Fussy*[2] the question arose whether certain persons were duly assembled as a select vestry. The meeting was held on an unusual day, and no notice was given to one of the members of the special vestry. The Court, accordingly, held that they were not duly assembled as a special vestry.

A public body entrusted with the performance of a public duty cannot hold an extraordinary meeting unless all the members be summoned who can be summoned, or the unsummoned members are actually present at such meeting. The proceedings at a meeting at which any individual is not present who might have been summoned and was not summoned are void, though the omission be accidental, or though the individual has given a general notice that he wishes not to be summoned[3] or the convening officer thought that a certain member was out of the summons.[4] It is competent, however, as, for example, in the case of companies, for the relevant rules to provide that certain classes of members need not be given notice of certain classes of meetings, and also that accidental omission to give a member notice of a meeting is not to invalidate the proceedings at that meeting. The right of an enemy at common law or under the Trading with the Enemy Act 1939 to notice of meetings of a company of which he is a member, is suspended, and a meeting is properly held though no notice has been given to such a person.[5]

In many cases provision is made for notice to be given by advertisement, and this is effective. Such advertisement may be required to be inserted in a newspaper or posted in some specified place. If the requirement is complied with, notice is duly given. This is of particular advantage where the persons entitled to notice are unknown, such as holders of bearer warrants, or are all the parishioners in a parish or some such body.

(2) *Notice not essential if all entitled to attend are present.*—But if all the persons entitled to attend are present and agree to what is

[1] *R. v. Mayor, etc., of Shrewsbury* (1735) Cas. *temp.* Hardw. 147.
[2] (1831) 7. Bing, 305.
[3] *R. v. Langhorne* (1836) 6 N. & M. 203.
[4] *R. v. Mayor, etc., of Shrewsbury* (*supra*).
[5] *Re Anglo-International Bank, Ltd.*, [1943] Ch. 233.

proposed, the proceedings cannot afterwards be invalidated on the ground of lack of notice. "The Court would never allow it to be said that there was an absence of resolution when all the shareholders have expressly assented to that which is being done."[1]

(3) *Absence beyond reasonable summoning distance (or possibly serious illness) of a person entitled to attend a meeting may sometimes be a good reason for not summoning him.*—"The election being by a definite body on a day of which, till summons, the electors had no notice, they were all entitled to be specially summoned, and if there was any omission to summon any one of them, unless they all happened to be present, or unless those not summoned were beyond summoning distance (as, for instance, abroad), there could not be a good electoral assembly, and even a unanimous election by those who did attend would be void."[2]

In *re Portuguese Consolidated Copper Mines*,[3] a director of a company, on being told a meeting would be held next week, said, "I cannot be there." It was held that this could not be relied on as a waiver of his right to notice, and as no notice was sent to him the meeting was declared invalid. "Perhaps if a member were at such a distance that it would be absolutely impossible for him to attend, then the secretary might be excused from sending a notice to him and the meeting would be properly convened. Possibly the same exception might hold good when a member was so dangerously ill that he could not be moved."[4]

It is desirable to send notices of meetings to all members in all circumstances, even to those who may be abroad, since it enables them to be kept fully informed of what is being done at meetings of bodies of which they are members.

In cases where the relevant rules so provide it is essential to the validity of a meeting that a notice should be sent to a member even though it cannot possibly reach him until after the meeting has taken place.

(4) *Notice should normally state nature of business: agenda.*—The notice convening the meeting should, in most cases, contain sufficient description of the nature of the business which the meeting is to transact, and the meeting cannot in ordinary cases go outside the business described in that notice.[5]

In some cases the practice is not to give any indication of the nature

[1] *Express Engineering Works*, [1920] 1 Ch. 466.
[2] *Smyth v. Darley* (1849) 2 H.L.C. 789, at 803.
[3] (1889) 42 Ch. D. 160.
[4] *Young v. Ladies' Imperial Club*, [1920] 2 K.B. 523.
[5] *Longfield Parish Council v. Wright* (1918) 88 L.J. (Ch.) 119.

of the business, unless there is something unusual to be considered. For example, notices of meetings of directors in many companies contain no agenda.

In other cases statute may specify what information should be given: thus in *Smith v. Deighton and Billington*[1] the following passage occurs:

"Undoubtedly it was the intention of the Legislature in framing this Statute to provide that due information should be given to all the parishioners of the special purpose for which their attendance is required. . . . As to the second part of the resolution—the making a rate for the general expenses of the parish—we are all clearly of opinion that the notice was wholly insufficient for that purpose [*i.e.* because the notice did not clearly apprise the parishioners of the special purposes for which the meeting was called] and that the provisions of the Statute have not been complied with."

In other cases the regulations governing the body concerned may provide that the nature of any business to be transacted, other than routine business, must be specified: see as regards companies under the Companies Acts, Chapter 14, *post*.

The object of requiring a proper notice of the purposes for which the meeting is to be held is to enable a member to exercise his own judgment as to whether he will attend or not. A notice may be good in part and bad in part, and it is not wholly invalid because it extends to something which cannot be done at the meeting.[2] The heading in a notice of "Any other business" will generally authorise the transaction of business of a purely formal nature but not business of any substantial importance. In *Young v. Ladies' Imperial Club*[3] it was held that as the notice of a meeting did not state the object of the meeting with sufficient particularity it was invalid and consequently the proceedings of that meeting were invalidated.

In the case of meetings of local authories and other meetings where the business consists of numerous items, the order and nature of business to be transacted is frequently stated on an agenda paper, more familiarly called "the agenda". It should, as a rule, be circulated with or as part of the notice to the members who are entitled to be present at the meeting, and often the notice and agenda form one document. The agenda should follow some common form, varying with the type of meeting and the business to be transacted. The order in which items of business should be taken is often regulated by standing orders and, if so, should not be departed from unless the

[1] (1852) 8 Moore P.C. 187.

[2] *Cleve v. Financial Corporation* (1873) L.R. 16 Eq. 363.

[3] [1920] 2 K.B. 523.

chairman, with the consent of the meeting, approves. No business should be placed on the agenda or transacted at a meeting unless it comes within the scope of the notice convening the meeting.

Agenda are often drawn up in the following order:

(1) Appointment of chairman (if there is no regular chairman).
(2) Verification of the correctness of the minutes of the previous meeting.
(3) Matters arising from previous meeting's minutes.
(4) Correspondence (a *précis* of ordinary and routine letters; important letters in full).
(5) Reports of committees and/or officers (reports are often given *in extenso*).
(6) Finance (consideration of accounts and financial questions).
(7) Any special business (the nature of which should be specifically and explicitly stated).
(8) Other motions which can properly be brought before the meeting.
(9) General business.
(10) Date of next meeting.

Under general business an opportunity may be taken to deal with any formal or unimportant matters, such as a resolution to pay a tradesman's bill. If, however, the relevant rules provide that notice must be given of the business to be transacted, no business of any real importance can be transacted under this head unless proper notice of it has been given.[1] In preparing the agenda, care should be taken to include therein all the business to be transacted, with sufficient detail to enable the members to grasp what it means.

An agenda should be clear and explicit, and in a summary form. It should enable the members to ascertain what matters will be discussed, and, if circulated before-hand, give them an opportunity of forming some opinion as to the course which they will adopt at the meeting. A properly drawn-up agenda prevents many questions being put to the chair, considerably shortens a meeting, and helps to get the sense of the meeting in an intelligent and expeditious manner. Further, a well-arranged agenda prevents much confusion and irritation through members speaking on insufficient facts. It is generally advisable to consult the chairman of the meeting in preparing the agenda.

If ordinary routine business is being transacted, notes of the decisions arrived at may be made on the agenda, particularly when a wide margin or space is left for that purpose; but it is generally

[1] *Longfield Parish Council v. Wright*, 88 L.J. (Ch.) 119.

advisable to have a rough minute book, so that, when necessary, a detailed and more correct record of the proceedings may be taken. The agenda should be filed and kept for reference.

(5) *Notices must be explicit.*—They must be frank, open, clear, satisfactory and free from "trickiness". A resolution passed on the basis of an unfair or inadequate disclosure of information in the notice is invalid.[1] "The Court does not scrutinise these notices with a view to exercise criticism, or to find out defects, but it looks at them fairly. I think the question may be put in this form: What is the meaning which this notice would fairly carry to ordinary minds? That, I think, is a reasonable test."[2]

(6) *In giving notice of a meeting it is necessary to give in detail the following particulars:* place, date, day, and time of meeting. If one meeting is to be held immediately after another, it is desirable to fix the time of the second meeting when it is thought the first meeting will end, adding the alternative "or at the conclusion or adjournment of the previous meeting".

A meeting may not be convened for a Sunday (Sunday Observance Act 1833).

The place at which the meeting is to be held must be one which is accessible to the persons entitled to be present. A majority cannot bind a whole corporation if a minority is deprived of its right of attending the meeting, *e.g.* by holding a meeting in a place to which some members have no access or where the place of meeting is so inconvenient or small that it is physically impossible for all to be present. Every corporate act must be done at a meeting properly convened, properly constituted, and properly held at a place of meeting at which every member has the right to attend. The date of the meeting must be sufficiently far ahead to comply with any relevant requirements as to the length of notice for that meeting, and in the absence of any such provisions the notice should be of a reasonable length.

(7) *Adjourned meetings.*—A meeting may be adjourned to complete unfinished business; no notice of the adjourned meeting need be given unless the relevant rules otherwise provide, but no business not specified in the notice of the meeting may be transacted at the adjourned meeting. In some cases, however, the relevant rules require a new notice (cf. Clause 57 of Table A, Companies Act 1948).

(8) *Clear days' notice.*—Where the rules specify a particular length of notice but contain no other provision this means that the notice

[1] *Kaye v. Croydon Tramways*, [1898] 1 Ch. 358.

[2] *Henderson v. Bank of Australasia* (1890) 45 Ch. D., at 337.

must be given that number of "clear days" before the meeting. See *re Railway Sleepers Supply Co.*[1] and the authorities there cited.

"Clear days" means days exclusive of the day of the notice of service and of the day on which the meeting is to be held: *e.g.* when 14 days' notice is required notice for a meeting to be held on the 16th of the month must be served on the 1st. It will be necessary in each case to see from the rules when service is deemed to be effected. Thus in Table A (Clause 131) of the Companies Act 1948, service is deemed to have been affected 24 hours after the letter containing the same is posted and where this applies and notice is being given by post the notice required to be served on the 1st of the month in the above example would have to be posted on the last day of the previous month, even if a Saturday or Sunday.

Similarly the phrase "not less than twenty-one days' notice" in Section 141 of the Companies Act 1948, means 21 clear days' notice, exclusive of the day of service and of the day on which the meeting is to be held.

Where notice is to be given by advertisement the clear days count between the day on which the advertisement calling the meeting appears in a newspaper and the day of the meeting, and such notice is effectual even though it may not reach members until some days afterwards.[2]

In the absence of any express provision to the contrary Sundays will be included in computing the length of the notice. The Municipal Corporations Act 1882 provides that in the case of meetings under that Act when the notice required is of not more than seven days, a Sunday, Christmas Day, Good Friday, Monday or Tuesday in Easter Week or a day appointed for a public fast, humiliation, or thanksgiving is not to be included in computing the number of days.

[1] (1885) 29 Ch. D. 204.

[2] *Mercantile Investment Co. v. International Co. of Mexico*, [1893] 1 Ch. 484*n*.

CHAPTER 3

Quorum and Appointment of Chairman

Quorum

Regulations will almost invariably exist specifying the minimum number of members who must be present at a meeting to enable it to transact business. The acts of a corporation, other than a trading corporation, are those of the major part of the corporation, corporately assembled. In the absence of any express regulation or special custom, the major part must be present at the meeting, and of that major part there must be a majority in favour of the act done or resolution passed.[1] In the above circumstances (*i.e.* where there is no express regulation or special custom) the quorum of, say, a corporation of thirteen to constitute a valid meeting would be seven, and the act or resolution of the majority of these seven or greater number will bind the corporation.[2] [A trading corporation frequently acts without a resolution of the company, *e.g.* by its directors or by some other agent, but presumably the same principle would, in the absence of express provisions in the articles, apply to acts done or resolutions passed by meetings of such a corporation.]

Regulations generally provide for a lesser quorum than this, and so soon after the time for which the meeting was convened as that number is present the meeting may proceed to business. Generally speaking it will not be competent for a quorum to be fixed at one, for one person cannot normally constitute a meeting.[3] Unless specially provided, persons represented by proxy cannot be counted as present in forming a quorum, and only those members can be counted towards a quorum who are competent to take part in the business before the meeting.[4]

A quorum having once been constituted it is occasionally the practice, when the business of the meeting has once been properly started, to continue it unless some member objects and calls the attention of the chairman to the absence of a quorum, as is done in the

[1] *Merchants of the Staple of England v. Bank of England* (1887) 21 Q.B.D. 160.
[2] *Hascard v. Somany* (1693) Freem. K.B. 504.
[3] *Sharp v. Dawes* (1876) 2 Q.B.D. 26.
[4] *Yuill v. Greymouth, etc., Railway Co.*, [1904] 1 Ch. 32.

House of Commons. Business so transacted will generally be invalid. The Twelfth Schedule to the Local Government Act 1972, provides that business is not to be transacted unless the quorum required by the Act is present. Table A in the Companies Act provides in Article 53 that no business shall be transacted unless a quorum is present at the time when the meeting proceeds to business.

Under this Article, when read in conjunction with Article 54 (which covers occasions when the quorum is not present within half an hour), it was decided in *re Hartley Baird*,[1] that provided that members sufficient in number to form a quorum are present when the meeting proceeds to business it will not cease to be a valid meeting if some persons withdraw so that those present fall below the number required to constitute a quorum. Upon Wynn-Parry J.'s reasoning it would appear that even in the absence of a provision in the terms of Article 54, Article 53 requires the quorum when the meeting proceeds to business, but not otherwise. A different decision was reached in Scotland in *Henderson v. James Louttit & Co.*,[2] which Wynn-Parry J. declined to follow.

In calculating a quorum of creditors present at a first meeting in bankruptcy, only those who have lodged proofs can be included; consequently, if there is only one creditor who has lodged a proof and he is present, he forms a quorum and constitutes a meeting;[3] also, one person can be constituted a committee.

In the case of companies, however, see Chapter 15, *post*.

Appointment of Chairman

If a person is present who has previously been duly elected chairman or has for some other reason a right to take the chair, that person must take the chair. If there is no such person or such person is not present, the election of a chairman is necessary, and it is desirable in such cases that a temporary chairman, who is not a candidate for the chairmanship, should be chosen, merely for the purpose of electing the chairman.

The chairman may be elected for a particular meeting, or annually, or for a fixed period of time, or sometimes for life. There is usually nothing to prevent a person proposing or seconding himself as chairman; in any event, he is entitled to vote for himself.

Often there is a deputy-chairman or vice-chairman who takes the chair in the absence of the regular chairman at the appointed time.

Should the chairman and, if there is one, the vice-chairman be

[1] [1955] Ch. 143.

[2] (1894) 21 R. (Ct. of Sess.) 674.

[3] *Re Thomas, ex parte Warner* (1911) 55 S.J. 482; see also *East v. Bennett Bros.*, [1911] 1 Ch. 163.

absent, it is open to the members present to elect one of their number to the vacancy, who will retain his position even if the laggard chairman or vice-chairman turns up afterwards. Usually, however, the ordinary chairman is allowed a few minutes' grace before another member is elected to the chair. As a matter of courtesy, though not of right, the chairman thus appointed often gives way to the regular chairman upon the arrival of the latter by vacating the chair. This operates as a virtual resignation.

A chairman should always be punctual and regular in his attendance, and whenever possible should send notice to the meeting when he is likely to be absent or unavoidably late.

The opening remarks of the chairman should be brief and to the point. He should direct and control rather than lead a meeting.

How elected.—A person nominated to take the chair must be duly proposed and if there is more than one candidate, the decision of the meeting should be taken either by show of hands or, if the relevant rules so provide and a poll is properly demanded, by a poll. The actual putting of the motion for the election of a chairman to the vote is generally done by the proposer or secretary, but it is much better for a temporary chairman to be appointed, especially when there is a contested election. It cannot in any case be done by the person proposed to be elected as chairman, for "No man can preside at his own election and return himself."[1]

Objection to appointment of chairman.—Any objection to the nomination of a chairman should be made there and then. If it is not it will be too late afterwards to attempt to raise the question. "It is alleged that there was an irregularity in nominating the chairman; but it appears on a balance of the evidence that he was nominated and seconded. However, Mr. Bluck took the chair, and the meeting acquiesced and adopted him as chairman. In that capacity he was bound to declare, according to his means of knowledge, the sense of the meeting—that is the duty of the chairman."[2]

Assuming that his appointment is regular and in order, the newly-elected chairman then takes the chair.

Qualifications of a Chairman

"It's the chair as is speaking," said Mr. Gape, who had a true Englishman's notion that the chair itself could not be called to order.—*Orley Farm*, by ANTHONY TROLLOPE.

The chairman is the person responsible for the actual conduct of the proceedings. "There is not, as far as I know, any case which has

[1] *R. v. White* (1867) L.R., 2 Q.B., at 561.
[2] *Cornwall v. Woods* (1846) 4 No. of Cas. 559.

ever arisen to guide us in deciding how far the powers of a chairman extend. . . . Public meetings must be regulated somehow; and where a number of persons assemble and put a man in the chair they devolve on him, by agreement, the conduct of that body. They attorn to him, as it were, and give him the whole power of regulating themselves individually. This is within reasonable bounds. The chairman collects, as it were, his authority from the meeting."[1]

Duties of the Chairman

The chairman should be well acquainted with the statutory rules, standing orders, or other relevant rules of the body over which he is presiding, and his decisions must be governed and controlled by them.[2]

The chairman should:

(i) See that the meeting is properly convened in accordance with the rules and properly constituted—*i.e.* that proper notice was given; that there is a quorum of members present; and that his own appointment is regular and in order.

(ii) Take care that all the requirements of the relevant rules are duly observed.

(iii) See that the items of business are taken in the order set out in the agenda paper, unless that order is altered with the consent of the meeting.

(iv) Take care that due and sufficient opportunity is given to those who wish to speak (and particularly the minority) to express their views on the subject under debate or discussion. Speakers should be called on by name. The chairman has no right to prevent discussion upon a matter which is included in the notice convening a meeting, and he should see that the sense of the meeting is properly ascertained with regard to any question which is properly before the meeting.

(v) Allow no discussion unless there is some motion before the meeting.

(vi) Prevent irrelevant discussion, and forbid a second speech on the same motion except in the case of a proposer, when under the rules he has a right of reply.

(vii) Take the sense of the meeting by putting the motions and

[1] *Taylor v. Nesfield; Wills on Vestries, 29n.*

[2] The method of addressing a woman in the chair varies. She is sometimes addressed as "Mr. Chairman", more usually "Madam Chairman", she is also referred to in the course of the proceedings variously as "Sir" and "Madam". In the House of Commons a chairman is always addressed by name and not as "Mr. Chairman".

> amendments in proper form. Unless the relevant rules otherwise provide, voting will be by show of hands in the first place. In the case of elections governed by the common law there is a right to demand a poll. "The right to demand a poll being, therefore, as it appears to us, by the common law, an incident to the popular election of a person to an office, we think the electors cannot be deprived of it without a special custom of election inconsistent with such right or expressly excluding it by negative terms—*viz.* that no such right exists in the particular parish."[1] A similar right may exist in the case of meetings of particular bodies if the relevant rules are silent on the point.

The chairman is not necessarily *functus officio* when he has declared the result of the voting.[2] Before declaring that a motion is lost or carried, a chairman has a right to have a recount if he is uncertain who has voted for or against the motion. He must also decide all emergent questions which necessarily require decision at the time.[3] In the exercise of his authority, the chairman must act *bona fide*, and in the best interests of the meeting. If he is empowered to demand a poll, he is under a duty to do so if he believes that there is a large number of proxies which may reverse the result on a show of hands.[4] His decisions, even when not strictly correct, will be upheld by the Court, unless there is evidence that some substantial injustice has arisen therefrom or that they were not made in good faith.

In *ex parte Mawby*,[5] where a chairman of a vestry meeting rejected votes which were admissible, but such rejection caused no difference in the result, the Court declined to interfere; and in *Shaw v. Thompson*,[6] though the Court held that the conduct of the chairman was erroneous and illegal, it refused to declare the election null and void, on the ground that there was no evidence that the poll was improperly conducted or that any voter was prevented from recording his vote.

As to the chairman's powers of preserving order at the meeting, see Chapter 8 (*infra*), and as to his power to adjourn the meeting in the event of disorder, *post* p. 46.

[1] *Campbell v. Maund* (1836) 5 A. & E. 865.

[2] *Hickman v. Kent or Romney Marsh Sheepbreeders Association* (1920) 36 T.L.R. 528; affirmed (1921) 37 T.L.R. 163.

[3] *Re Indian Zoedone Co.* (1884) 26 Ch. D., at 77.

[4] *Second Consolidated Trust Ltd. v. Ceylon, etc., Estates Ltd.*, [1943] 2 All E.R. 567.

[5] (1854) 3 E. & B. 718.

[6] (1876) 3 Ch. D. 233.

The Casting Vote

In the absence of express provision a chairman has no second or casting vote, but this privilege may of course be conferred by the relevant rules which govern the meeting.

Where a chairman has a second or casting vote, if he intends to exercise both his votes he should give his first vote while the vote of the other members is being taken and before the result of the voting is apparent. It would be quite wrong for a chairman to reserve his votes and give, if the numbers proved uneven, *i.e.* eight Ayes and seven Noes, first to the Noes his vote as member, and then his casting vote as chairman. It is not usually desirable for a chairman who wishes to maintain a reputation for impartiality to exercise his casting vote, as he is thereby bringing into being something which exactly one-half of those voting is opposed to. A chairman has only a casting vote if there is an *equality of votes,* which means an equality of valid votes. He may exercise his ordinary vote one way and his casting vote another, but he may decline to vote at all, and, in case of equality of votes, if he declines to vote, the motion is lost. He may give a contingent or hypothetical casting vote, to come into operation if, in the course of subsequent proceedings, it should appear that there has been an equality of valid votes.[1]

For further details of the chairman's position, see Chapter 15, below.

[1] *Bland v. Buchanan,* [1901] 2 K.B. 75.

CHAPTER 4

Conduct of Meetings

The conduct of a meeting should be governed by the relevant rules. The nature of the rules depends upon the character of the body holding the meetings, but they should be clear, explicit, and free from any ambiguity. They should be fair and reasonable, and interpreted in an impartial manner. From them the chairman obtains most of his power, and, if properly drawn up, they form an invaluable authority to which the chairman can appeal. But the chairman must know the rules and understand their purport and meaning, otherwise it may lead to unnecessary conflict with members of the meeting.

The rules which local authorities make for the regulating of their proceedings and business are called Standing Orders. These are permanent regulations which cannot usually be varied or abrogated without notice of definite character, *e.g.* six months. Any member may direct attention to a breach of them.

Usually some provision is made for the suspension of standing orders for urgent or special purposes. Statutes or standing orders which limit or extend common law rights, *e.g.* those which modify the rules of meetings, must be expressed in clear and unambiguous language.

Where there are no standing orders or where standing orders are inadequate, then either the practice of the House of Commons or the usual practice of previous meetings may be followed. In a simple case, however, the difficulty may be overcome by the chairman exercising his common sense and bearing in mind that it is his duty to ascertain the views of the meeting.

Rules should safeguard the general rights of the members of the meeting, and should not crush the rights of minorities. When once agreed to, any alteration should be made only after proper notice has been given to the persons concerned—in fact, there should be a standing rule that any such alteration should require notice of a definite length or should take place only at certain meetings.

Standing orders are of great assistance to chairman, members, and officials alike; they prevent misapprehension of the powers of the meeting, avoid confusion and disorder, and facilitate the dispatch and conduct of business.

Some societies adopt the rules of the House of Commons, *mutatis mutandis*, but these are somewhat complex and unworkable for ordinary meetings. "It appears to me that meetings of this kind (*i.e.* of a limited company) are not bound to model all their proceedings on the rules of the House of Commons. Those rules are very useful; they are the result of long experience, and when those rules are understood they work out admirably. But they are too complex for the apprehension of ordinary shareholders. . . . I think the chairman is not to be caught suddenly by an expression of opinion, when he, without very much experience (of course, I am speaking of chairmen in general, not of this chairman), on the spur of the moment, has to come to some conclusion upon some proposal before the meeting; and I am prepared to hold—and do hold—that he is allowed to express his opinion in a deliberative way."[1] But it is not necessary that a member should persist in disputing the chairman's decision thus given in order to entitle him to impeach afterwards the validity of such ruling. The chairman should know his business, and if he improperly deprives a member of a right to which he is legally entitled, the validity of the proceedings may be afterwards impeached.

The meeting open to all the members of any particular body is generally the ultimate authority for all the business transacted by that body. Unless there is an express or statutory delegation of authority to a committee or some other body no reports or resolutions of delegated bodies are binding until they have been confirmed by the delegating body. In some cases, however, much of the important business is often delegated to committees.

A committee may consist of one person but normally consists of several. "A committee means a person or persons to whom powers are committed which would otherwise be exercised by another body."[2] It exercises limited powers, which may be modified or withdrawn by its appointing authority. Its decisions are usually in the form of *recommendations* which require the adoption or approval of its appointing authority. A committee may, however, be given power to act on behalf of the whole body, and not merely to make recommendations. A committee may thus be set up by a local authority to deal with particular subjects—*e.g.* finance, highways, education, and so forth. In committee the proceedings are less formal, and discussion tends rather to elucidate the opinions of the members, and so to form some *consensus ad idem*, rather than to be

[1] *Henderson v. Bank of Australasia* (1890) 45 Ch. D. 330.
[2] *Re Taurine Co.* (1883) 25 Ch. D., at 132.

directed at the long-suffering reporter as is often the case at public meetings of a local authority itself. The powers of committees should be clearly set forth in their appointment. The chairman and the members of a committee are normally members of the appointing body. It is competent for a particular body if its rules so provide to delegate most of the powers to a committee in such a way that those powers can no longer be exercised by the delegating body. Such delegation is generally made by companies to their boards of directors. In such cases unless the articles otherwise provide the exercise by the directors of the powers delegated to them cannot be controlled by the company in general meeting, and to enable the company to do this it would be necessary to alter the articles (see p. 69, *infra*).

In turn, the committee may appoint sub-committees to deal with some specific branch of its work. A *sub-committee* stands in the same relation to the committee as the committee does to the whole body of persons by which it is appointed, and can only act within the limits prescribed by its appointing authority, *i.e.* the committee. Delegating to a sub-committee does not imply a parting with the powers granted by the delegating committee, but confers an authority to do things which otherwise the committee would do itself. Such powers delegated to the sub-committee can be resumed at any time by the appointing committee.[1] Such sub-committee must report to the committee; the existence of a sub-committee expires with the existence of its creating body.

A committee may come into existence and have certain powers even without being expressly appointed. In such a case the powers and jurisdiction of the committee will be implied. An example of such a committee, and the limits on its jurisdiction, is found in the trade union case of *Abbott v. Sullivan.*[2]

In some cases a body has no power to delegate; for instance, the National Dock Labour Board, a statutory body.[3]

The rules, or the contract between the members, of the body may exclude the power to delegate, as in *Bonsor v. Musicians Union,*[4] where a power delegated to a committee was purported to be exercised by the secretary of the committee and such exercise was invalid and void, since the committee had no power to delegate its authority to the secretary.

A delegating body may also at any time revoke the power of a

[1] *Huth v. Clarke* (1890) 25 Q.B.D. 391.

[2] [1952] 1 K.B. 189.

[3] *Barnard v. National Dock Labour Board,* [1953] 2 Q.B. 18; *Vine v. National Dock Labour Board,* [1956] 1 All E.R. 1.

[4] On this point, [1954] Ch. 479.

single member of a committee and his appointment to such committee.[1]

Revocation of the powers of a committee or of any of its members may be made arbitrarily and even capriciously (*ibid.*).

Standing Orders

Standing Orders[2] will usually deal (*inter alia*) with the following matters:

(1) Place, day, and time of meeting, and provision as to the convening of special meetings.
(2) The order in which business is to be transacted, *e.g.*:
   (1) Reading the notice of the meeting. This is sometimes agreed to be taken as read.
   (2) Minutes and their confirmation.
   (3) Correspondence.
   (4) Reports of committees and officers.
   (5) Finance.
   (6) Motions for debate (if proper notice has been given) in the order in which they appear on the agenda paper.
(3) Motions.
   (1) Notice and withdrawal of motions and amendments thereto.
   (2) How motions may be properly interrupted (see *post*, Chapter 5, Procedural Motions).
(4) Questions—in what circumstances they may be put and how to be answered.
(5) Rules of debate.
   (1) Motions to be proposed and seconded.
   (2) Speaker to stand except when in committee and to address the chair.
   (3) Length of speeches. If a time limit is set for speeches, provision should be made for an extension of such time with the special permission of the meeting.
   (4) No second speech to be allowed on the same question, unless by way of explanation, which must not introduce a new topic—this power to be left to the discretion of the chairman.
   (5) Irregular or improper conduct. The meeting should have power to deal with this, by *e.g.* resolving that the

[1] *Manton v. Brighton Corporation*, [1951] 2 K.B. 393.

[2] A model form of Standing Orders for local authorities is published by H.M. Stationery Office entitled *Model Standing Orders* (SBN 11 750113 1).

offending member be not further heard. The chairman should have the power in case of disorder or obstruction of suspending the meeting.

(6) Adjournments of debate or meetings.

(7) Rescission of resolutions, stating requisite time and notice.

(8) Voting.

 (1) Voice.

 (2) Show of hands.

 (3) Division.

 (4) Poll: how and when to be demanded, and regulations as to taking a poll.

(9) Appointment of committees and their powers.

(10) How and when standing orders or rules may be altered.

(11) Suspension of standing orders or rules. Provision is usually made for this in special circumstances, and it generally requires a certain specified majority of the members present.

Articles of companies, on the other hand, will not generally contain rules governing meetings of the company in such detail as this. They will generally only deal with the matters dealt with in (1), (6), (8) and (9) above and in addition will deal with the method of appointing the chairman of meetings and define his powers, and will also prescribe the requisite quorum for meetings. In the case of local authorities these matters are governed by the statutory provisions applicable thereto (see Part Four, *post*).

Discussion and Debate

The conduct and control of the discussion or debate is mainly in the hands of the chairman, who must be discreet, impartial, and tactful in its management. The following rules are, it is suggested, appropriate:

(1) Every member who so desires should, where practicable, have an opportunity of speaking upon each motion; no second speech to be allowed except that the mover of the original motion should have the right of reply, the advocates and the opponents of the question before the meeting to speak alternately. Members should usually stand whilst speaking, except when in committee. Every speech should be addressed to the chairman, and as far as possible reference to persons by name should be avoided. Every member who speaks should direct his speech strictly to the motion under discussion, or to an explanation, or to a question of order. Sometimes a

time limit to length of speeches is fixed, which may be varied by the consent of the meeting.

(2) The order in which members should speak is determined by the chairman, who should endeavour to ascertain either the implied or express wishes of the meeting thereon, any conflict of opinion being settled by vote of the meeting. The chairman should call each member, whom he wishes to speak, in turn and by name. According to custom, the member who is entitled to address the meeting is the one who first rises to speak and who is observed by the chairman; in that event, to prevent uncertainty, the chairman announces the member's name. If a meeting declines to accept the choice of the chairman as to who shall speak, *e.g.* when several members rise simultaneously to address the meeting, it is open to the meeting to resolve this matter by formal motion, *e.g.* that Mr. A. be now heard. But deference to the chairman is a principle which should be invariably observed. It is not open to the majority to prevent the views of the minority being put forward.[1]

(3) The chairman should impartially allow supporters and opponents of a motion equal opportunities of speaking, and have regard to the rights of minorities.

(4) The chairman should insist on members refraining from unseemly interruptions or making a running commentary on the remarks of the speaker, and from holding informal sub-committees or private conversations *sotto voce* during debate, or any other conduct tending to disturb the meeting. He should call a member to order for repetition, unbecoming language, or any breach of order, and may direct such member, if speaking, to discontinue his speech.

(5) Points of order which may be raised by any member, whether he has previously spoken or not, should be taken immediately they are brought to the notice of the chairman. Explanations, which should be brief and to the point must not introduce new topics. The chairman should not allow a speech or debate to follow an explanation, and unless he is firm about this a wrangle and possible disorder generally follows. The chairman's decision on points of order is final, and in it he should have the loyal support of the meeting.

(6) Members should realise that support of the chairman and the maintenance of order expedite the transaction of business, and that the conduct of a disorderly member, if unchecked, may

[1] *Const v. Harris* (1824) T. & R. 496; *Wall v. London and Northern Assets Corporation*, [1898] 2 Ch. at 480.

result in a disorderly and ineffective meeting. A want of support for the chairman often makes the subject of discussion a vehicle for personalities, to the detriment of good feeling and good taste.

(7) Discussion must be relevant to the subject under debate. Members who ignore this rule, or who use offensive language, or impute improper motives to colleagues, should be sharply dealt with by the chairman, and, in the event of persistent disregard of the authority of the chair, should be requested to retire from the meeting, and, if necessary, removed therefrom.

(8) The rising of the chairman should be accompanied by silence, and any member speaking should immediately resume his seat.

CHAPTER 5

Motions (or Resolutions) and Voting

A motion, as its name implies, is a proposal moved by a member. If resolved upon, it becomes a resolution. It is thus inaccurate, though not uncommon, to speak of submitting a resolution to a meeting, *e.g.* in Section 141 (3) of the Companies Act 1948.

All motions should be:

(1) In writing, signed by the mover, and handed to the chairman of the meeting, unless they are procedural motions (see *infra*).

Every motion and consequently, if successful, the resulting resolution should begin with the word *That*, and should generally be affirmative, not negative, in form.

(2) Relevant to the business for which the meeting is called, within the scope of the notice convening the meeting, and within the powers of that meeting.

(3) Duly proposed and, where it is the practice of the meeting or is required by the rules, seconded; and

(4) In compliance with any particular requirements of the relevant rules.

In the House of Commons a motion or amendment does not require to be seconded. The Speaker habitually acts on the mover's proposal of a motion or of an amendment without calling for a seconder and also puts of his own accord questions to the House. Where the relevant rules do not otherwise provide it will be sufficient if the motion or amendment is moved but not seconded, or if the chairman himself puts a proposal to the meeting.[1]

Motions are in the control of the meeting, and cannot be withdrawn unless with the unanimous consent of the members present. Motions which are not moved by the person who has given notice therefor, or by some other member for him, are dropped motions and cannot be revived without a new notice. Motions should be discussed in the order in which they appear on the agenda paper, unless the members present wish otherwise. In case of conflict of opinion, the question should be decided by vote. A motion which has

[1] *Re Horbury Bridge Coal Co.* (1879) 11 Ch. D. 109.

been negatived may not be brought forward again at the same meeting, but may, subject to the relevant rules, be brought forward again at a future meeting.

When there is no amendment to a motion, it is put to the meeting for its opinion, and if agreed to becomes the resolution of the meeting. When there is an amendment to the motion (and it is better to have only one amendment at a time), it should be put to the meeting first; if not carried, other amendments in turn may be put, and if all amendments are lost, the original motion is put to the meeting for its decision. A mover of a motion may vote for an amendment thereof. By doing so he would in effect withdraw at least *pro tanto* his original motion. He is not tied by his original motion.

A resolution rescinding a former resolution is governed by the same principles as any other resolution but sometimes the relevant rules prohibit the rescission of a resolution for a certain period.

Amendments

Unless the relevant rules otherwise require, ordinary amendments can be moved without previous notice, provided they are relevant to the motion and not outside the scope of the notice convening the meeting, and do not involve such a substantial alteration of the motion as to make it a new motion. See, however, p. 125, *post*, for the position in the case of company meetings.

Amendments generally seek to do one or more of the following things:

(1) To omit certain words.
(2) To omit certain words and insert others.
(3) To insert certain words.

Amendments should be dealt with separately and should be taken in their logical order. The effect of one or more amendments being carried will be to alter the original motion, which should then be put to the meeting again as altered without being again proposed or seconded: if this substantive motion be not carried, no resolution results. It would not, of course, be necessary to put the original motion more than once unless it were altered by amendment.

Amendments are a fruitful source of trouble to the chairman, who often forgets that he collects his authority from the meeting and not from himself, unless of course the relevant rules give him express powers. If the chairman is uncertain whether an amendment is in order, he should allow it to be moved so as to save the resolution, as failure to admit germane and relevant amendments will nullify a resolution. In one case, where the chairman's refusal to put the amendment had withdrawn a material and relevant question from the meeting, the Court set aside the resolution passed thereat.[1]

Chairmen sometimes refuse to admit amendments on the ground that they have not been seconded, but, unless standing orders expressly provide, the chairman has no alternative but to allow the amendment to be put. "In my opinion, if the chairman put the question *without its being proposed or seconded by anybody*, that would be perfectly good."[2] Of course the mere fact of there being no seconder may indicate that it is the amendment of a small minority and will therefore be lost.

An Amendment

(1) Must not merely negative the motion. A person wishing to move such an amendment can achieve the same result by voting against it;

(2) Should, if the rules so provide, be formally moved and seconded;

(3) Must come strictly within the scope of the notice convening the meeting.

Amendments substantially altering the motion cannot usually be put without proper notice. "How is it possible for the Court to know how many shareholders abstained from attending the meeting, being satisfied that the arrangement, *as it was proposed*, was advantageous to them, and being quite content to exercise no voice about it?"[3] Any amendment without notice which substantially alters the motion of which notice is required is out of order, as is also any amendment which is merely obstructive or dilatory;

(4) Should preferably be in writing, clearly stating the proposed alteration, signed by the mover, and given to the chairman;

(5) May be moved and seconded by members who have not already spoken on the motion; after which all members have a right to speak, unless the relevant rules otherwise provide:

(6) Must not be moved after the question is put:

(7) Gives no right of reply to the mover;

(8) Cannot be withdrawn without the consent of the meeting:

(9) If there is an equality of votes, and the chairman does not exercise his casting vote, is, in the same way as a motion requiring to be passed by a simple majority, deemed not carried.

[1] *Henderson v. Bank of Australasia* (1890) 45 Ch. D. 330.
[2] *Re Horbury Bridge Coal Co.* (1879) 11 Ch. D. 109.
[3] *Clinch v. Financial Corporation* (1868) L.R., 5 Eq., at 481.

No member can move more than one amendment to the same motion, unless the rules otherwise provide. The meeting must not be asked to vote on two or more amendments at the same time. The chairman should, therefore, allow only one amendment to be before the meeting at a time. When several amendments are before the meeting, it is generally the practice to take them in the order in which they will affect the main question, and not in the order in which they were moved. It is, however, usual not to allow an amendment of an amendment. If an amendment of an amendment is allowed, it generally leads to confusion. No amendment should be allowed relating to those parts of an original motion which have already been agreed upon as forming part of the amended motion. If the amendment is not carried, the original motion remains to be further amended or discussed.

When an amendment has been put to the meeting and carried, it must be put a second time, embodied in a substantive motion, which supersedes the original motion. This substantive motion can be amended and discussed as if it were the original motion. Any amendment which so amends the substantive motion that it becomes again the original motion should not be allowed. It sometimes happens that where an amendment has been carried the substantive motion incorporating that amendment is lost, in which case the original motion, is not revived. This is a device which is used to get rid of the whole subject under discussion.

It is not essential to follow the rules of the House of Commons in dealing with amendments. The observance of strict formality in putting motions and amendments thereon to meetings at which there is no recognised practice is unnecessary; it is enough if conflicting propositions are put to the meeting in such a way that those present understand what it is that they are called on to decide.[1]

Amendments when motion is withdrawn.—Sometimes a motion to which an amendment is proposed to be moved is withdrawn, and if it is properly withdrawn, which usually requires the consent of the meeting, the amendment, *ipso facto*, falls to the ground and can no longer be moved. But if the original motion could have been moved without notice, a new motion incorporating the amendment, if it is one not requiring notice either, can be moved.

Procedural Motions

When a motion has been duly moved and seconded, discussion thereon may be interrupted by motions for amendment (*supra*) or

[1] *Ex parte Stevens, in re The Vestry of Hammersmith* (1852) 16 J.P. 632.

by some or all of the following further motions, no notice of which is required and which need not be in writing.

(1) To move the previous question [That the question be *not* now put].
(2) To proceed to the next business.
(3) To move the closure [That the question be now put].
(4) To adjourn the debate.
(5) To adjourn the meeting.
(6) To refer a recommendation of a committee back for further consideration and report.

(1) *To move the previous question.*—When the main question, but not an amendment thereto, is under discussion, it is competent for any member who has not spoken on the main question to move the "Previous Question", in order to get rid of a motion which is considered inconvenient or on which it is thought unwise for any decision to be taken. If duly seconded, discussion may follow. The previous question takes precedence of all amendments, and may take the form of "That the question be now put"; in which case the supporters of the "Previous Question" (which is a device for shelving the matter for the time being) vote *against* it, and if successful the main question is got rid of as regards that meeting. The more general way of putting the previous question is in the form: "That the question be not now put." If this motion is not carried, the main question is then put to the vote at once without further discussion. On the other hand, if it is carried, the main question cannot be put at that meeting, though it may be brought up at a subsequent meeting. The object of the previous question is to avoid the putting of the original resolution to the vote by considering whether or not the original resolution shall be put to the vote at all. No amendment may be moved to the "Previous Question", though it may be superseded by a motion for adjourning the meeting.

(2) *To proceed to the next business.*—This motion, which has the same effect and object as the "Previous Question", *i.e.* to prevent a decision being obtained on the motion under discussion, may generally be moved at the close of any speech, and, if seconded, is put forwith without speech or debate. If carried, the subject under discussion drops; if lost, there is generally a limit of time—*e.g.* half an hour—before this motion can be moved again concerning the same subject of debate.

(3) *The closure*, is generally moved in the form: "That the question be now put." This is moved and put in the same way as the preceding motion. If carried, the motion under discussion is put to the vote.

The object of this motion may be either to stifle discussion or to get a decision on a question which has been reasonably or sufficiently debated. "As to the closure, I think if we laid it down that the chairman, supported by a majority, could not put a termination to the speeches of those who were desirous of addressing the meeting, we should allow a small minority, or even a member or two, to tyrannize over the majority. The case has been put . . . as the terrorism of the majority. If we accepted this proposition, we should put this weapon into the hands of the minority, which might involve the company in all-night sittings. That seems to me to be an extravagant proposition, and in this particular case there seems to have been nothing arbitrary or vexatious on the part of the chairman or of the majority."[1]

When the views of the minority have been reasonably heard, it is competent to the chairman, with the sanction of a vote of the meeting, to declare the discussion closed, and to put the question to the vote. Not everybody is entitled to speak who wants to speak, nor should a member be allowed to speak at an undue length. The purpose of a meeting is to get things done, to come to a decision on certain matters, and discussion must be relevant, and reasonable, and subordinate to the main object of the meeting. The editors consider that, unless the relevant rules otherwise provide, the chairman has a discretion whether or not to accept a motion for the closure, which is an antidote to obstruction or delay. He should use it to defeat mere obstructive tactics, but at the same time have regard to the rights of minorities.

(4) *To adjourn the debate.*—The mover of the original motion is usually allowed the right of reply to this motion, after which no further debate is permitted. It is often the practice to give the person who successfully carries this motion the right of reopening the debate when it is resumed at the same or the next meeting.

(5) *To adjourn the meeting.*—This motion may be moved at the close of any speech or conclusion of any business. The mover of the question under debate at the time is allowed some right of reply. If the motion to adjourn is carried it is usual to resume the debate or business thus interrupted at the next ordinary meeting, unless another time is fixed, but it is desirable to have this point clearly dealt with by the resolution.

If a motion for adjournment of the debate or of the meeting is defeated, it may be moved again after the debate or meeting has gone on for a reasonable time.

[1] *Wall v. London and Northern Assets Corporation*, [1898] 2 Ch. 469, at 483.

(6) *To refer the recommendation of a committee back to the committee.*—When a motion emanates from a committee whose province it is to make recommendations on certain defined subjects, it is sometimes referred back to the committee for further consideration, having regard to more recent information which may not have reached the committee, or it may be that other circumstances have intervened since the committee met which may render it inadvisable to adopt the recommendation. Further, the recommendation may not meet with the approval of the parent body, which latter may not possess the requisite knowledge to amend the motion. In any case, it is more courteous to give the committee an opportunity of submitting another recommendation. Reference back may in some cases be tantamount to rejection, and is a useful method of negativing a recommendation.

In every case the relevant rules relating to motions of this kind must be complied with. In the case of adjournments, either of a particular discussion or of a meeting, the question of giving notice of the business to be transacted at the adjourned meeting will be governed by the relevant rules.

Voting

The usual methods of obtaining the sense of a meeting are:

(1) Voice. This is only adopted when it is obvious that the meeting is practically unanimous. The chairman in this case usually reads the motion to the meeting, exclaims "As many as are of that opinion, say 'Aye'," and listens to the voices given in the affirmative. Then he says, "As many as are of the contrary opinion, say 'No'," and pauses to receive the voices given in the negative. By the volume of the voices he judges whether the Ayes or the Noes are in the majority. Then he announces "The Ayes (or the Noes) have it." This gives an opportunity for anyone present to demand a vote by show of hands.

(2) By show of hands, which is generally adopted in the first instance, each person having one vote. Voting by show of hands means the ascertainment of the views of those persons present who are entitled to vote and who in fact do hold up their hands. If the chairman's declaration as to the result is challenged, a second show of hands should be demanded. Generally, the relevant regulations provide that the declaration of the chairman as to the correctness of the result is decisive, and any objection as to its accuracy should be made at once.

(3) By a division: *i.e.* a regular count of the members for and

against the motion. In this case members separate themselves by going into different rooms or lobbies, the counting of members being delegated to tellers, one or two being appointed for each side of the question.

(4) By a poll, *i.e.* providing an opportunity for every member to cast his vote.

In the absence of special provisions a vote will first be taken on a show of hands at the end of which any voter may probably demand a poll.

"I am clearly of opinion that the demand for a poll must be made at once, as soon as the preliminary show of hands is over. Where an election is taken by a show of hands, the chairman is to form a judgment at once, to the best of his opinion, as to who is elected; and if it is the intention to test his decision in a more formal manner, this must be done at once."[1]

"The common law right on that subject is generally understood to be that any voter, however satisfied with the correctness of the declaration on the show of hands, yet may appeal from it to the whole body of electors, and keep a poll open till all have had the opportunity of attending to record their suffrages."[2]

A demand for a poll probably cannot be withdrawn after if has been accepted and the meeting has come to an end.[3] The demand for a poll is an abandonment of the result of voting by show of hands, and the voting proper begins with the poll.[4] The chairman is the proper person to grant a poll and to make arrangements therefor.

The cases above referred to are all cases of elections governed by the common law, but it is at least likely that a similar right to a poll exists in other cases where voting takes place and where the relevant rules do not deal expressly with the question.

In one case it was held that it is no objection to the proceedings at an election by a vestry that the chairman directed a poll without first taking a show of hands, although a show of hands was demanded and the poll was not demanded but was objected to.[5]

Declaration of poll.—One of the duties of the chairman is to declare the poll. If no time is fixed for closing the poll, as should in all cases be done, it cannot be closed so long as any votes are coming in, but it may be closed a reasonable time after votes have stopped

[1] *R. v. Vicar of St. Asaph* (1883) 52 L.J., Q.B. 672. See also *R. v. Thomas* (1883) 11 Q.B.D. 282.

[2] *R. v. The Vestry of St. Pancras* (1839) 11 A. & E. 26.

[3] *R. v. Mayor of Dover*, [1903] 1 K.B. 668.

[4] *Anthony v. Seger* (1789) 1 Hagg. Cons., p. 13.

[5] *R. v. Rector, etc., of Birmingham* (1837) 7 A & E. 254.

coming in, although if any voter is improperly excluded the poll will be invalidated.[1]

When a motion is put to a meeting a person present may take one of three courses.—He may vote for or against it, or he may abstain from voting at all. A person who is present and abstains may affect the result where, for a motion to be passed, there is required to be cast in its favour a proportion of the votes of those present. It is otherwise where the proportion is of those voting. In *Labouchere v. Wharncliff*[2] a motion was put which required a two-thirds majority *of those present*. Of the 117 persons present 77 voted for, 38 voted against and 2 abstained. The motion was lost.

There is no necessity for any particular formality in recording a vote. "A man may give his vote in divers ways, either by writing, or by hand, or by voice, or by conduct, *e.g.* by nod. The form in which acquiescence is given matters not, if acquiescence be actually indicated."[3]

Circumstances in which a vote may be taken twice on the same resolution.—When a chairman has not formally declared the result of a vote or is in doubt as to whether his declaration is right or wrong, he is entitled if he thinks well to take a second vote on the matter, especially if he considers that through some misunderstanding the first vote did not properly represent the sense of the meeting. In *Hickman v. Kent or Romney Marsh Sheepbreeders' Association*,[4] the articles governing the association required in the circumstances twelve voting in favour to four against before a certain resolution could be properly carried. The chairman, having put the resolution, counted and found eleven in favour and four against. As he had not voted himself and was doubtful whether one or two persons had in fact voted, he put the resolution again, and it was carried by fourteen to four. It was objected that "when the chairman had counted eleven for and four against he declared the motion carried, and he was then *functus officio* and could not validly have a recount. I do not agree. I think that if he had said that the motion was carried but was in doubt as to whether he was right or wrong, he was entitled immediately to have the votes counted again."[5]

As to the chairman's vote, see *ante*, p. 17.

[1] *R. v. Lambeth* (1838) 8 A. & E. 356.
[2] (1879) 13 Ch. D. 346.
[3] *Everett v. Griffiths*, [1924] 1 K.B. 941, at 953.
[4] (1920) 36 T.L.R. 528; affirmed (1921) 37 T.L.R. 163.
[5] 36 T.L.R., at 533.

CHAPTER 6

Speeches and Defamation

Introduction

Speeches made at meetings and reports submitted in connection therewith come under the general law relating to defamation. Generally speaking, a person making statements at meetings or in reports has little to fear from the law of defamation provided that he acts with reasonable care, and avoids making unsupportable attacks on characters and reputations.

(1) A defamatory statement is one which tends to lower a person in the estimation of right-thinking members of society generally,[1] or which tends to make them shun or avoid that person. It does not necessarily have to expose that person to hatred or contempt.[2]

(2) A defamatory statement may be either libel or slander. Libel is in written or some other permanent form whereas slander is in oral or some other transient form. Defamatory statements made on television and radio are libel and not slander.

Defences

Statements which are at first sight defamatory can often be made with impunity because of the various defences which may be available in libel proceedings.

(1) *Justification*

The maker of a defamatory statement can plead justification and say that the statement is substantially true. It is not enough to have an honest belief in the truth of the charges if they transpire subsequently to be untrue. For this reason, it is a difficult defence to rely on; especially as the onus of proving the truth of the charges rests on the maker of the statement. It is, therefore, essential to take the greatest care to check the truth of any statement to be made.[3]

[1] *Sim v. Stretch*, [1936] 2 All. E.R. 1237.

[2] *Drummond-Jackson v. British Medical Association*, [1970] 1 W.L.R. 691.

[3] A person's conviction for a criminal offence is now proof that he committed that offence; see Civil Evidence Act 1968 s. 13.

Justification, if successful, is a complete defence, even if the defendant was motivated by malice in making the speech or report.

(2) *Fair Comment*

It is a defence if it can be established that the statement consisted only of fair comment on a matter of public interest. This defence can in turn be defeated by proof that the statement was made maliciously.

(a) Matters of public interest include, *inter alia*, the public conduct of everyone taking part in public affairs, the administration of public institutions and local affairs. Normally, the defence is more likely to apply to proceedings of meetings of public bodies than with meetings of private bodies such as societies and limited companies, but the conduct of societies and limited companies, whether public or private, can constitute a matter of public interest in some circumstances. The scope of public interest extends to "whenever a matter is such as to affect people at large, so that they may be legitimately interested in or concerned at, what is going on; or what may happen to them or to others".[1] Thus, a company's conduct towards its employees[2] and the contents of a prospectus issued to the public[3] have been held to be matters of public interest. In the editors' opinion, the defence of fair comment should extend to all prospectuses and any documents filed at the Companies' Registry for public inspection.

(b) In addition, the statement must satisfy the following conditions:

(i) It must be comment and not asserted as fact. Express or implied statements of fact upon which the comment is based must be accurate.[4] If a defamatory statement of fact is made, the only defences available are justification or qualified privilege.

(ii) It must be such comment as, in the opinion of the jury, constitutes fair criticism fairly arising out of the facts.[5]

(iii) It must be strictly relevant to the true facts, and

[1] *London Artists Ltd. v. Littler*, [1969] 2 Q.B. 375.

[2] *South Hetton Coal Co. v. North-Eastern News Association* (1894) 1 Q.B. 133.

[3] *Lotinga v. Edward Lloyd Ltd., The Times*, 5th Dec., 1910.

[4] *Kemsley v. Foot*, [1952] A.C. 345.

[5] *Slim v. Daily Telegraph Ltd.*, [1968] 2 Q.B. 157.

(iv) It must not impute to the person defamed discreditable or improper motives unless the imputation is a reasonable inference from the facts.[1]

(c) It is not necessary to prove the truth of all the allegations of fact provided that the statement is fair comment in the light of those allegations of fact which are proved (Defamation Act 1952 Section 6).

(3) *Malice*

As mentioned on page 35 above, the defence of fair comment can be defeated by proof of malice. The same is true of the defence of qualified privilege. Malice may be proved from the contents of the statement:

(i) As long as the maker of the statement honestly believes in the truth of what he says and is not reckless, not caring whether what he says is true or false, malice cannot be inferred from the fact that his belief is unreasonable, prejudiced or unfair. Mere inadvertence, forgetfulness, careless blundering, negligence, want of sound judgment, honest indignation or strong words are not evidence of malice. The test is whether the statement was made without any honest belief in its truth.[2]

(ii) Malice may be established also by showing that the maker of the statement was actuated in making it by some improper or extraneous motive, such as spite.

(4) *Qualified Privilege*

A statement made on a privileged occasion, however, defamatory or untrue, is protected unless the maker was motivated by malice in the case of qualified privilege. Privilege is either absolute, such as statements made in the Houses of Parliament or in the administration of justice, for example, or qualified.

(i) Qualified privilege applies whenever the person making the statement has an interest, or a legal, social or moral duty to make it to the person to whom it is made, and the person to whom it is so made has a corresponding duty or interest to receive it.[3]

(ii) In respect of qualified privilege, unnecessary publication may also be evidence of malice, and the publication might be wider than is justified in the circumstances by the privilege.[4]

[1] *London Artists Ltd. v. Littler*, [1969] 2 Q.B. 375.
[2] *Horrocks v. Lowe*, [1972] 1 W.L.R. 1625 C.A.
[3] *Adam v. Ward*, [1917] A.C. 309.
[4] *Cutler v. McPhail*, [1962] 2 Q.B. 292.

The presence of the Press or other third parties at the making of the defamatory statement does not necessarily prove malice. There is a distinction between three situations:

(a) The defence of qualified privilege is not lost if the Press or other third parties happens to be present at a meeting (*i.e.* in accordance with the regular custom of the meeting) where a defamatory statement is made[1], or if the maker of the statement calls in a third person, such as his solicitor, to hear what he says as a reasonable precaution to protect his own interests.[2]

(b) The defence may be lost if the Press or other third parties are expressly invited to attend the meeting by the person making the defamatory statement.[3] An opportunity should not be sought for making a defamatory statement in front of third parties which might have been made in private.[4]

(c) If several persons make the defamatory statement at an occasion protected by qualified privilege, the defence is lost only by those against whom express malice is proved.[5] An agent's malice may bind his principal,[6] but an agent is not liable for publishing his principal's defamatory statement if express malice is proved only against his principal.[7]

(5) *Newspaper Reports*

Under the common law, a report of a public meeting, a company meeting or of other bodies was not privileged.[8] The Defamation Act 1952 extended the defence of qualified privilege to fair and accurate reports in newspapers of matters of public concern in meetings of a number of bodies. The full list of such bodies is to be found in Part II of the Schedule to the Defamation Act 1952.

(a) The list includes meetings and reports of local authorities, commissions of inquiry, lawful public meetings and general meetings of public companies. General meetings of private companies are not included, and newspapers must rely on

[1] *Pittard v. Oliver*, [1891] 1 Q.B. 474.
[2] *Taylor v. Hawkins* (1851) 16 Q.B. 308.
[3] *Pittard v. Oliver*, [1891] 1 Q.B. 474.
[4] *Toogood v. Spyring*, 1 Cr. M. & R. 181.
[5] *Longdon-Griffiths v. Smith*, [1951] 1 K.B. 295.
[6] *Angel v. H. H. Bushell & Co. Ltd.* (1968) 1 Q.B. 813.
[7] *Eggar v. Viscount Chelmsford*, [1965] 1 Q.B. 248.
[8] *Ponsford v. Financial Times* (1900) 16 T.L.R. 248.

the common law defences of justification or fair comment in respect of any defamatory reports of such meetings.

(b) In addition, the statutory privilege extends only to publication which is for the public benefit, and the privilege is destroyed if the person making the report has been requested by the plaintiff to publish in the same newspaper a reasonable letter or a statement by way of explanation or contradiction and he has not done so (Defamation Act 1952 s. 7(2)). A general letter demanding an apology and withdrawal is not a request in accordance with the sub-section.[1]

Companies

In most cases, statements made in a company meeting, in a board meeting and in reports and circulars to the shareholders are protected by qualified privilege. Evidence of malice destroys the privilege.

(1) *Meetings*

Qualified privilege protects persons making statements in good faith in a company meeting on a subject in which the members are interested, *i.e.* where the person making the statement has an interest or a legal, social or moral duty to make it to the members, and the members have a corresponding duty or interest to receive it; the privilege may be lost if the statement is made privately after the determination of the meeting instead of as part of the proceedings of the meeting.[2]

Statements about the auditors, particular employees, or the directors are examples of subjects in which the members are interested.

Providing that the person making the defamatory statement has not sought the presence of the Press or other third parties at the meeting, the privilege is not destroyed merely through their presence.

(2) *Reports and Circulars*

Reports and circulars sent to members of the company by the company[3] or by some other members[4] are privileged in the absence of malice.

Those drafting reports and circulars must ensure that they have an honest belief in the truth of the contents and that there is no unnecessary publication.

[1] *Khan v. Ahmed*, [1957] 2 Q.B. 149.
[2] *Martin v. Strong* (1836) 5 A. & E. 535.
[3] *Lawless v. Anglo-Egyptian Cotton Co.* (1869) L.R. 4 Q.B. 262.
[4] *Quartz Hill Gold Mining Co. v. Beall* (1882) 20 Ch. D. 501.

(3) *Board Meetings*

Directors of a company have a duty to discuss the affairs of their company and they are entitled to discuss the conduct of their officials so long as they do so honestly.[1] Statements made by a director to an official or a member of a company or to the company's solicitor are normally privileged.[2] This privilege may be lost by unnecessary publication. Thus, in *Watt v. Longsdown*,[3] it was held that the defendant director was under a duty to communicate to his chairman a letter of complaint about the conduct of the plaintiff employee, but that he was under no duty to communicate the contents of the letter to the plaintiff's wife.

Local Authorities

In the absence of malice, statements made to a local authority on a matter with which the authority is competent to deal are protected by qualified privilege.

Local Authorities are bound to exhibit publicly notices convening Council Meetings (Local Government Act 1972 Twelfth Schedule). These notices are protected by qualified privilege. They must specify with sufficient clarity the purposes for which the meetings are convened, but need not set out any reports which are to be considered at the meeting. Consequently, if a report set out in a notice which is publicly exhibited, is defamatory it will not be protected by the defence of qualified privilege.[4]

The publication of the agenda for a local authority meeting to the Press or to a member of the public, with or without further particulars indicating the nature of any item, is privileged in the absence of malice.[5] This protection is now extended to the agenda of certain committee meetings of local authorities as well as council meetings.[6]

Parties

There is a distinction between defaming a corporation as opposed to its officers.

(1) *Companies*

A company cannot commence proceedings for any words which reflect not upon the company but solely upon its individual

[1] *Allan v. Clarke, The Times*, 17th Jan. 1912, p. 16.
[2] *M'Gillivray v. Davidson* (1934) S.L.T. 45.
[3] [1930] 1 K.B. 130.
[4] *De Buse v. McCarthy*, [1942] 1 K.B. 156.
[5] Public Bodies (Admissions to Meetings) Act 1960 s. 1(5).
[6] Local Government Act 1972 s. 100.

officers or members. A trading company has a trading character to protect which can be injured by statements made at meetings or in reports. A company can sue one of its own directors or members for defamation.[1]

Thus, it may be defamatory to make a statement reflecting on the conduct of a company's trade[2] or on its financial stability.[3] If the statement does not reflect on the company's trading character, it will not be defamatory.

(2) *Non-trading Corporations*

A non-trading corporation has a "governing character" to protect as distinct from the reputations and character of its members and officials. A local authority[4] and a trades union or employees' association[5] may bring proceedings to protect its reputation against injury.

[1] *Metropolitan Saloon v. Hawkins* (1859) 4 H. & N. 87.

[2] *D. and L. Caterers Ltd. and Jackson v. d'Ajou*, [1945] K.B. 364.

[3] *Irish People's Assurance Society v. City of Dublin Assurance Co. Ltd.* (1929) I.R. 25.

[4] *Bognor Regis U.D.C. v. Campion*, [1972] 2 W.L.R. 983.

[5] *National Union of General and Municipal Workers v. Gillian*, [1948] K.B. 81. See also Trade Union and Labour Relations Act 1974 ss. 2 and 3.

CHAPTER 7

Admission to Meetings (including the Press)

One of the matters that sometimes requires to be decided in connection with meetings is who should be invited to attend.

Obviously in the case of a public meeting held in a public place no one can be excluded. In the case of a public meeting on private premises, however, the organisers can decide who may come to the meeting.

Generally speaking, in the case of private meetings there is no right in the public or Press to attend, but the meeting itself may decide whether outsiders of any kind shall be permitted to be present. Large public companies, for example, generally desire that their general meetings shall be reported in the papers, and so invite the attendance of reporters, but they are not of course bound to do so.

At common law the public have no right to attend meetings of local authorities. In *Mayor &c. of Tenby v. Mason*[1] the defendant, a burgess and ratepayer of a town, asserted his right to be present at meetings of the council of the borough (other than committee meetings) in his capacity of (1) ratepayer of the borough; (2) reporter of a newspaper owned by him and published in that town; and in the alternative, as a member of the public. The corporation of the town claimed a declaration of the council's right to exclude persons not members of the council (which the defendant was not) from their meetings; and for an injunction restraining the defendant from trespassing and being present at meetings of the council. It was held that a meeting of the council of a municipal corporation was not a public meeting in the sense that any member of the public had a right to attend; that there was no ground for implying against a municipal corporation a right which was not expressed in any statute nor supported by any authority; and that the defendant had therefore no such right as was asserted by him either as a burgess or as a member of the public; nor had he the right to attend as a newspaper reporter without the express or implied permission of the council. The effect of this decision was greatly modified by the Local Authorities (Admission of the Press to Meetings) Act 1908. This Act has now

[1] [1908] 1 Ch. 457.

been repealed and replaced by The Public Bodies (Admission to Meetings) Act 1960. The latter Act provides that any meeting of a local authority or other body exercising public functions (the Schedule to the Act containing a list of bodies to which the Act applies) shall be open to the public. The public may be excluded by resolution of the body whenever exclusion is considered advisable in the public interest by reason of the confidential nature of the business or other special reasons.

Public notice of any meeting which is to be open to the public must be given three clear days before the meeting, and copies of the agenda must, on request, be supplied to newspapers. Newspaper reporters must also be given reasonable facilities for taking their report and (if possible) for telephoning it.

The Act applies to committees of bodies whose members consist of or include all members of the body and was extended by Section 100 of the Local Government Act 1972 to certain other committees (see p. 167, *post*). In practice the Press and public are generally excluded from committee meetings other than those which they are entitled to attend. It is at committee meetings that the real work of a local authority is normally done.

It is often much better to admit the Press and public to meetings which they have no statutory right to attend than for garbled reports or one-sided statements to be communicated to the newspapers by irresponsible members; in fact, unless there is unanimity of opinion against their admission, it is preferable to admit the representatives of the Press, otherwise there is almost inevitably a "leakage" of information of an imperfect character.

On the other hand, it is often desirable to exclude the Press and public when business rather than propaganda work is the object of the meeting, especially when the deliberations of that meeting are reported to a parent body or society to whose meetings they are invited. The presence of the Press often retards the progress and business of the meeting, since members are apt to indulge in talk rather than engage in business, more particularly when elections are imminent, and there is on such occasions a natural tendency to play to the gallery *via* the newspapers. Moreover, there are times when matters of a confidential or delicate nature, or plans that are immature or undeveloped or of such a nature that they should in the first instance be discussed privately, are being considered, and the presence of the Press would naturally prevent free and open discussion.

CHAPTER 8

Expulsion from Meetings

When a meeting of a body or society takes place in premises which are private property or to which a stranger has no right of access, a stranger may only remain so long as his presence is not objected to, and when he is requested to leave for good reason or no reason and refuses to do so he becomes a trespasser and may thereupon be ejected with such reasonable force as may be necessary.

The expulsion, however, of a member of a meeting (*i.e.* of a person who is entitled to attend thereat) except for disorderly conduct of a serious nature is illegal unless standing orders otherwise provide, and such standing orders are within the powers of the constitution governing the meeting.

"The power, therefore, of suspending a member guilty of obstruction or disorderly conduct during the continuance of any current sitting, is . . . reasonably necessary for the proper exercise of the functions of any legislative assembly of this kind; and it may very well be, that the same doctrine of reasonable necessity would authorise a suspension until submission or apology by the offending member; which, if he were refractory, might cause it to be prolonged (not by the arbitrary discretion of the assembly, but by his own wilful default) for some further time."[1]

Similarly in *Doyle v. Falconer*[2] it was said that if a member of a colonial House of Assembly was guilty of disorderly conduct in that House while sitting, he might be removed or excluded for a time or even expelled, and that if the conduct of the members was not such as to secure order and decency of debate, the law would sanction the use of that degree of force which might be necessary to remove the person offending from the place of meeting and to keep him excluded, and that the same rule would apply *a fortiori* to obstructions caused by a non-member. In either case if the violation of order amounted to a breach of the peace recourse might be had to the ordinary courts.

[1] *Barton v. Taylor* (1886) 11 App. Cas. 197, at p. 204, a case concerned with the New South Wales Assembly.

[2] L.R. 1 P.C. 328, at 340.

It is the duty of the chairman to preserve order at the meeting, and consequently, in the event of a member of a meeting being so disorderly as to interfere unduly with the reasonable conduct of the meeting or to prevent the proper transaction of business, the chairman may order him to withdraw. If he refuses to comply with this order he may be ejected with reasonable force. If he resists ejection he may commit a breach of the peace. It is usually desirable, however, that the chairman should be supported by the majority of the meeting before he orders a member to withdraw, and he should take care not to give instructions for ejection—which should be delegated to a stalwart official—unless he is quite sure such instructions will be expeditiously and efficiently carried out.

Expulsion from Societies and Clubs

When the governing body of a club or society resolves on the expulsion of a member the resolution must, in order to be valid, have been duly passed in accordance with the rules at a meeting of the body properly convened and held, and in addition the following conditions must be fulfilled:

(1) The body must have the power to expel under the rules.
(2) These rules must not be contrary to natural justice.
(3) If the decision to expel is founded on the alleged commission of some act by the member, he must be given an opportunity of defending himself.
(4) The resolution must be *bona fide.*

In *Lee v. The Showmen's Guild of Great Britain*[1] a committee of a trade union purported to expel a member. The Court of Appeal affirmed the decision of Ormerod J. that on the true construction of the rules the conduct upon which the expulsion had been based could not be unfair competition (the sole grounds for the committee's decision) and accordingly that the fine imposed and subsequent expulsion were *ultra vires* and void.

A wrongful expulsion may give rise to a claim for damages, even against a trade union.[2]

Probably the principles of natural justice are inapplicable to companies incorporated under the Companies Acts. Certainly these principles can be made not to apply to such a company.[3]

[1] [1952] 2 Q.B. 329.
[2] *Bonsor v. Musician's Union,* [1956] A.C. 104.
[3] *Gaiman v. National Association for Mental Health,* [1971] 1 Ch. 317.

CHAPTER 9

Adjournments

If the chairman leaves the meeting before the business is completed, or if he purports to adjourn the meeting without authority, the meeting may, if a quorum still remains, appoint another chairman and proceed with the business, for the chairman has no right to adjourn the meeting without the consent of the meeting itself unless the business for which it was convened has been done or an express power in that behalf is given him by the relevant rules. "In my opinion the power which has been contended for is not within the scope of the authority of the chairman—namely, to stop the meeting at his own will and pleasure. The meeting is called for the particular purposes of the company. According to the constitution of the company, a certain officer has to preside. He presides with reference to the business which is there to be transacted. In my opinion, he cannot say, after that business has been opened, 'I will have no more to do with it; I will not let this meeting proceed; I will stop it; I declare the meeting dissolved, and I leave the chair.' In my opinion that is not within his power. The meeting by itself can resolve to go on with the business for which it has been convened, and appoint a chairman to conduct the business which the other chairman, forgetful of his duty or violating his duty, has tried to stop because the proceedings have taken a turn which he himself does not like."[1]

In *R. v. Winchester*,[2] where there was no regular presiding officer at an election, it was held that the control thereof devolves at common law upon the electors themselves.

The relevant rules often make provision for adjournments. When they do not, a meeting may resolve upon an adjournment.[3] When the relevant rules make no special provision and no quorum is constituted for a particular meeting, that meeting is ineffective. Table A of the Companies Act 1948, however, provides in such a case for an automatic adjournment to the same day in the next week.

[1] *National Dwellings Society v. Sykes*, [1894] 3 Ch. 159.
[2] (1806) 7 East 573.
[3] *R. v. Grimshaw* (1847) 11 Jur. 965.

Even if the relevant rules do not give the chairman power to adjourn the meeting, he may do so in the event of disorder. Such an adjournment must be for no longer than the chairman considers necessary and the chairman must, so far as possible, communicate his decision to those present.[1]

Postponement of Meetings

A properly convened meeting cannot be postponed. The proper course to adopt is to hold the meeting as originally intended, and then and there adjourn it to a more suitable date. If this course be not adopted, members will be entitled to ignore the notice of postponement, and, if sufficient to form a quorum, hold the meeting as originally convened and validly transact the business thereat.

[1] *John v. Rees*, [1970] Ch. 345.

CHAPTER 10

Minutes

The minutes of a meeting comprise a record of what was done at the meeting: *e.g.* resolutions and decisions of the meeting should be minuted, but not the speeches or arguments in connection therewith. The minutes may be drawn up during the meeting and put up for approval at the end of the meeting, but the more usual course is to approve them at the next meeting. Any inaccuracy in the minutes is fatal to their value and usefulness.

The minutes should be:

(1) An exact account of what was actually agreed upon.
(2) Sufficiently detailed and complete, so that a member who was absent could fully understand what was done at that meeting.
(3) Concise.

The minutes should contain, *inter alia*:

(1) In the case of meetings of a local authority and where the meeting is of a comparatively small body, *e.g.* of the board of directors of a company or of a committee, the names of the members present. It is usual in the meetings of small bodies to record in the minutes the names of those persons who vote against a specific resolution, if they request this to be done.
(2) Full and exact details of all contracts and questions involving financial considerations.
(3) The exact words of all resolutions which have been passed.
(4) Appointments, salaries, powers, and duties of officials (these should be very explicit).
(5) Instructions to officials, and all transactions authorised at that meeting.

Minutes, when lengthy, should be carefully indexed, and when not in actual use should, if possible, be kept in a fire-proof safe. Where the business transacted at a meeting is of some importance, copies of the minutes of that meeting may be circulated with the notice of the next meeting. It is important that the minutes should be signed by the chairman, either of the meeting at which they were taken or of that at which they were verified—generally the latter. There are certain statutory provisions as to the evidential value of minutes when so signed in the cases of companies and local authorities, and these are discussed respectively in Parts III and IV. The relevant rules may, however, provide that the minutes shall be conclusive evidence of the facts therein stated and such a provision will be good in the absence of fraud.[1]

Any discussion on the minutes, except as to their accuracy, is out of order, and the chairman should rule accordingly. Questions arising out of the minutes are permissible with the consent of the meeting if only for information and not for discussion.

It is unwise for a chairman to sign the minutes without getting them verified as correct by a meeting. The usual method is to bring up the minutes at the next succeeding meeting, when they are read if not previously circulated. The chairman then asks whether in the opinion of the meeting they are a correct report of the proceedings, and, if the answer is in the affirmative, he formally signs them. It is not necessary that he should have been present at the meeting at which they were taken.

If there is a conflict of opinion as to their accuracy, an amendment to the motion of their correctness, embodying the suggested alteration, should be put to the meeting and it is obvious that those who were not present at the preceding meeting should not take part in the discussion or vote. The approval of the minutes by a meeting *merely verifies their accuracy*; it does not necessarily mean that such minutes are adopted or that the resolutions therein are confirmed or ratified.

[1] *Kerr v. John Mottram*, [1940] Ch. 657.

PART TWO

Public Meetings

CHAPTER 11

Public Meetings

This chapter deals only with the holding of public meetings, that is the kind of meeting defined as a public meeting in the Public Order Act 1936.

Section 9(1) of the Public Order Act 1936 contains for the purpose of that Act the following definitions:

"Meeting" means a meeting held for the purpose of the discussion of matters of public interest or for the purpose of the expression of views on such matters.

"Public meeting" includes any meeting in a public place and any meeting which the public or any section thereof are permitted to attend, whether on payment or otherwise.

"Public place" means any highway, public park or garden, any sea beach, and any public bridge, road, lane, footway, square, court, alley or passage, whether a thoroughfare or not; and includes any open space to which, for the time being, the public have or are permitted to have access, whether on payment or otherwise.

Where Meetings may be Held

Meetings may be convened for any lawful purpose on any day, at any time, and in any place, provided that it is not unlawful for the persons attending to occupy that place, and that that place complies with any statutory enactment or bye-laws which may have been made affecting the safety of those attending. The Trade Union Act 1913, s. 3, however, restricts the application of trade union funds for the holding of political meetings.

Public Highways.—There is no right to hold meetings for any purpose on public highways, since a highway exists only for the purposes of passage.

"A claim on the part of persons so minded to assemble in any numbers, and for so long a time as they please to remain assembled, upon a highway, to the detriment of others having equal rights, is in its nature irreconcilable with the right of free passage, and there is, so far as we have been able to ascertain, no authority whatever, in favour of it. It was urged that the right of public meeting, and the right of occupying any unoccupied land or highway that might seem appropriate to those of Her Majesty's subjects who wish to meet there, were, if not synonymous, at least correlative. We fail to appreciate the argument, nor are we at all impressed with the serious consequences which it was said would follow from a contrary view. There has been no difficulty experienced in the past, and we anticipate none in the future, when the only and legitimate object is public discussion, and no ulterior and injurious results are likely to happen. Things are done every day, in every part of the kingdom, without let or hindrance, which there is not and cannot be a legal right to do, and not unfrequently are submitted to with a good grace because they are in their nature incapable, by whatever amount of user, of growing into a right."[1]

"The primary and over-ruling object for which streets exist is passage. The streets are public, but they are public for passage, and there is no such thing as a right in the public to hold meetings as such in the streets. . . . Streets are for passage, and passage is paramount to everything else. That does not necessarily mean that any one is doing an illegal act if he is not at the moment passing along. It is quite clear that citizens always meet in the streets, and may stop and speak to each other. The whole thing is a question of degree, and nothing else. . . . The right of free speech is to promulgate your opinions by speech so long as you do not utter what is treasonable, or libellous, or make yourself obnoxious to the statutes that deal with blasphemy or obscenity. But the right of free speech is a perfectly separate thing from the question of the place where that right is to be exercised. . . . Open spaces and public places differ very much in their character, and before you could say whether a certain thing could be done in a certain place, you would have to know the history of the particular place. . . . Here we are dealing with a street proper. . . . It is a thoroughfare. . . . In such a place there is not the slightest right in any one to hold a meeting as such. . . . The magistrates . . . have got to consider two things; first, whether what is going on in the streets is at all likely to interfere with . . . the right of passage; and, secondly, whether what is going on is likely to lead to a breach of the peace."[2]

In *Aldred v. Miller*[3] it was held, on the assumption that a public street may be lawfully used as a place for public meeting, that such meeting must be conducted so as not to interfere with other public uses of the street. "There is no such thing as a private right in any

[1] Wills J. in *ex parte Lewis* (1888) 21 Q.B.D. 191 at 197.
[2] *M'Ara v. Magistrates of Edinburgh*, [1913] *S.C.* at 1073.
[3] [1924] S.C. 117.

individual to make use of any public street for holding public meetings. If the thing is done at all, it must be done with due regard to the equal participation of all the members of the public in the various uses for which public streets are kept open. The duty of the police is to vindicate public right, and not to facilitate abuse of the street by any individual of his own."

Whilst there is no right to hold such a meeting, the fact that a public meeting is held upon a highway does not necessarily make the meeting unlawful. Whether it is unlawful or not depends upon the circumstances in which it is held, *e.g.* whether or not an obstruction is caused. "The justices had no right to assume that simply because the meeting was held on a highway, it could be interrupted not withstanding the provisions of the Public Meeting Act 1908."[1]

Other Places.—No public meeting of more than fifty persons can be held for certain purposes within one mile of Westminster Hall during a Session of Parliament (Seditious Meetings Act 1817).

Local authorities often permit public meetings to be held in certain defined parts of the areas under their control and make bye-laws for their regulation, which if within the scope of the authority conferred on them by Statute, are enforceable.[2]

No right on the part of the general public to hold meetings on a common is known to the law,[3] and consequently a bye-law prohibiting public meetings on a common is valid. There is no right to hold public meetings in the Royal Parks unless specific regulations so provide.[4] Similarly there is no right to hold public meetings in Trafalgar Square, except in accordance with regulations made by the Department of Environment.[5]

In *Hampstead Garden Suburb Trust v. Denbow*,[6] it was held that a company had a right to restrain a public meeting being held in a private road on their land which was not dedicated to the public and along which there was no public right of way.

Advertisement

If the proposed meeting is one at which the attendance of the general public is desired, adequate notice should be given. There

[1] *Burden v. Rigler*, [1911] 1 K.B. 337 at 340.
[2] *Slee v. Meadows* (1911) 75 J.P. 246.
[3] *De Morgan v. Metropolitan Board of Works* (1880) 5 Q.B.D. 155.
[4] *Bailey v. Williamson* (1873) L.R. 8 Q.B. 118.
[5] Trafalgar Square Regulations 1952.
[6] (1913) 77 J.P. 318.

are many methods of advertising a meeting, each having certain advantages with corresponding drawbacks. Among those ommonly used are the following:

(1) *Distribution of handbills*—This has the merit of cheapness. However, handbills delivered from door to door may be unwelcome.
(2) *Bill-posting*—This method will now generally be impracticable for it is subject to strict control under the Town and Country Planning Act 1971 and the statutory instruments made thereunder. These Regulations (*inter alia*) make fly-posting an offence punishable on summary conviction by a fine.
(3) *Newspaper or television advertisement*—The most effective media of advertising are undoubtedly the newspapers and television, provided sufficient space or time is taken to make an impact.

The General Conduct of a Public Meeting

The platform should be carefully planned—one person, one reserved seat; a few spare seats are always useful in case of unexpected visitors. The supporters of the chairman should know the position of their seats, some person being appointed to see that they get them.

With regard to the chairman, the usual custom is for the conveners to select their own chairman beforehand and may announce his name on the notice or advertisement of the meeting.

The chairman on rising should open the meeting with a few remarks merely by way of introduction as to the purport of the meeting or the chief speakers. He should remember that "brevity is the body as well as the soul of wit", and modify his speech accordingly. When the loquacious chairman is told to "sit down" he should, while blandly ignoring the interruption, take an early opportunity of resuming his seat.

The order of the meeting should proceed exactly as prearranged, the speeches being few and none of them long, except that of the principal speaker. At such meetings there is no obligation on the part of the chairman to allow anyone to speak, or to ask questions. The speakers and procedure are determined by the chairman and the conveners of the meeting.

Resolutions which are generally put to the vote at such meetings comprise:

(1) Declaration of principles or policy.
(2) Resolutions embodying such principles or policy to be sent to some authority or persons.
(3) Votes of thanks to principal speaker and chairman.

Disorder at Public Meetings

Disorder at public meetings generally arises from one or more of the following causes:

(1) *Irrelevant or violent interruptions* require to be dealt with in a firm and tactful manner by the chairman. Some interruptions are welcomed. They agreeably vary the monotony of a meeting, and often give the speaker an opportunity of relieving his speech by a well-delivered retort. But unless kept within due bounds, disorder generally follows.

    The chairman should use his discretion, and insist on questions being asked at the close of the speech, and also see that sufficient and proper time is allowed therefor. Sometimes he should allow an opponent to reply, but it all depends on circumstances and the temper of the audience.

(2) *Organised opposition* is very difficult to deal with, especially when the conveners of the meeting are unprepared for it. Generally, there is some indication beforehand, when it is folly not to be fully ready for it. People who come merely to disturb a meeting held on private premises generally prefer the back of the room, so that, should their courage fail them, there is a convenient exit for escape in time of trouble. It is a good plan to put probable disturbers in the front of the room, keeping them apart as much as possible. If they know there is a stronger force in the rear, they will often come to the conclusion that discretion is the better part of valour. Again, if the disturbers are all together it impedes the work of the "chucker-out", and his advent generally leads to a free fight, uproar, and disorder. Stewards of public meetings should be men of good physique, good temper, and not afraid of a row. They should know their business thoroughly, and it is wise for them to meet and have some preliminary understanding on the matter.[1]

[1] Statutory recognition is given to the position of stewards by s. 2(6) of the Public Order Act, which provides that nothing in that section, the main object of which is to prohibit quasi-military organisations, is to prohibit the employment of a reasonable number of persons as stewards to assist in the preservation

(3) *A weak and tactless chairman* may cause disorder at a meeting. If he is not fair, firm, competent, or impartial, trouble may easily arise. He should carefully observe the spirit and temper of his audience, and act accordingly; quelling at the instant any signs of incipient disorder.

All persons who attend public meetings on private premises, whether admission is free or otherwise, are bound to observe the rules laid down by the conveners of the meeting, and submit to their reasonable control. A person who has paid for his admission cannot, at any rate so long as he behaves himself properly, be ejected. This proposition can, it is conceived, be collected from the decision in *Hurst v. Picture Palaces.*[1] In that case it was held that a visitor to a theatre who has paid for his seat has a right to retain the seat so long as he behaves himself and keeps within the regulations laid down by the management. In the Court of Appeal, Buckley L.J. said: "A licence, coupled with an agreement not to revoke it for good consideration, conferred an enforceable right, and the grant of a right to enter upon premises and see the spectacle included a contract not to revoke till the performance was ended." See *Winter Garden Theatre (London) Ltd. v. Millennium Productions Ltd.*[2]

Where, however, there is no charge for admission, the licence to attend may be revoked at any time, and any person whose licence has been revoked becomes a trespasser and must withdraw.

Upon refusal to withdraw he may, after reasonable interval, be ejected, and such reasonable force as may be necessary to effect his removal is lawful. Excessive force if used will entitle the person ejected to damages. In *Hawkins v. Muff*[3] the plaintiff, who was ejected with violence from a political meeting by two stewards (causing fracture of his knee) for interjecting a remark during a speech by Mr. Churchill, brought an action against the chairman of the meeting and fifteen other persons, and was awarded by a jury £100 damages for assault.

Thus where a meeting is held on private premises, a person who has not paid for his admission can at any time be com-

---

of order at any public meetings held upon private premises—or their being furnished with badges or other distinguishing signs.

[1] [1915] 1 K.B. 1.

[2] [1948] A.C. 173 at 189.

[3] *The Times*, 24th March, 1911.

pelled to withdraw, and even if he has paid can be compelled to go if he behaves in a disorderly manner. In order, however, to justify his arrest his conduct must amount to a breach of the peace.

"Proof of annoyance and disturbance, such as crying 'Hear, hear', and putting questions to the speaker, and making observations on his statements would not be a sufficient justification of the defendant's conduct (i.e. giving such person in charge to the police); but, in order to find a verdict for the defendant, they must be satisfied that what was done by the plaintiff amounted to a breach of the peace."[1]

The conveners of a meeting in a public place have no power to compel an interrupter to withdraw.

The Powers of the Police

Section 1 of the Public Meeting Act 1908 provides that any person who at a lawful public meeting acts in a disorderly manner for the purpose of preventing the transaction of the business for which the meeting was called together shall be guilty of an offence. It also provides that any person who incites others to commit an offence under this section shall be guilty of a like offence.

By Section 84 of the Representation of the People Act 1949, a person who acts in a disorderly manner or incites others so to act for the purpose of preventing the transaction of business at a public meeting, which is a political meeting held in a parliamentary constituency between the date of issue of a writ for the return of a Member of Parliament for such constituency and the date at which a return to the writ is made or a meeting held with reference to a local government election in the electoral area for that election on, or within three weeks before, the day of election, is guilty of an illegal practice.

If a constable suspects an offence has been committed by any person under Section 1 of the Public Meeting Act or Section 84 of the Representation of the People Act, he may, if so requested by the chairman, require the person concerned to give his name and address. Failure or the giving of a false name is an offence; if he fails or refuses or the constable reasonably suspects he has given a false name and address, the constable may arrest him without warrant. This provision was added to the Public Meeting Act by Section 6 of the Public Order Act (p. 58 below).

The Metropolitan Police view of the Act of 1908 was stated in

[1] *Wooding v. Oxley* (1839) 9 C. & P. 1 at 5.

May, 1913, as follows: The Public Meeting Act gives no additional power to and imposes no additional duties on the police, but it makes the deliberate interruption of public meetings an offence cognisable by the law. The view taken by the police is that they are not required to take any initiative under the Act, and are not empowered to arrest interrupters. It is not their business to secure a hearing for speakers. It is for the speakers to get on such good terms with their audience that they can secure a hearing for themselves. The police ought not to interfere except to prevent a breach of the peace, and it may and must often happen that an act constituting a breach of the peace is committed where it is not observed by a police officer, or if done in his sight it may not be in his power to arrest the particular wrongdoer.

It has been held that police officers are entitled to enter and to remain on private premises where a meeting is being held, at any rate when the public generally have been invited to enter, if they have reasonable grounds for believing that if they are not present an offence or a breach of the peace will be committed.[1]

The Public Order Act 1936

The principal object of this Act was to help to control the disorders that had for some time prior to its passing been fomented by Fascist organisations.

Section 1 prohibits the wearing of uniforms in connection with political objects. Section 2 prohibits "Quasi Military Formations", and Section 3 confers powers on the police to enable them to preserve public order in connection with public processions. Apart from Section 2(6) (see *ante*, p. 55) these sections do not come within the scope of this book.

Section 4, however, makes it an offence for any person while present at a public meeting or on the occasion of a public procession to have with him an offensive weapon (not defined in the Act) otherwise than in pursuance of lawful authority, and Section 5 makes it an offence for any person in any public place or at any public meeting to use threatening, abusive, or insulting words or behaviour with intent to provoke a breach of the peace or whereby a breach of the peace is likely to be occasioned. In *Jordan v. Burgoyne*,[2] the conviction was upheld of the leader of a Fascist Group arising out of a meeting held in Trafalgar Square where the speaker had said "Hitler was right" and made insulting references to the

[1] *Thomas v. Sawkins*, [1935] 2 K.B. 249.

[2] [1963] 2 Q.B. 744.

Jews. The Divisional Court said that a speaker must take his audience as he finds them and the offence is committed if he uses words that are "threatening, abusive or insulting" to the audience although they might not be such, for example, to an audience consisting solely of the speaker's supporters. Section 7 of the Race Relations Act 1965 amended this provision so that it is now also an offence if any person in any public place or at any public meeting distributes or displays any writing, sign or visible representation which is threatening, abusive, or insulting with intent to provoke a breach of the peace or whereby a breach of the peace is likely to be occasioned.

The maximum penalty for an offence under the Public Order Act, other than one under Sections 2 and 5, is three months' imprisonment or a fine of £50 or both. Under the Act a constable is given a power of arrest without warrant of any person reasonably suspected by him of committing an offence under Sections 1, 4, or 5.

By Section 1 of the Public Order Act 1963, the maximum penalties for offences under Section 5 of the 1936 Act and Section 1 of the 1908 Act were increased: they are now—

(a) on summary conviction, three months' imprisonment or a fine of £100, or both;
(b) on conviction on indictment, twelve months' imprisonment or a £500 fine, or both.

Dispersal of Public Meetings

An unlawful assembly is an assembly of three or more persons with intent either to commit a crime by open force or to carry out any common purpose, lawful or unlawful, in such a manner as to give firm and courageous persons in the neighbourhood of such assembly reasonable grounds to apprehend a breach of the peace in consequence of it.[1]

"Any meeting assembled under such circumstances as, according to the opinion of rational and firm men, are likely to produce danger to the tranquillity and peace of the neighbourhood is an unlawful assembly. You will have to say whether, looking at all the circumstances, these defendants attended an unlawful assembly, and for this purpose you will take into your consideration the way in which the meetings were held, the hour of the day at which the parties met, and the language used by the persons assembled and by those who addressed them. Everyone has a right to act in such

[1] Stephen, *Digest of Criminal Law*, 8th ed., p. 77.

cases as he may judge right, provided it be not injurious to another, but no man or number of men has a right to cause alarm to the body of persons who are called the public. You will consider how far these meetings partook of that character, and whether firm and rational men having their families and property there would have reasonable ground to fear a breach of the peace."[1]

To take part in an unlawful assembly is a common law offence punishable by fine and imprisonment, and the police are entitled and bound to disperse such assemblies.

An assembly originally lawful does not become unlawful because it will incite unlawful opposition. "What has happened here is that an unlawful organisation has assumed to itself the right to prevent the appellants and others from lawfully assembling together, and the finding of the justices amounts to this, that a man may be convicted for doing a lawful act if he knows that his doing it may cause another to do an unlawful act. There is no authority for such a proposition."[2] Similarly, in *R. v. Londonderry Justices*[3] it was said: "If danger arises from the exercise of lawful rights resulting in a breach of the peace, the remedy is the presence of sufficient force to prevent that result, not the legal condemnation of those who exercise those rights."

This principle is, however, subject to the limitation that if it is impossible to preserve order by any other means than dispersing a lawful assembly the police may call upon the persons taking part to disperse, and if they do not do so they commit the offence of obstructing the police in the execution of their duty.

D was about to address a number of people in a street when a police officer, who reasonably apprehended that a breach of the peace would occur if the meeting were held, forbade her to do so. D persisted in trying to hold the meeting and obstructed the police officer in his attempts to prevent her doing so. Neither D nor any of the persons present at the meeting committed, incited, or provoked a breach of the peace. It was held that, as it is the duty of a police officer to prevent breaches of the peace which he reasonably apprehends, D was guilty of wilfully obstructing the officer when in the execution of his duty.[4]

So, too, in *Humphries v. Connor*,[5] it was held that a police officer was justified in removing a provocative emblem from the person of

[1] *R. v. Vincent* (1839) 9 C. & P. 91 at 109.

[2] *Beatty v. Gillbanks* (1882) 9 Q.B.D. 308 at 314. [3] (1891) 28 L.R. Ir. at 450.

[4] *Duncan v. Jones*, [1936] 1 K.B. 218. The offence is now embodied in the Police Act 1936, s. 51.

[5] 17 Ir. C.L.R. 1.

a lady, thereby protecting her from the threatened violence of a hostile crowd, and thus preserving the public peace which would otherwise have been broken. The moment at which a police officer becomes entitled to prevent a person from doing an otherwise lawful act must depend on questions of fact in each case. The dividing line is a difficult one to draw. In view of the state of the authorities the position must be regarded as obscure but the police are entitled to call upon innocent persons to disperse if that appears to be the only way that a breach of the peace can be avoided. Professor de Smith has pointed out that "the citizen cannot be sure of his rights, and the policeman is also in an invidious position. Whether he protects an unpopular speaker against the crowd (for example, by arresting abusive interrupters and charging them with insulting or threatening words or behaviour likely to cause a breach of the peace), or tries to dispserse a gathering in order to preserve the peace, he can expect to be criticised for taking sides or stifling freedom of expression. If he intervenes too precipitately, he may be sued or prosecuted for assault and will incur the displeasure of his superiors."[1]

If the people constituting an unlawful assembly take steps towards executing their intentions they are guilty of the offence of *rout* and if they do execute their intentions in a violent manner, alarming a person of reasonable courage, they are guilty of *riot*. No one can be guilty of riot unless it is established that the accused intended to assist one another by force if necessary. Any property owner suffering loss as a result of a riot has a claim on police funds under the Riot (Damages) Act 1886.

The Court of Appeal held in *R. v. Caird*[2] that an assembly becomes riotous *at least* when alarming force or violence begins to be used and that anyone who actively encourages or promotes an unlawful assembly or riot, whether by words, by signs or by actions or by participating in it, is guilty of an offence. 300–400 students and others had gathered outside the Garden House Hotel, Cambridge, and forced their way into the hotel in order to break up a dinner "with a Greek flavour". There was considerable violence to property and to the person. Seven convictions for riotous or unlawful assembly were upheld.

Anyone who *arranges or addresses* a meeting of three or more persons to support the I.R.A. or other proscribed organisation is guilty of an offence under the Prevention of Terrorism Act 1974. It is also an offence to wear clothes or display articles in public demonstrating support for the I.R.A. or other proscribed organisation.

[1] de Smith, *Constitutional and Administrative Law* (2nd ed. 1973), pp. 509–10.
[2] (1970) 54 Crim. App. Rep. 499.

Justices have jurisdiction to bind over to be of good behaviour a person who, in addressing meetings in public places, although he does not directly incite the commission of breaches of the peace, uses language the natural consequences of which is that breaches of the peace will be committed by others, and who intends to hold similar meetings, and use similar language in the future.[1]

Persons taking part in meetings held on the highway may, of course, commit the offence of obstruction and be dealt with accordingly.[2]

Defamation

So far as the speaker at a public meeting is concerned he is liable for defamatory statements made by him in exactly the same way as he would be liable for statements made on any other occasion.

It is, however, provided by the Defamation Act 1952 that a fair and accurate report on a matter of public concern in a newspaper (as defined in the Act) of the proceedings at any public meeting held in the United Kingdom, unless the publication is proved to be made with malice, is privileged subject to explanation or contradiction; that is to say it is privileged unless upon the request of any person defamed thereby that a reasonable letter of explanation or contradiction be published in the same newspaper the defendant has refused or neglected to comply with the request (Defamation Act 1952, Section 7 and Part II of the Schedule).

The schedule defines a public meeting as any meeting *bona fide* and lawfully held for a lawful purpose, and for the furtherance or discussion of any matter of public concern, whether the admission thereto is general or restricted.

Religious Meetings

These meetings are protected from disturbance by the Places of Religious Worship Act 1812, Section 12 of which provides that any person wilfully and maliciously or contemptuously disquieting or disturbing any meeting or congregation of persons assembled for religious worship, or disturbing, molesting or misusing any preacher, teacher or person officiating at such meeting or congregation, or any person there assembled, upon proof before any justice by two or more credible witnesses, is to find two sureties, to be bound in the sum of fifty pounds to answer for such offence, and in default to be committed to prison till the next Crown Court, and upon

[1] *Wise v. Dunning*, [1902] 1 K.B. 167.
[2] *Arrowsmith v. Jenkins*, [1963] 2 Q.B. 561.

conviction to forfeit the sum of forty pounds. See also the Religious Disabilities Act 1846, s. 4, by which the section referred to above was extended to include all meetings lawfully assembled for religious worship.

PART THREE

Meetings of Companies Incorporated under the Companies Acts

CHAPTER 12

The Control and Management of Companies

Part III of this book deals with the various meetings that are held in connection with companies incorporated under the Companies Acts. The general principles dealing with meetings of all kinds have already been discussed in Part I, and in many places in that Part reference has been made for an illustration of those principles to cases concerned with companies registered under the Companies Acts. This Part, however, is confined to a consideration of the meetings held in connection with such companies.[1]

The Companies Act 1948[2] provides that certain things may only be done by a company with the authority of a *special* resolution, certain other things may only be done with the authority of an *extraordinary* resolution, and that certain other things may be authorised by the company in general meeting, *i.e.* by *ordinary* resolution. All these resolutions must be passed by a general meeting, *i.e.* a meeting of the shareholders entitled to vote, and, except in the case of ordinary resolutions, require, in order to be passed, a three-fourths majority of the votes cast at the meeting. The Articles of Association of a company usually provide what acts may be done by the directors and what by a special, extraordinary or ordinary resolution of the company in general meeting. These provisions cannot, however, have the effect of relaxing the provisions of the Act.

If the Act requires that certain things be done by special resolution, such as reducing capital, the articles may not provide for them to be

[1] Previous editions of this book referred briefly to companies incorporated by royal charter or by statute. The former are comparatively rarely met with, and the latter, which comprise railway companies and public utility companies, are diminishing in number as the result of nationalisation. In the case of a statutory company the special Act incorporating it normally provides that the provisions of the Companies Clauses Consolidation Acts shall apply, in which case the relevant provisions as to meetings will be found in those Acts. Subject to those provisions and any provisions in the incorporating Act, the principles discussed in Part I will apply to meetings of such companies.

[2] This Act is referred to in this Part as "the Act", and references in this Part to sections will, unless otherwise stated, be to sections of this Act.

done by a less stringent resolution: on the other hand, anything which may be done by ordinary resolution, or in general meeting (which means the same thing), can be done by a more stringent resolution, either extraordinary or special since the greater includes the smaller. Similarly if the articles specify how any particular act may be done, or who has the power to do it, this can be altered by altering the articles by special resolution: the new provision must, of course, not purport to contravene the Act.

If articles contain complex provisions for any particular act, such as a capitalisation of profits, it is normally prudent, in exercising the power thereby given, to do so by special resolution even if the article permits an ordinary or extraordinary resolution. The special resolution will itself constitute an *ad hoc* alteration of the articles so that the risk of technically failing to comply with some provision of the article is obviated.

Unless the Act or the articles otherwise provide, a company can authorise any act by an ordinary resolution, *i.e.* one passed at a general meeting by a bare majority of votes. "Unless some provision to the contrary is to be found in the charter or other instrument by which the company is incorporated, the resolution of a majority of the shareholders, duly convened, upon any question with which the company is legally competent to deal, is binding upon the minority, and consequently upon the company, and every shareholder has a perfect right to vote upon any such question, although he may have a personal interest in the subject-matter opposed to, or different from, the general or particular interests of the company."[1]

This is, however, limited to matters which the company is legally entitled to transact. Even if all the shareholders agree to the company doing something which is illegal or beyond its powers, this is inaffective and the company does not thereby acquire the power necessary for that purpose.

Further, the majority will not be able to control the acts of the company in so far as the control of any particular class of act has been removed from it by the articles, except by altering the articles which requires a special resolution. Articles usually provide that the business of the company shall be managed by the directors, in which case the powers of the members in general meeting are very limited. But if the directors wish to waive their power, or are unable to exercise it because of conflicting personal interests, or if their exercise of the power is challenged as not having been exercised in good faith for the purpose for which the power was given, the company in general

[1] *North-West Transportation Co. v. Beatty* (1887) 12 App. Cas. 589, at 593.

meeting may by ordinary resolution exercise or ratify the exercise of the power.[1]

Under most articles it is the directors who are to manage the company's business and affairs. Regulation 80 of Table A[2] provides that the business of the company is to be managed by the directors, who may exercise all such powers of the company as are not, by the Act or the articles, required to be exercised by the company in general meeting, subject, nevertheless, to the articles, to the provisions of the Act and to such regulations, being not inconsistent with the articles or the Act, as may be prescribed by the company in general meeting. The Regulation further provides that no regulation made by the company in general meeting shall invalidate any prior act of the directors which would have been valid if that regulation had not been made. The wording of this Regulation is not a happy piece of drafting; it is not easy to understand what is meant by the words "subject to such regulations, being not inconsistent with the articles, as may be prescribed by the Company in general meeting". It seems to the editors that any such regulations must be restricted to matters which are not concerned with the management of the company's business (since that is a power and duty of the directors) and for which there is nothing laid down in the articles. The words are a snare and should not be relied upon, since their effect must be uncertain. If it is desired to make regulations controlling the directors, these should be adopted by special resolution.

If the members of a company disapprove of the action of its directors on a matter which is within the powers of the directors, they cannot, by passing a resolution, annul the directors' decision. The members can remove the directors by ordinary resolution (*post*, p. 119) or, by special resolution, control the directors for the future by altering the articles.

If the directors purport to act outside their own powers, but *intra vires* the company, the company in general meeting may ratify their action;[3] but the Court will, at the instance of a single

[1] *Bamford v. Bamford*, [1970] Ch. 212; *Barron v. Potter*, [1914] 1 Ch. 895; *Foster v. Foster*, [1916] 1 Ch. 532.

[2] References to Table A are to the Table A in the First Schedule to the Act. Articles of Association of a company may adopt all or any part of Table A and in the case of companies limited by shares registered after the commencement of the Act, if the Articles do not exclude the provisions of Table A these provisions will constitute the regulations of the Company (Section 8). The various Regulations in Table A dealing with meetings are referred to as examples of the kind of Articles now frequently met with.

[3] *Grant v. United Kingdom Switchback Railway Co.* (1888) 40 Ch. D. 135.

shareholder, restrain a company from purporting or attempting to do an act which is illegal or outside the powers of the company.

If the act is only irregular on the part of the directors and is such that the company could ratify it, or is one which the company has done irregularly when it might have done it regularly, a minority cannot obtain the interference of the Court.

In *MacDougall v. Gardiner*[1] it was said: "In my opinion, if the thing complained of is a thing which in substance the majority of the company are entitled to do, or if something has been done irregularly which the majority of the company are entitled to do regularly, or if something has been done illegally, which the majority of the company are entitled to do legally, there can be no use in having litigation about it, the ultimate end of which is only that a meeting has to be called, and then ultimately the majority gets its wishes."

"It is most important that the Court should hold fast to the rule[2] upon which it has always acted, not to interfere for the purpose of forcing companies to conduct their business according to the strictest rules, where the irregularity complained of can be set right at any moment."[3] In the ordinary way the directors are the persons entitled to institute proceedings on behalf of the company, but when the majority of the shareholders desire to protect the company's rights they are entitled to start proceedings in the name of the company.[4] As a result of the rule stated above it has long been the law that in any action complaining of an act by or on behalf of a company which is capable of ratification by the company in general meeting the company must be the plaintiff. If the majority are not prepared to launch proceedings in respect of the act in question, they would be certain to ratify it at a general meeting, when the act, though originally irregular or unauthorised, would become valid and any proceedings launched by a minority would be bound to fail.

This rule of procedure does not apply where the act complained of would require for its ratification the passing of a special or extraordinary resolution. If it did, a bare majority, by refusing to bring proceedings in the name of the company to avoid the act, would be able effectively to ratify an act which by virtue of the Act or the constitution of the company required to be authorised by a resolution passed by a three-quarters majority.[5]

[1] (1875) 1 Ch. D. 13, at 25.

[2] The rule is often referred to as The Rule in *Foss v. Harbottle* (1843) 2 Hare 461.

[3] *Browne v. La Trinidad* (1887) 37 Ch. D. 1, at 17.

[4] *Pender v. Lushington* (1877) 6 Ch. D. 70.

[5] *Baillie v. Oriental Telephone Co.*, [1915] 1 Ch. 503.

Minority shareholders may also bring actions complaining of the acts of the company where those acts are alleged to be a fraud on, or oppressive of minorities.[1]

[1] *Atwool v. Merryweather* (1867) L.R. 5 Eq. 464*n.*

CHAPTER 13

Meetings of Members, including Classes of Members and of Debenture-Holders

Statutory Meeting

Every company which is incorporated as a public company limited by shares is required to hold a statutory meeting (Section 130). This is a tiresome procedure, and nowadays is commonly circumvented by the simple expedient of incorporating a company as a private company, and almost immediately thereafter converting it into a public company. Section 130 sets out the time within which the statutory meeting must be held, the notice required, and the information to be given. This information is contained in the "statutory report" and the information so to be given is of a nature which will give members at an early date an opportunity of ascertaining the precise position and prospects of the company.

The statutory report covers such matters as the financial position, shares allotted, names of directors, auditors and officers and contracts which are to be modified (see below). The statutory report is certified by two directors, and certain information therein is also certified by the auditors: it has to be delivered to the Registrar of Companies for registration. At the meeting a list of members has to be produced (Sub-section (6)).

Notices convening a meeting under this section must comply with the same provisions as notices of other general meetings and must also state that it is to be the statutory meeting.[1] Under Section 133 the articles may not provide for a shorter notice of any meeting than 14 days and this will generally be the length of notice required by the articles. The notices can then be accompanied by the statutory report required by the section which must be sent to the members at least 14 days before the day on which the meeting is held (Sub-section (2)).

All members, whether or not under the articles they are entitled to receive notice of or to attend or vote at general meetings, are to be sent the statutory report.

[1] *Gardner v. Iredale*, [1912] 1 Ch. 700.

Modification of Contracts.—By Section 42 a company bound to hold a statutory meeting may not previously to the statutory meeting vary the terms of a contract referred to in the prospectus, or statement in lieu of prospectus, except subject to the approval of the statutory meeting.

Hence where the company has varied the terms of a contract referred to in the prospectus the approval of the statutory meeting will be necessary in order to make such variation valid, and this is the reason for the requirement of paragraph (*e*) of Section 130(3).

Discussion.—Unlike ordinary meetings, any topic may be discussed which is relevant to the incorporation of the company or the statutory report, whether notice has been given of it or not, but no resolution may be passed unless proper notice thereof has been given in accordance with the articles (Sub-section 7).

Adjournment under Sub-section (8): The *meeting* may adjourn from time to time, and this puts the power of adjournment into the hands of the *majority of the meeting* (unanimity is not necessary) whether or not the articles give the majority this power in the case of general meetings independently of the chairman. The adjourned meeting has the same powers as an original meeting and, unlike ordinary meetings, it may consider any resolution of which notice of a proper length has been given, whether it was given before or after the original meeting (Sub-section 8), *e.g.* notice of a statutory meeting is given on the 1st January for the 16th. On this day it is adjourned to the 16th February, and it will then be possible to consider a special resolution at the adjourned meeting if notice of it is given on the 25th January. This would not be so in the case of other general meetings.

Default in complying with the provisions of the Section.—By Sub-section (9), a penalty of £50 may be imposed on every director who knowingly and wilfully is a party to the default. Default in delivering the statutory report under Sub-section (5), or in holding the statutory meeting also results in the company being liable to be wound up by the Court (Section 222(*b*)). In *re Kent Outcrop Coal Co.*[1] the first compulsory winding-up order was made under this paragraph. Only a shareholder may present a winding-up petition on this ground (Section 224). Where a petition for winding up is presented on this ground the Court may, instead of making a winding-up order, direct that the statutory report shall be delivered or that a meeting shall be held (Section 225(3)).

The statutory meeting is a general meeting and, subject to the

[1] (1912) W.N. 26.

special provisions above referred to, the rules relating to general meetings will apply to it.

Annual General Meetings

Section 131 contains provisions relating to annual general meetings. Sub-section (1) provides that every company shall in each year hold a general meeting as its annual general meeting in addition to any other meetings in that year, and shall specify the meeting as such in the notices calling it; and that not more than 15 months shall elapse between the date of one annual general meeting of the company and that of the next. But a relaxation is made by the provision that, so long as a company holds its first annual general meeting within 18 months of its incorporation, it need not hold it in the year of its incorporation or in the following year.

Failure to hold a meeting in the calendar year and not holding it within 15 months from the preceding meeting are separate offences. The former offence is not committed until after 31st December, even though the period of 15 months has already elapsed.[1]

If an annual general meeting is not held in compliance with this Sub-section the Department of Trade may, on the application of a member, direct the calling of a general meeting (Sub-section (2)). Such a meeting is, subject to any directions given by the Department, to be regarded as an annual general meeting. If, through default in holding a meeting in one year, the Department orders a meeting to be held and it is so held in the following year, the meeting is not to be treated as the annual general meeting for the year in which it is held unless at that meeting it is so resolved (Sub-section (3)). The Department does not exercise its powers under the Act as readily as might be hoped and expected.

Default either in holding an annual general meeting or in complying with any directions given by the Department under Sub-section (2) renders the company and any officer in default liable to a fine of £50 (Sub-section 5)).

The articles usually specify what is to be usual business at an annual general meeting. It normally consists of the consideration of the accounts and reports, the declaration of a dividend, the election of directors, and the fixing of the remuneration of the auditor. Sometimes the directors' remuneration is also fixed at this meeting. Regulation 52 of Table A provides that all business is to be deemed special that is transacted at an extraordinary general meeting, and also all that is transacted at an annual general meeting, with the exception of declaring a dividend, the consideration of the accounts, balance

[1] *Smedley v. Registrar of Companies*, [1919] 1 K.B. 97.

sheets, and the reports of the directors and auditors, the election of directors in the place of those retiring and the appointment of, and the fixing of the remuneration of, the auditors.

Whatever the provisions of the articles, the business at an annual general meeting includes by virtue of Section 140(6) the consideration of any resolution of which notice has been given on a requisition under that section (p. 76, *post*).

Section 159 also provides that every company must at each annual general meeting appoint an auditor to hold office until the conclusion of the next annual general meeting. Under Sub-section (2) of that section a retiring auditor will be automatically reappointed without any resolution being passed unless he is not qualified for appointment or has resigned or a resolution has been passed appointing someone in his place, or providing that he shall not be reappointed. Any such resolution will require special notice, in accordance with Section 142 (p. 120, *post*).

In the absence of fraud, the directors have a right to select the place of meeting if acting *intra vires* and *bona fide*.[1] The power of the directors to select the place of meeting is, of course, a fiduciary power which must be exercised in the interests of the company. If it were called at a place or time which would be inconvenient for shareholders so as to have the effect of restricting the attendance this would be a wrongful exercise of their power, and could be challenged.[2]

During the whole of the annual general meeting the register of the interests of directors of the company in shares or debentures of the company and related companies required to be kept by Section 27 of the Companies Act 1967 is by Section 29(11) required to be open to the inspection of the members. It must also be produced at the commencement of the meeting.

Extraordinary General Meetings

General meetings of the shareholders, other than annual general meetings and the statutory meeting, are called "extraordinary general meetings"; Regulation 48 of Table A; these meetings are held for the transaction of some business which cannot wait until the next annual general meeting. They will usually be convened by the directors, but in some cases may be requisitioned by the members: see Section 132 and Regulation 49.

The articles provide who may call meetings. For example, Regulation 49 of Table A provides that such meetings be called by

[1] *Martin v. Walker* (1918) 145 L.T.N. 377.
[2] *Cannon v. Trask* (1875) L.R. 20 Eq. 669.

the directors, but in addition members may themselves convene such meetings where either—

(1) There has been a requisition for a meeting and the directors fail to comply (see next paragraph); or
(2) There are too few directors in the United Kingdom to form a quorum.

Whatever the provisions of the articles may be, the directors are bound under Section 132 to call such a meeting on the requisition of a specified proportion of the members, in which case the requisitionists must state the objects of the meeting, but the directors may fix the time and place of the meeting.

The requisition must be signed by the requisitionists and deposited at the registered office; it may consist of several documents, each signed by one or more requisitionists (Sub-section (2)). For this purpose it is generally accepted in practice that a requisition sent through the post is due compliance with the requirement to deposit.

Where a requisition is made by holders of shares held jointly, such requisition must be signed by all the joint holders.[1] Where the requisition consists of several documents the requirement that they shall be in "like form" does not mean that they must be in exactly the same form.[2]

If the directors do not proceed within 21 days to convene a meeting, the requisitionists may themselves do so in the same manner, as nearly as possible, as that in which meetings are convened by the directors (Sub-sections (3) and (4)).

If on receipt of a requisition the directors give a proper notice as to part only of the business specified in the requisition, the requisitionists may convene a meeting for the purpose of considering the business omitted from the notice sent out by the directors.[3]

The company must pay the reasonable expenses of requisitionists incurred in themselves convening a meeting but may retain the amount out of remuneration falling due to the defaulting directors.

Section 132 does not specifically provide that the meeting so requisitioned must be convened by the directors for a date falling within a specified period. But the duty and power of the directors under the Section are fiduciary, and must be exercised in good faith. Accordingly they could not purport to call a meeting to be held, say, in six months: this would not be reasonable or justifiable, and would not be compliance with the Section. Indeed, if, in order to let the

[1] *Patent Wood Keg Syndicate v. Pearse* (1906) W.N. 164.
[2] *Fruit & Vegetable Growers Association v. Kekewich*, [1912] 2 Ch. 52.
[3] *Isle of Wight Railway Co. v. Tahourdin* (1883) 25 Ch. D. 320.

proposals contained in the requisition have effect, the meeting had to be held quickly, the directors would not be complying with the Section if they deliberately fixed a date too far away, even though for other purposes such a date might have been suitable. If the directors fail to act responsibly on receipt of a requisition, the requisitionists are probably best advised to apply to the Court for a declaration that the directors have not complied with the Section, coupled with an alternative application under Section 135.

Class Meetings

Under the Articles.—Where the capital of a company is divided into shares of different classes, the articles usually provide for the alteration of the rights attached to a class with the consent of the holders of a specified majority of the shares of that class. The purpose of such an article is to enable changes to be made even if the consent of every member of the class cannot be obtained.

For example, in Regulation 4 of Table A, it is provided that if at any time the share capital is divided into different classes of shares, the rights attached to any class (unless otherwise provided by the terms of issue of the shares of that class) may, whether or not the company is being wound up, be varied with the consent in writing of the holders of three-fourths of the issued shares of that class, or with the sanction of an extraordinary resolution passed at a separate general meeting of the holders of the shares of the class. The article makes the provisions of the articles relating to general meetings apply to such separate general meetings except that it states expressly that the necessary quorum shall be two persons at least holding or representing by proxy one-third of the issued shares of the class and that any holder of shares of the class present in person or by proxy may demand a poll.

In the absence of such a provision it may well be impossible to alter the special rights of a class except with the unanimous consent of the holders of that class or by means of a Scheme of Arrangement sanctioned by the Court under Section 206 (see below).

If any alteration is made with the consent of the requisite majority under an article such as this, the holders of not less than 15 per cent of the issued shares of that class may apply to the Court to have the alteration cancelled on the ground that the variation would unfairly prejudice the class in question (Section 72).

Under an article in the form of Regulation 4, if the necessary quorum is not present at the meeting, *i.e.* "two persons at least holding or representing by proxy one-third of the issued shares of the class", such quorum will still be required at the adjourned meeting and no smaller quorum will suffice, even if the articles relating to general meetings include an article in form similar to Regulation 54 of Table A.[1]

Under the directions of the Court.—The meetings above referred to are convened by the company in the same way as meetings of the company are convened, but there is another kind of class meeting which may be held. This is under Section 206. Under this section where a compromise or arrangement is proposed between a company and its creditors or any class of them or between the company and its members or any class of them, the Court may, on the application of the company or of any creditor or member of the company, or, in the case of a company being wound up, of the liquidator, order a meeting of the creditors or class of creditors, or of the members of the company or class of members, as the case may be, to be summoned in such manner as the Court directs. If a majority in number representing three-fourths in value of the creditors or class of creditors or members or class of members, as the case may be, present and voting either in person or by proxy at the meeting, agree to any compromise or arrangement, the compromise or arrangement, if sanctioned by the Court, becomes binding on all the creditors or the class of creditors, or on the members or class of members, as the case may be, and also on the company or, in the case of a company in the course of being wound up, on the liquidator and contributories of the company.

Any company liable to be wound up under the Act is a "company" within Section 206. This will include most companies carrying on business or incorporated in the United Kingdom, including companies incorporated by charter or registered under Part VIII of the Act. It will also include all overseas companies as defined in Part X of the Act, that is, companies incorporated abroad but which have established a place of business in the United Kingdom. The Court having the jurisdiction to hear a petition to sanction a scheme under Section 206 must be the Court in that part of the United Kingdom where the company is liable to be wound up. In some cases, *e.g.* where an overseas company having a place of business in, and has registered under Section 407, in Scotland and England, Courts in either country have jurisdiction. A company carrying out operations on the continental shelf but otherwise not registered or having a place of business in Scotland or England will not fall within the Court's jurisdiction for this purpose. The expression "arrangement" includes a reorganisation of the share capital of the company by the consolida-

[1] *Hemans v. Hotchkiss Ordnance Company*, [1899] 1 Ch. 115.

tion of shares of different classes or by the division of shares into shares of different classes or by both those methods.

By Section 207 a company proposing a Scheme of Arrangement under Section 206 is required to give certain specified information regarding the effect of the Scheme and the interests of directors and debenture stock trustees. This statutory requirement is itself not normally adequate, and does not derogate from the requirement that shareholders or creditors must be given all relevant information, whether favourable or adverse, which might influence their judgment. These principles are discussed at length in *Carruth v. Imperial Chemical Industries*, [1937] A.C. 707: for a fuller discussion of this aspect see *Gore-Browne on Companies*, 42nd ed., pp., 872–4, and relevant section in Second Supplement thereto.[1] Section 207 also contains provisions relating to the convening of the meetings, and notices for this purpose.

This is a useful provision enabling all the members and creditors to be bound by a scheme of which the majorities of the various classes approve.

There are sometimes difficult questions of what constitutes a separate class: generally speaking, if either—

(a) certain shares have different rights from other shares, and those rights are relevant for consideration of the scheme

or (b) certain shares are treated differently under the scheme from others,

separate classes exist for the purpose of the Section.

The meetings are summoned by Order of the Court and in accordance with its direction. Under modern practice, the Court does not require notice to be sent to any but the first-named of joint holders, unless the articles require notice of general meetings to be sent to all joint holders. The Court requires that proxies be accepted at any time up to and including the meeting itself.

The meetings are conducted under the chairmanship of a person appointed by the Court by name: if no such person is present the meeting cannot take place, since he is directed by the Court to report the result to the Court. Accordingly it is prudent to name three alternative chairmen, so that exigencies of mortality or natural hazards are not likely to frustrate the meeting. The chairman so appointed makes a full report of the meeting, including how votes were cast, the numbers and shareholdings present or represented and whether any proxies or votes were rejected (and why). If there is opposition it is also sensible for the chairman, by affidavit, to indicate

[1] Published by Jordan & Sons Limited.

its nature and extent. It may also be necessary to indicate if any shareholders of the class hold conflicting interests as holders of another class, if the treatment of the two is different.

The class meetings themselves do not constitute general meetings of the company: if the scheme requires either the consent of the company in general meeting, or some corporate act which has to be performed in general meeting, such as an increase or reduction of capital, then an extraordinary general meeting must be convened for this purpose; such a meeting is convened by the directors in the ordinary way, and is not called on the direction of the Court. Inclusive forms of proxy for a class meeting are settled by the Court, whereas those for the general meeting will be separate and will follow the form required by the articles: see further, *post*, regarding time for deposit of Court proxies.

As to class meetings that may be required to be held in connection with compensation to directors for loss of office, see *post*, p. 92.

Meetings of Debenture Stock Holders

Akin to class meetings are meetings of debenture stockholders. These will be convened and conducted in accordance with the provisions contained in the debenture stock Trust Deed. Under trust deeds made some years ago, the provisions for calling meetings of debenture stockholders are often inadequate for modern requirements. The quorum requirements are often so high that in practice they are difficult to attain, and these requirements often extend through to a meeting adjourned from the original date, through lack of quorum, to a later date. A second defect is often the very restricted powers for amendment of the Deed: frequently they cannot be used to enable the substitution of a similar debenture stock of another company in place of that under the Trust Deed. Such substitution is often very desirable in the case of a take-over bid for the company concerned, or if the parent company in a group wishes to rationalise the financial structure and borrowings of the group.

If the provisions under the Trust Deed are inadequate, the company has to have recourse to a scheme under Section 206.

Where a meeting of debenture holders is held, each holder may vote in his own interests, but if he has conflicting interests in a capacity as shareholder of the company, or as a creditor of a different class, he must not vote in favour of the other interest, or, if he does, his vote may be open to challenge.[1]

A person may be entitled to vote at a meeting of debenture holders if debentures have been allotted to him, his name is in the register of

[1] *Re New York Taxicab Co.*, [1913] 1 Ch. 1.

debenture holders, and he has the right to call for duly sealed debentures and is bound to accept them.[1]

Debentures are often issued on the terms that the rights of the holders may be varied with the consent of a certain proportion of the holders or with the consent of a resolution passed by a particular majority at a meeting of the holders. Any such variation must, to be valid, be one strictly in accordance with the terms of the debentures. A power of this kind to vary rights will not justify abandoning rights and a power to compromise can only be exercised if there is some dispute to compromise[2] or if there is some compromise (but not abandonment) of rights.[3]

[1] *Dey v. Rubber & Mercantile Corporation*, [1923] 2 Ch. 528.
[2] *Mercantile Investment Co. v. International Co. of Mexico*, [1893] 1 Ch. 484*n*.
[3] *Re N.F.U. Development Trust Ltd.*, [1972] 1 W.L.R. 1548.

CHAPTER 14

Notice of Meetings

A company is not corporately assembled so as to be able to transact any business unless the meeting is convened by a proper notice given in accordance with the provisions of the Act and the company's articles and stating the time and place of the meeting. The notice must also state the nature of the business to be transacted except where such business is of a kind of which under the articles notice is not required.

Any defect in this notice will, however, be cured if all the members entitled to be present attend and agree on the course proposed,[1] and if all the members agree, either expressly or tacitly, it is not even necessary in an ordinary case that there should be an actual meeting.[2]

Private companies frequently adopt an article in terms similar to Regulation 5 of Part II of Table A. This provides that, subject to the provisions of the Act, a resolution in writing signed by all the members entitled to attend and vote at meetings, shall be as valid and effective as if it had been passed at a general meeting. In the view of the editors a resolution in writing, signed by all the members entitled to attend and vote, is as effective as a special or extraordinary resolution and falls to be registered under Section 143(4).[3]

The provisions of the Act referred to in the opening words are those which require an act to be performed by the company at a meeting, *e.g.* increase of capital (Section 61) or the passing of special and extraordinary resolutions. In those cases a meeting being required the clause would not apply and an actual meeting would have to be held: but see *re Express Engineering Works*[4] and *re Oxted Motor Co.*[5]

The general principles affecting notices of all classes of meetings are discussed fully *ante*, Chapter 2. The following remarks concern the particular law and practice governing meetings of shareholders.

[1] *Baroness Wenlock v. River Dee Co.* (1883) 36 Ch. D. 681*n*.

[2] *Parker & Cooper v. Reading*, [1926] 1 Ch. 975. *Bailey Hay & Co. Ltd.*, [1971] 1 W.L.R. 1357.

[3] *Re Pearce Duff & Co. Ltd.*, [1960] 1 W.L.R. 1014, and *Bailey Hay & Co. Ltd.*, [1971] 1 W.L.R. 1357.

[4] [1920] 1 Ch. 466.

[5] [1921] 3 K.B. 32.

(1) *General Provisions as to Notice*.—The notice must state the hour, date, and place of meeting, all of which, although usually left by the articles to the discretion of the directors, must be reasonably convenient for the shareholders.

Although the Court will not interfere with the powers and duties of directors in their management of the internal affairs of a company, directors will be restrained from fixing a particular date for holding the annual general meeting of the company for the purpose of preventing shareholders from exercising their voting powers.[1]

The articles generally provide for a certain length of notice, but the Act contains certain provisions which require that at least 21 days' notice be given of the annual general meeting (Section 133) and of any meeting at which a special resolution is to be proposed (Section 141) and at least 14 days of any other meeting (or 7 days in the case of an unlimited company). If, however, shorter notice is agreed to, in the case of an annual general meeting by all the members entitled to attend and vote or, in the case of any other meeting, by a majority in number of such members having between them 95 per cent of the total voting rights at the meeting, the meeting will be valid (Section 133(3)).

The number of days must be clear[2] so that for this purpose there must be 21 days excluding the day when the notice is given or is deemed to be given and the day when the meeting is to be held. If the meeting is to be on, say, a Wednesday and the articles provide that notice is deemed to be given on the day following that on which it is posted, or (as in Table A, Regulation 131, 24 hours after posting), the notice must be posted on the Monday 23 days before the date of the meeting (if the annual general meeting or one for passing a special resolution) or 16 (9 if the company is unlimited) days before the date of any other meeting.

If the articles provide that general meetings are to be convened by notice through the post, a notice by advertisement would be irregular, and vice versa. Table A, Regulation 131, provides that service of a notice of a meeting if sent by post is deemed to have been effected at the expiration of 24 hours after the letter containing the same is posted. Some articles purport to provide that notice is deemed to be given on the date of posting. The validity of such an article is doubtful and the only concession on which reliance can be placed is that which is contained in Table A: since Table A is statutory it must be legal.

[1] *Cannon v. Trask* (1875) L.R. 20 Eq. 669.

[2] *Mercantile Co. v. International Co. of Mexico*, [1893] 1 Ch. 484*n*.; *Hector Whaling Co.*, [1936] Ch. 208.

Where debentures are secured by a trust deed or are in a series, provisions for the convening of meetings of the debenture holders will normally be set out in the trust deed or in the debentures. If no such regulations are set out, advertisement in suitable newspapers convening a meeting will be sufficient notice, and will be given on the day on which the advertisement appears.[1]

The articles usually prescribe the method by which notices are to be served: see, for example, Regulation 131 of Table A.

Where by the articles, a notice of a call on a member may be served by sending it through the post in a letter addressed to such member at his registered place of abode, it is not necessary to follow literally the address on the register, but a substantially accurate designation of the registered place of abode is enough.[2] The same principle would apply in the case of notice of a meeting.

Notices must be issued by the proper authority.—It is usually the directors who are responsible for convening the annual general meeting and empowered to convene extraordinary meetings (cf. Regulation 49 of Table A).

The power to convene meetings is a power of the Board, not of some only of the directors,[3] unless acting as a duly constituted Board or as a duly appointed committee with power to do so.

A notice issued by the secretary without the authority of a resolution of the directors duly assembled at a board meeting is invalid,[4] and even where a meeting is requisitioned under Section 132, the secretary cannot validly summon a meeting without the authority of the Board of Directors.[5] A notice issued without such authority, either because no instructions have been given by the board for its issue or because the instructions were given by an improperly constituted board, may become a good notice if adopted and ratified by a proper board meeting held prior to the general meeting. "The question is whether, although the notice was not authorised beforehand, it has been so ratified now as to make it a good and valid notice. In my opinion it has. The principle of the cases, which I do not propose to go through, is that the ratification of an act purporting to be done by an agent on your behalf dates back to the performance of the act."[6]

Regulation 105 of Table A provides that all acts done by any

[1] *Sneath v. Valley Gold Ltd.*, [1893] 1 Ch. 477.
[2] *Liverpool Marine Insurance Co. v. Haughton* (1875) 23 W.R. 93.
[3] *Browne v. La Trinidad* (1887) 37 Ch. D., at p. 17.
[4] *Re Haycraft Gold Reduction Co.*, [1900] 2 Ch. 230.
[5] *Re State of Wyoming Syndicate*, [1901] 2 Ch. 431.
[6] *Hooper v. Kerr* (1900) 83 L.T. 730.

meeting of directors or by any person acting as a director shall, notwithstanding that it be afterwards discovered that there was some defect in the appointment of any such director or person acting as aforesaid or that they or any of them were disqualified, be as valid as if every such person had been duly appointed and was qualified to be a director. An article in this form may validate a meeting held on notices sent out by an irregularly constituted board.[1] As to the extent to which such an article will be effective, see *Morris v. Kanssen*.[2]

Notices should be signed by the secretary, qualified by the words "By Order of the Board", and the secretary should see that the board meeting, which has authorised the convening of a general meeting, was itself properly convened and that a quorum of directors was present. Where, however, the articles make no provision for the calling of meetings, two or more members holding not less than one-tenth of the issued share capital, or if the company has not a share capital, not less than 5 per cent in number of the members of the company, may call a meeting (Section 134(b)).

As to the power of members to give notice of a meeting in certain circumstances, see Chapter 13.

Subject to any limitations in the articles, all members on the register are entitled to receive notice of meetings, and if notice is not sent to any person entitled to receive it, the meeting is irregular and its proceedings invalid.[3] Articles normally provide that accidental failure to give notice will not invalidate a meeting or the proceedings.[4] But if the failure to send a notice is deliberate, where, for example, the company believes that notice to the address in the register will not reach the member and accordingly does not send one to him, the saving of the article will not operate: the failure to send the notice is not accidental.[5]

If, however, a meeting is irregularly convened, a person who attends and takes part may be unable subsequently to complain of the irregularity. At an adjourned general meeting, of which adjournment notice was given by circulars sent to the shareholders, but not by advertisement, as required by the deed of settlement, it was resolved to make a call. A shareholder who was present and voted at the adjourned meeting was held not entitled to take advantage of the irregularity of the notice.[6]

[1] *Transport Ltd. v. Schomburg* (1905) 21 T.L.R. 305.
[2] [1946] A.C. 459.
[3] *Smyth v. Darley* (1849) 2 H.L.C. 789.
[4] *West Canadian Collieries*, [1962] Ch. 370.
[5] *Musselwhite v. C. H. Musselwhite*, [1962] Ch. 965.
[6] *Re British Sugar Refinery Co.* (1857) 26 L.J. Ch. 369.

Articles, however, often prescribe that certain classes of members shall not be entitled to receive notice: *e.g.* the holders of preference shares in cases where the preference shares do not confer the right to vote or members who are in arrears with their calls. If the preference shares do not confer the right to vote, the holders will not necessarily be entitled to notice even though there is no such special provision.[1] To exclude all doubt, articles which provide that certain classes of members are not to have a vote also often provide that they shall not be entitled to receive notices of or attend meetings. Except as provided by the articles, all members entitled to vote are entitled to receive notices of, and attend, general meetings.

In the case of joint holders all must be given notice unless the articles, as they almost invariably do, provide that this shall not be necessary. Regulation 132 of Table A provides that notice to joint holders may be given to the first named in the register.

In the absence of any provision in the articles, the executors or administrators of a member when not themselves registered as members are not entitled to notice, for they are not members of the company. Regulation 134 of Table A, however, provides that notice is to be given to a personal representative of a member if the member but for his death would have been entitled to receive the notice. Articles, however, frequently provide that notice need not be given to such persons. Similarly, a member who becomes bankrupt remains a member and is able to exercise the votes attributable to his shares, notwithstanding that by taking appropriate steps under the appropriate provisions the trustee in bankruptcy might be able to secure registration of himself in respect of the shares.[2] A company cannot, therefore, treat a member who is known to be bankrupt in any other manner than they treat other members, whether in connection with sending notices to him or accepting his votes.

The mere presence at the meeting of persons not entitled to be present, not objected to by those who are so entitled, does not by itself invalidate a meeting.[3]

The auditor is entitled to attend any general meeting and to receive all notices and other communications relating thereto. He is also entitled to be heard on any part of the business affecting him as auditor (Section 162(4)).

Under Section 5 notice of a resolution for altering the objects clause of a memorandum has to be given to the holders of any

[1] *Re Mackenzie*, [1916] 2 Ch. 450. See *Warden v. Hotchkiss*, [1945] Ch. at p. 278, but see Section 134(*a*).

[2] *Morgan v. Gray*, [1953] Ch. 83.

[3] *Carruth v. Imperial Chemical Industries*, [1937] A.C. 707.

debentures which entitle their holders to object to any such alteration, *i.e.* debentures secured by a floating charge and issued before the 1st December, 1947, or debentures so secured forming part of the same series as any debentures issued before that date. In default of provisions as to giving notice to the holders of such debentures it is to be given in the same way as notice is given to members of the company.

Service of notices.—Articles usually provide for the method of serving notices on the members. In so far as they do not make any provision for service of notices of meetings, every such notice must be served on every member of the company (not merely, it will be noted, those entitled to vote) in the manner in which notices are required to be served by the Table A for the time being in force (Section 134(*a*)). These provisions are found in Regulations 131 to 133, to which reference has already been made in this chapter, and Regulation 134. One important feature of this article is the provision for the giving of notice to a person who has no registered address in the United Kingdom, by sending the same to an address in the United Kingdom supplied by that member for the purpose.

Where the articles do not provide, as Table A does, that notice need not be given to members whose only address is outside the United Kingdom but also provide that a notice will be deemed to be delivered when the letter containing it will be delivered in the ordinary course of post, notice need not be given to members with registered addresses abroad.[1] The decisions which establish this are, in the view of the editors, somewhat surprising.

The right of a person who is an enemy at common law or under the Trading with the Enemy Act to receive notices is suspended so long as he remains an enemy, and meetings are properly convened though no notice has been served upon a person who, if he were not an enemy, would be entitled to notice.[2]

Notices must state the real nature of the business to be transacted.—The notice of a general meeting must disclose all facts necessary to enable the shareholder receiving it to determine in his own interest whether or not he ought to attend the meeting. The vote of the majority at a general meeting, as it binds both dissentient and absent shareholders, must be a vote given on proper information. Not only must the matter be fairly put before the meeting but the meeting itself must be conducted in the fairest possible manner.[3]

A notice must give at any rate a fair, candid and reasonable

[1] *Re Warden and Hotchkiss, Ltd.*, [1945] Ch. 270.

[2] *Re Anglo-International Bank*, [1943] Ch. 233.

[3] *Tiessen v. Henderson*, [1899] 1 Ch. at p. 861.

explanation of the business intended to be transacted.[1] In *Normandy v. Ind Coope & Co.*,[2] it was held that notice of a resolution to alter the articles (*inter alia*) in various ways favourable to the directors and increasing their powers was not satisfactory, there being no mention of those alterations in the notice, although the notice stated that the proposed new articles might be seen at the company's office and that a copy would be forwarded to shareholders on application.

Giving facilities for obtaining information is not equivalent to giving the information. It is sometimes found that rather than attempt to summarise proposals or changes, companies will set out in full the relevant provisions, often by way of appendix. In the view of the editors this procedure is not a proper course for directors to follow: even though it may contain, for a diligent and informed reader, all the relevant material, it is in so indigestible a form as to be an unfair presentation. The proper procedure is for the notice to summarise the proposals and, if these involve changes from existing provisions, to summarise the differences: shareholders can then be offered the full details for inspection if they wish, but they will at least know what they are seeking. Such a procedure is not liked by directors, who feel cautious lest some provision may, unwittingly, be summarised incorrectly or overlooked, but on principle the information should be presented fairly in this way.

Notice of an annual general meeting is not, however, required to specify any business declared by the articles not to be special business (see Chapter 15). A meeting has no power to pass any resolution outside the scope of the notice.

Notice of an annual general meeting must specify the meeting as such (Section 131), and when it is proposed to pass a special or extraordinary resolution at any meeting, the notice of the meeting must specify the intention to propose the special or extraordinary resolution as a special or extraordinary resolution as the case may be (Section 141), and since it has to specify this intention in regard to "the resolution" the words of the proposed resolution must be set out in the notice. The view generally held is that no amendment can be made to any such proposed resolution, for if the resolution as passed is different from the one specified in the notice, notice of the intention to propose the resolution actually passed will not have been given as required by Section 141, and it will not therefore be a special or extraordinary resolution, even if passed by the required majority.[3] Nevertheless if there is a typographical error, or other flaw, which

[1] *Kaye v. Croydon Tramways*, [1898] 1 Ch. 358.
[2] [1908] 1 Ch. 84.
[3] *McConnell v. Prill & Co.*, [1916] 2 Ch. 57.

would be obvious in the light of the proposal and the information given, the resolution can be passed in its proper form and will be effective: it is not necessary to re-convene the meeting. The Courts have, on various occasions, acted on this principle when confirming reductions of capital.

An ordinary resolution need not be passed in the exact terms of the notice, and under all ordinary forms of articles there is no need to specify a proposed ordinary resolution. It is sufficient to specify the nature of the business. In *Betts & Co. v. Macnaghten*[1] the notice stated that the meeting was for the purpose of considering the following resolution with such amendments and alterations as should be determined upon at that meeting. "That A, B, and C be appointed directors." The notice was taken as read at the meeting and A, B, C and two other persons were appointed directors. It was held that the notice sufficiently indicated the special business to be transacted, and that the particularity of the names did not put greater restriction upon the meeting than there would have been had the notice been in general terms: and accordingly all five were properly appointed. So, too, an amendment to an ordinary resolution which has been set out in the notice will not invalidate the resolution. But this will only apply if the amendment renders the resolution less, and not more, onerous to the company or its members, *e.g.* where the remuneration to be paid to directors is, under the amended resolution, less than that proposed in the notice.[2] The reason for this is that shareholders may have given proxies, or desisted from voting, because they were content with the stated proposal, but might have had a different attitude had the more onerous proposal been proposed originally.

An annual general meeting may transact special business if the notice provides for it[3] and there is nothing in the regulations confining special business to extraordinary meetings. Unless the purport of the special business to be transacted is stated in the notice convening the meeting, the meeting is invalid so far as the special business is concerned.[4]

The transaction at a meeting of some business outside the objects specified in the notice will not make the whole meeting irregular.[5]

[1] [1910] 1 Ch. 430.

[2] *Torbuck v. Westbury (Lord)*, [1902] 2 Ch. 871. The resolution in this case was a Special Resolution; but the section of the Companies Act 1862 relating to Special Resolutions differed from Section 141 (above).

[3] *Graham v. Van Diemen's Land Co.* (1856) 26 L.J.Ex. 73.

[4] *Lawes' Case* (1852) 1 De G. M. & G. 421; *Kaye v. Croydon Tramways Co.*, [1898] 1 Ch. 358.

[5] *British Sugar Refinery Co.* (1857) 26 L.J.Ch. 369.

Where the notice deals with two separate resolutions the failure of the one will not invalidate the other, even in cases where they are closely associated.[1] If it is intended that one proposal should take effect only if another does, they should either be put in a single resolution or made interdependent in their terms.

Once a resolution for a member's voluntary winding up has been passed the company can without notice appoint a liquidator. Consequently where a notice was given of a resolution to wind up and to appoint A as liquidator and the winding-up resolution was passed but B was appointed liquidator, that appointment was good.[2]

Notice of an adjournment of a meeting, where it is adjourned to a fixed date, is not necessary, unless the articles otherwise provide, for it is merely a continuation of the original meeting and will be confined to business specified in the original notice.[3] Regulation 57 of Table A provides for fresh notice to be given if the adjournment is for 30 days or more: the same length of notice must in such cases be given as in the case of an original meeting unless, as is common (but not in Table A), the articles expressly provide the length of such further notice. If, therefore, the meeting is not the annual general meeting, and if no business remains which requires a special resolution, 14 days' notice will be required: if the meeting is the annual general meeting, or any remaining business includes a special resolution, 21 days' notice will be required.

When a meeting is adjourned it is customary to fix the day and time for the adjourned meeting. When the articles do not provide that notice must be given of an adjourned meeting or when the adjournment does not exceed the time specified in the articles, fresh notice is not necessary.

An adjourned meeting may only transact business which was unfinished at the first meeting or which could have been transacted within the terms of the notice of that meeting. To transact other business a separate meeting should be convened to be held immediately after the adjourned meeting.

But as regards the statutory meeting Section 130(8) provides that notice may be given either before or after the former meeting of any resolution to be considered at the adjourned meeting, and such resolution may be passed if such notice has been given in accordance with the articles.

Authentication of notices.—A notice must be properly authenticated. Section 36 provides that a document requiring authentica-

[1] *Cleve v. Financial Corporation* (1873) L.R. 16 Eq. 363.
[2] *Trench Tubeless Tyre Co.*, [1900] 1 Ch. 408.
[3] *Kerr v. Wilkie* (1860) 1 L.T. 501.

tion by a company may be signed by a director, secretary, or other authorised officer of the company, and need not be under its common seal. Section 455 provides that a document includes a notice.

Meeting ordered to be held by the Court.—If for any reason it is impracticable to call or to conduct a meeting of a company, the Court may order one to be convened and held, and may give such directions as to the calling and conduct as it thinks expedient (Section 135). The directions may include a provision that one member present in person or by proxy shall constitute a meeting. The Court may call a meeting notwithstanding the opposition of some members.[1] This power may also be useful if there is a dispute as to who are the duly constituted directors able to call a meeting.

Annual general meetings may be ordered to be held by the Department of Trade, but experience shows that it is very difficult to persuade the Department to act (Section 131).

Notice of resolution, etc., circulated on requisition of members.—In the ordinary case the business specified in the notice will be that which the conveners of the meeting think ought to be transacted.

Now, however, Section 140 provides for the giving of notice of resolutions and the circulation of statements relating to business proposed to be transacted at the instance of persons other than the conveners of the meeting. It permits persons other than the conveners of a meeting, at their own expense, to require the company

(a) to give notice of a resolution which may properly be moved and is intended to be moved at the next annual general meeting; and
(b) to circulate any statement with respect to any matter to be dealt with at any forthcoming general meeting. The statement must not be more than one thousand words.

The meeting itself can, however, decide that any such notice or statement shall not be at the expense of the requisitionists. Requisitionists are therefore well advised to include in their resolutions one which puts the expenses on the company.

As appears from the foregoing summary, the requisitionists can have notice of a resolution given only for an annual general meeting; they can, however, secure the circulation of a statement relating to any proposal which is to be considered at any general meeting; whether or not an annual general meeting.

The requisition must be given by the holders of not less than one-twentieth of the total voting rights exercisable at the meeting to which the requisition related or by not less than one hundred members

[1] *Re El Sombrero, Ltd.*, [1958] Ch. 900.

holding shares in the company on which there has been paid up an average sum, per member, of not less than £100 (Sub-section (2)).

Sub-sections (3) and (4) provide for the method of serving the notice or statement, the manner and time in which the requisition must be made, and also for the deposit or tender with the requisition of a sum reasonably sufficient to meet the company's expenses in giving effect thereto.

The company will not, however, be required to circulate a statement if it or any other person who claims to be aggrieved by the terms of any such statement applies to the Court and the Court is satisfied that the rights conferred by the section are being abused to secure needless publicity for defamatory matter. (Sub-section (5)).

Notice of proposal to pay compensation to directors.—The Act contains stringent provisions as to disclosing proposals to pay compensation for loss of office to directors. Under Section 191 a company may not make any payment to a director in compensation for loss of office or in consideration of or in connection with his retirement from office unless the particulars as to the proposed payment and the amount are disclosed to the members of the company and the proposal for the payment is approved by the company. When any such payment, therefore, is proposed, a meeting of the company will have to be held and the notice will have to contain the particulars required by this Section. It will be noticed that the Section provides for resolutions to be validly moved at annual general meetings: this provision overrides any limitation found in the Article on the business which may be dealt with at annual general meetings (Sub-section (6)). This enables members to have the company circulate their views, but on the whole it is little used: the requisitionists have to pay the expenses, and they usually prefer to control the distribution, printing and timing themselves, rather than hand their case to the board.

Section 192 requires similar disclosure of particulars and approval by the company of any payment made to any director of compensation for loss of office or as consideration for or in connection with his retirement from office when any such payment is proposed to be made in connection with the transfer of the whole or any part of the undertaking and property of the company. The section applies whether the proposed payment is by the company itself or some other person, *e.g.* a bidder for the shares.

Section 193 deals with the situation when a similar payment is proposed to be made to a director in connection with transfers of shares in the company resulting from certain classes of offers to purchase the shares mentioned in the Section which include (*inter alia*) offers conditional on acceptance to a given extent. In such cases it is the duty of the director to see that the particulars and amount of the proposed payment are disclosed in the offer to purchase the shares. Further, under this Section any such proposed payment must be approved by a meeting of the holders of all the shares to which the offer relates and of all other shares of that class or those classes of shares.

Sub-section (5) of the Section provides that if at a meeting summoned for the purpose of approving such a payment a quorum is not present on the original day and after one adjournment, the payment shall be deemed to have been approved. Such disclosures as are required by Sections 192 and 193 would be obligatory under the law even if statute had not so provided:[1] but the statutory requirements probably ensure that the matter is not overlooked.

[1] *Re George Newman & Co.*, [1895] 1 Ch. 674.

CHAPTER 15

Quorum and Appointment of Chairman

Quorum

Articles generally make provision as to the number of members which will constitute a quorum: *i.e.* the number of members who are entitled to transact business of the meeting so as to bind all the members. If the articles do not lay down the number of members necessary to form a quorum at meetings of a company, it is provided by paragraph (*c*) of Section 134, that in the case of a private company two members, and in the case of any other company three members, personally present shall be a quorum.

Only persons entitled to vote are counted in a quorum.[1]

If the articles so permit, a person present by proxy may be counted towards the quorum. Regulation 4 of Table A, Part II, which is applicable to private companies and is alternative to Regulation 53 of Part I, does so permit. Under this Regulation two members present in person or by proxy shall be a quorum.

Articles normally state what is to happen if no quorum is present when the meeting is due to begin. A common example is that found in Regulation 54 of Table A, Part 1, which provides that if within half an hour no quorum is present, the meeting is dissolved if convened upon the requisition of members: but in any case other than a meeting requisitioned by members, it stands adjourned for one week exactly and to be held at the same place, or to such other date, time and place as the directors may determine. This distinction between the two types of meeting is, in the editors' view, unnecessary and rather silly. It may even be an unfair protection for directors if, for example, one large shareholder requisitions a meeting but is unable to get a quorum because the directors do not attend. At the adjourned meeting, the Regulation provides that the members present shall be a quorum: it does not, for this purpose, distinguish presence in person from presence by proxy, so that presence by proxy is effective. A question can arise whether two joint holders, present personally or by proxy, can be counted for the purpose of a

[1] *Young v. South African, etc., Syndicate*, [1896] 2 Ch. 268, cf. *re Greymouth-Point Elizabeth Railway Co.*, [1904] 1 Ch. 32.

quorum, the question being due to the Article normally found (see Table A, Regulation 63) which has the effect that the first named in the register in respect of a holding may so vote as to exclude the votes of the other. On principle, however, the answer must be that both can be counted for a quorum: both are members, and both are entitled to vote: the votes of the second named would be excluded if the first-named were to vote all the jointly-held shares, but he is not bound to do that and will not necessarily do so.

For the purpose of a quorum, a corporation which is itself a member of a company and which has authorised some person to act as its representative at any meeting of the company, under the provisions of Section 139 of the Act, is regarded as personally present, not as present by proxy.[1] Restrictions imposed upon a proxy do not apply to such a representative. A corporation includes a foreign company. A person present by his attorney is not present in person: nor is an executor of a deceased member counted for the purpose of a quorum if the Article requires the members to be personally present,[2] even if the executor is entitled to be on the register though not yet entered.

Effect of transacting business without a quorum.—The prescribed quorum—whatever it may be—must be present before a meeting can proceed to business. Regulation 53 of Table A provides that no business shall be transacted at any general meeting unless a quorum of members is present at the time when the meeting proceeds to business. Under this article, when read in conjunction with Article 54 (which covers occasions when the quorum is not present within half an hour) it was decided in *re Hartley, Baird*,[3] that provided that members sufficient in number to form a quorum are present when the meeting proceeds to business it will not cease to be a valid meeting if some persons withdraw so that those present fall below the number required to constitute a quorum. Upon Wynne-Parry Js'. reasoning it would appear that even in the absence of a provision in the terms Article 54, Article 53 requires the quorum when the meeting proceeds to business, but not otherwise. A different decision was reached in Scotland in *Henderson v. James Louttit & Co.*[4] which Wynn-Parry J. declined to follow.

The Hartley-Baird decision is not only clearly correct as a matter of construction but is also a desirable result: it avoids the possibility that persons who find the decisions of a meeting going against them

[1] In *re Kelantan Coco Nut Estates, Ltd.* (1920) W.N. 274.
[2] *Bowling & Welby's Contract*, [1895] 1 Ch. 663.
[3] [1955] Ch. 143.
[4] (1894) 21 R. (Ct. of Sess.) 674.

may be able, by walking out, to end the proceedings. Any resolution passed at a meeting where no quorum is present is ineffective.[1]

Normally one person cannot constitute a meeting: it is a contradiction of the meaning of the word. This was decided in a case where at a meeting of a company only one shareholder attended, holding the proxies of other shareholders.

He took the chair and concluded the proceedings by proposing a vote of thanks to himself. There being no "meeting" it followed that all resolutions "passed" thereat were invalid. "It is clear that, according to the ordinary use of the English language, a meeting could no more be constituted by one person than a meeting could have been constituted if no shareholder at all had attended."[2] In *re Sanitary Carbon Co.*,[3] it was held, following *Sharp v. Dawes*, that a meeting of a company attended by one shareholder only, he being the proxy of all the other members, is not validly constituted. See *Daimler & Co. v. Continental Tyre Co.*[4] This would seem to follow in the case of a private company to which Regulation 4 in Part II of Table A and Regulation 54 in Part I applied because the quorum required for the adjourned "meeting" is clearly intended to be something less than that for the original "meeting"; only by permitting one person to constitute a quorum can any meaning be given to the two Regulations read together. Accordingly since Table A recognises the possibility of a "meeting" where only one person is physically there, and since the Courts have accepted that one person may constitute a "meeting", it follows that "meeting" can have a special meaning so as to take the provisions outside the reasoning of *Sharp v. Dawes*. That being so, the special meaning would apply throughout the article and *Sharp v. Dawes* would no longer be followed. For the same linguistic reason no meeting will exist if, on an adjournment for lack of quorum, there is only one person present at the place and time to which the meeting is adjourned: even though, usually, articles provide that singular includes the plural and vice versa, there can, in ordinary English, be no meeting unless at least two persons are there: it is, however, arguable that "meeting" does not carry its ordinary meaning, but a special meaning for the purpose of enabling certain statutory and constitutional formalities to be satisfied.

If the articles allow a member present by proxy to count towards a quorum, the presence of one member and one non-member holding

[1] *Howbeach Coal Co. v. Teague* (1860) 5 H. & N. 151.

[2] *Sharp v. Dawes* (1876), 2 Q.B.D., p. 29. *Re London*, [1969] 1 W.L.R. 711.

[3] (1877) W. N. 223; followed *in re Keyes*, [1949] 3 D.L.R. 299.

[4] [1916] 2 A.C., at 324.

proxies would constitute a meeting where a quorum consisted of two persons.

But it is now recognised that one person can, in exceptional circumstances, constitute a valid meeting. The rule to the contrary does not, for instance, apply to the meetings of a class of shareholders. This was decided in the case of a company which under its memorandum, required the sanction of a resolution of a separate meeting of preference shareholders before an increase of capital could validly be made. All the preference shares were held by one person, who signed a document in the Minute Book recording his assent to the issue. It was held that the word "meeting" in the memorandum must be taken to have been used not in its strict sense, but as applicable to the case of a single shareholder. "In an ordinary case I think it is quite clear that a meeting must consist of more than one person. . . . I think I may very fairly say that where one person only is the holder of all the shares of a particular class, and as that person cannot meet himself, or form a meeting with himself in the ordinary sense, the persons who framed this memorandum having such a position in contemplation must be taken to have used the word meeting not in the strict sense in which it is usually used, but as including the case of one single shareholder."[1]

In the opinion of the editors the result could have been reached more easily by applying basic principles: since the association between members *inter se* is contractional, the one shareholder who held all the preference shares could quite simply have agreed to the proposal. That agreement would have been effective and binding on him, and would have been registrable as a resolution under what is now Section 141.

Once the conclusion is reached that one person can constitute a meeting, as that word is sometimes used, it must follow that even a general meeting of a company may consist of one person. The reasoning for this conclusion is that there is no hindrance, in law, to all the voting shares being held by one person. In such a case that person could constitute a "meeting": but on the reasoning quoted above of *East v. Bennett Bros.*, this would only be the result in the special circumstances of there being no other shareholder with a vote. This would apply if some voting shares were temporarily disenfranchised, *e.g.* by death of the holder.

In the case of general meetings there are, moreover, two statutory exceptions to the rule that one person cannot constitute a meeting, but it is noteworthy that the Section uses the word "deemed", thereby recognising that this is not in truth a meeting. Under Section

[1] *East v. Bennett Bros.*, [1911] 1 Ch. 163.

131(2) where the Department of Trade direct the calling of a general meeting of the company the directions given may include a direction that one member present in person or by proxy shall be deemed to constitute a meeting.

Under Section 135 a similar direction may be given by the Court when the Court orders a meeting of a company to be held when it is impracticable to conduct a meeting in the manner prescribed by the articles or the Act.[1]

Special class quorum.—In the case of class meetings the articles usually provide that the provisions of the articles as to general meetings shall apply but so that a quorum shall be two persons holding or representing by proxy at least one-third of the issued shares of the class. See Regulation 4 of Table A.

So high a quorum is not always easy to assemble. Where this quorum is specified it also applies at adjourned meetings, unless the articles specifically provide otherwise. Even if articles contain a provision similar to that of Regulation 54 of Table A as to the quorum at general meetings adjourned for want of a quorum in the first instance, that provision will not apply to class meetings merely by virtue of the general provision that the regulations as to general meetings are to apply to class meetings.[2] According to that decision no valid meeting of the class can be held until the quorum prescribed by the Article dealing with class meetings is present.

Appointment of Chairman

In the absence of any provision in the articles as to who is to be chairman of a meeting any member elected by the members present may be chairman (Section 134(*d*)).

(1) *Appointment.*—The articles generally provide who is to take the chair at meetings. Articles normally provide that the Chairman of the Board of Directors is to preside as chairman at every general meeting. If he is not present within 15 minutes of the time fixed for holding the meeting, or if he is unwilling to act, the directors are to elect one of themselves to be chairman of the meeting: but if no director is willing, or if none is present within 15 minutes, the members present may choose one of themselves. See Regulations 55 and 56 of Table A.

(2) *Authority.*—The authority which a chairman has is usually delegated to him by the company by its articles or by that meeting by which he is appointed. Where a number of persons assemble and put a man in the chair they confer on him by agreement the conduct of that body. The person presiding over a general meeting of share-

[1] *Re El Sombrero Ltd.*, [1958] Ch. 900.
[2] *Hemans v. Hotchkiss Ordnance Co.*, [1899] 1 Ch. 115.

holders is in his capacity as chairman of the meeting, acting as representative of the members present at the meeting, not that of the directors. His authority, which is collected from the meeting, enables him to do everything required to ascertain the opinion of the majority and to allow a proper discussion of the questions to be decided, and to ensure that the proceedings are conducted in accordance with the articles. He must, of course, act fairly and allow all members who wish to speak to a motion to have a reasonable opportunity to do so, even if there is clearly a majority who have already made up their minds.

(3) *Duties.*—It is the duty of the chairman to preserve order; to conduct the proceedings in a proper manner; and to take care that the sense of the meeting is properly ascertained with regard to any question which is properly before the meeting.[1]

The real object of a meeting is not so much to discuss matters, as to come to a decision on any question which is properly before it. "It is on him" (the chairman) "that it devolves both to preserve order in the meeting, and to regulate the proceedings so as to give all persons entitled a reasonable opportunity of voting. He is to do the acts necessary for these purposes on his own responsibility, and subject to being called upon to answer for his conduct if he has done anything improperly."[2]

In the absence of express provisions in the regulations, "the details of the proceedings must be regulated by the persons present and by the chairman, and if his decision is quarrelled with it must be regulated by the majority of those present".[3] But where the articles expressly provide for the conduct of meetings, the provisions contained therein must be followed.

(4) *Powers.*—The chairman must exercise his powers impartially. It is his duty to conduct the meeting in such a way that the business thereof may be facilitated and the results clearly and well defined. It is the duty of a chairman to maintain his ruling on points of procedure. But if the chairman's ruling be wrong he is, of course, subject to being called upon to answer for his conduct, and legal proceedings may follow which result in the proceedings being declared invalid.[4]

The chairman of a general meeting has *prima facie* authority to decide all incidental questions which arise at such meeting and necessarily require decision at the time.[5]

[1] *National Dwellings Society v. Sykes*, [1894] 3 Ch. 159.
[2] *R. v. D'Oyly* (1840) 12 A. & E. 139.
[3] *Wandsworth Gas Light Co. v. Wright* (1870) 22 L.T. 404.
[4] *Henderson v. Bank of Australasia* (1890) 45 Ch. D. 330.
[5] *Re Indian Zoedone Co.* (1884) 26 Ch. D. 70.

"Where a chairman frustrates the business of a meeting by wilfully and without good reason preventing that business from being considered, the meeting may in view of his gross violation of duty supersede him as chairman and go on to transact the business. But if in good faith the chairman gives a decision upon a matter of difficulty, such as has arisen in connection with the notice in this case, I am not prepared to hold that his decision can be ignored and overturned there and then. In my opinion in such a case his decision must stand until it is set aside by the Court, or by a general meeting properly convened for that purpose."[1]

The chairman has the following powers:

(a) *To regulate the course of the proceedings at the meeting.*—In case of dispute he is entitled to determine who should address the meeting, and protect the speaker from interruption. He is also entitled to prevent discussion taking place which is not relevant to the business of the meeting.

The business transacted must come within the scope of the notice given, and he should refuse to allow any proposed resolution to be put to the meeting which does not come within the scope of the notice; but he is bound to allow the proposal of all legitimate and germane resolutions and amendments, and a refusal to do so will invalidate that part of the proceedings, because such refusal may amount to the withdrawal of a material and relevant question from the meeting. "I think, then, that the chairman was entirely wrong in refusing to put the amendment, and that the resolutions which were passed cannot be allowed to stand, because the chairman, under a mistaken idea as to what the law was which ought to have regulated his conduct, prevented a material question from being brought before the meeting."[2]

Amendments to resolutions must also come within the scope of the notice convening the meeting and conform to any provisions of the articles as to notice or other requirements. Much difficulty may arise from amendments. Notice of an amendment to an ordinary resolution is not necessary, at any rate so long as the amendment cuts down the effect of the resolution notice of which was originally given or if the notice stated that the resolution might be passed with such alterations

[1] These words are believed to have been used by Lord Wark in *Melville v. Graham-Yooll*, an unreported case referred to in [1936] S.L.T. 54. The editors agree with the views contained in the extract.

[2] Cotton L.J., in *Henderson v. Bank of Australasia* (1890) 45 Ch. D., at 346.

as should be agreed upon.[1] No amendment radically altering the originally proposed resolution should be accepted. When the chairman rules an amendment out of order there is no obligation on the part of the mover of the amendment to contest that ruling or to leave the meeting. It is not necessary for the latter to keep up an altercation with the chairman, nor does he lose his right by acting under the ruling of the chairman.[2]

It is generally considered that no amendment should be accepted to a special or extraordinary resolution (see Chapter 17).

Where notice has been given of several resolutions, each resolution must, if any member so requires, be put separately and not *en bloc*; the poll thereon must in any event be taken separately.[3]

By Section 183 except in the case of a private company a motion for the appointment of two or more directors cannot be made by a single resolution unless that course is resolved upon by the meeting without a dissentient. If it is not so resolved the appointment of each director must be resolved upon by a separate resolution.

If there is the slightest doubt as to whether an amendment is in order or not, it should be allowed to be put; this will safeguard the ultimate resolution if it turns out in the end that the amendment is in fact relevant and germane to the resolution. The chairman has often to make up his mind at once upon the validity of amendments, and when he is fairly certain that the amendment will be lost there is no real harm done in allowing an amendment which he thinks not covered by the notice of the meeting. A chairman should not reject an amendment, if proposed, on the ground that it has no chance of success. To do so would endanger the original resolution on the ground of a technical objection, which may have no substance in fact.

(b) *To apply the closure with consent of meeting.*—When the views of the minority have been heard, it is competent to the chairman, with the sanction of a vote of the meeting, to declare the discussion closed, and to put the question to vote.[4] This procedure can be important if a minority are wasting time and repeating arguments or digressing into irrelevances.

[1] *Betts & Co. v. MacNaghten*, [1910] 1 Ch. 430.
[2] *Henderson v. Bank of Australasia, supra.*
[3] *Blair Open Hearth Furnace Co. v. Reigart* (1913) 108 L.T. 665.
[4] *Wall v. London & Northern Assets Corporation*, [1898] 2 Ch. 469.

(c) *To adjourn the meeting.*—See Chapter 19.

(d) *To make arrangements for taking a poll and to receive or reject proxies.*—His decision as to the rejection of proxies will be decisive until reversed by the Court.

(e) *To give a casting vote.*—The chairman has no casting vote unless it is so provided in the articles. Table A, Regulation 60 so provides. A casting vote may be exercised only if there is an equality of votes, *i.e.* equality of valid votes. If the chairman does not exercise his casting vote, the motion, of course, is not carried. A chairman may also have an ordinary vote if he is a member of the company, as he usually is. A chairman may give a contingent or hypothetical vote, to come into operation if in the course of subsequent proceedings it should appear that there has been an equality of valid votes.[1]

Since a casting vote is conferred on the office, and not on the individual, it must be exercised as a fiduciary power in what the chairman considers to be the interest of the company as a whole.

(f) *To declare the result of voting.*—The chairman's declaration on a show of hands that an extraordinary or special resolution is carried is conclusive unless a poll is demanded (Section 141(3)). Regulation 58 of Table A goes further and provides that unless a poll is demanded in one of the ways provided for by the clause a declaration by the chairman that a resolution has on a show of hands been carried or carried unanimously, or by a particular majority, or lost, and an entry to that effect in the book containing the minutes of the proceedings of the company shall be conclusive evidence of the fact without proof of the number or proportion of the votes recorded in favour of or against such resolution.

The chairman's declaration, if properly made, will, under articles in this form, be conclusive, and will prevent the question being reopened in legal proceedings even if evidence is forthcoming that the chairman's declaration was wrong,[2] unless there is an apparent error, *e.g.* where he states the number of votes given and they are insufficient,[3] or it is plain on the face of the proceedings that the requisite majority has not been obtained,[4] or there being no apparent opposition to a proposal he omits to put it to a show of hands.[5]

[1] *Bland v. Buchanan*, [1901] 2 K.B. 75.
[2] *Arnot v. United African Lands*, [1901] 1 Ch. 518.
[3] *Re Caratal (New) Mines*, [1902] 2 Ch. 498.
[4] *Re Clark & Co.*, [1911] S.C. 243. [5] *Citizens Theatre Ltd.*, [1946] S.C. 14.

Where articles provided that if votes were not disallowed at the meeting they should be good for all purposes, it was held in *Wall v. London & Northern Assets Corporation* (No. 2)[1] that in the absence of bad faith or fraud the resolution could not be afterwards impeached on the ground that votes were improperly received. In *Wall v. Exchange Investment Corporation*[2] it was held that the decision of the chairman who, in the *bona fide* exercise of the power conferred upon him by the articles, had refused to disallow a vote by proxy to which objection had been taken at the meetings, was final and would not be reviewed by the Court.

No decision will be conclusive, even under such articles, if the resolution was not in accordance with the notice of the meeting. Accordingly in *Betts & Co. v. MacNaghten*,[3] it was held that notwithstanding a declaration by the chairman, the notice of the meeting is part of the proceedings and may be looked at to see if the resolution is in accordance with the notice. If it is not, the chairman's declaration that the resolution was passed is not conclusive. Neither is a chairman's declaration conclusive where there is no quorum, since there would be no properly constituted meeting.

[1] [1899] 1 Ch. 550.
[2] [1926] Ch. 143.
[3] [1910] 1 Ch. 430.

CHAPTER 16

Voting at Meetings

The Articles of Association usually set out the rights of voting attached to shares. In so far as they do not, Section 134(*e*) of the Act applies and gives members, in the case of a company originally having a share capital, one vote for each share or £10 of stock, and in any other case one vote for every member.

The Act contemplates voting by a show of hands in the first instance,[1] and consequently this statutory provision could only apply on a poll.

The manner of voting is, however, invariably determined by the articles, which often provide that on a show of hands every member present in person and holding shares entitled to votes at the meeting shall have one vote, and on a poll every such member shall have one vote for each share of which he is the holder—see, for example, Regulation 62 of Table A.

On a show of hands one person can only give one vote. Even if the articles provide that a member present by proxy may vote on a show of hands his proxy will only have one vote whether he is a member of the company or not.[1]

Articles frequently provide that certain classes of shares, *e.g.* preference shares, shall confer no vote at general meetings or shall confer a right to vote at such meetings only on certain specified matters or when the preference dividend is in arrear for a certain period. Most forms of articles also contain a restriction on the right of a member to vote unless all calls or other sums presently payable by him in respect of shares in the company have been paid—as in Regulation 65 of Table A.

It used to be not uncommon to find provisions in articles that a member was not entitled to exercise his votes in respect of shares until he had held them for a specified period. In other cases voting rights were exercisable by a member only upon a limited number of shares: if he held more than that number he had no (or reduced) voting rights in respect of the excess. Neither of these restrictions is common today, but they are still found on occasion.

[1] *Ernest v. Loma Gold Mines,* [1897] 1 Ch. 1.

As between the company and a member, a member may vote as he pleases. Even if the company is aware that the member is, or may be, under a contract with a third person (including another member) to vote in a certain way or as that other person directs, the company is not entitled to question or reject a vote cast by a member in accordance with the articles.[1] Where a member holds shares in which another person has an interest, there may be a question as between him and that other person as to how he may vote. In the absence of a contract a person in whose name shares are registered (*e.g.* a mortgagee) can vote as he pleases, but where the mortgagee of shares agrees for a valuable consideration to vote at general meetings of the company in accordance with the wishes of the mortgagor, the Court will enforce the agreement by mandatory injunction.[2] Similarly an agreement made by a shareholder on a sale of shares held by him that he will vote in a particular way until the transfer is registered is valid and can be enforced,[3] and a member who holds shares as nominee or bare trustee for another is bound to vote as the beneficial owner directs.[4] In the absence of express provisions to the contrary an unpaid or partly paid vendor of shares remaining registered in respect of them retains the right to decide how those shares should be voted.[5]

The right of an alien enemy of voting personally or by proxy in respect of shares in an English company is suspended during war.[6]

A shareholder's vote is a right of property. The general principle is that he may use it as he pleases, and his motive is immaterial. "There is no obligation on a shareholder of a company to give his vote merely with a view to what other persons may consider the interest of the company at large. He has a right, if he thinks fit, to give his vote from motives or promptings of what he considers his own individual interest."[7] This rule is, however, subject to the qualifications that a majority of the members will not be allowed by the exercise of their votes to commit a fraud on the minority.[8] This means, in effect, that he must not vote so as to give himself, or to himself and others, something which belongs to or ought to belong to the company;[9] or which benefits him, or him and others, in their

[1] *Siemens Bros. v. Burns*, [1918] 2 Ch. 324.
[2] *Puddephatt v. Leith, No. 1*, [1916] 1 Ch. 200.
[3] *Greenwell v. Porter*, [1902] 1 Ch. 530. [4] *Wise v. Lansdell*, [1921] 1 Ch. 420.
[5] *Musselwhite v. C. H. Musselwhite*, [1962] Ch. 965.
[6] *Robson v. Premier Oil &c. Co.*, [1915] 2 Ch. 124.
[7] *Pender v. Lushington* (1877) 6 Ch. D., at p. 75.
[8] *Menier v. Hooper's Telegraph Co.* (1874) L.R., 9 Ch. 350.
[9] For examples see *Menier v. Hooper's Telegraph Co., supra. Cook v. Deeks*, [1916] 1 A.C. 554.

capacity as members in a way which is detrimental to the interests of other members or which differentiates them, unless, of course, the other members all agree. This qualification on the general rule becomes of greater significance in the case of meetings of a class of members. "While usually a holder of shares or debentures may vote as his interest directs, he is subject to the further principle that where his vote is conferred on him as a member of a class he must conform to the interest of the class itself when seeking to exercise the power conferred on him in his capacity of being a member."[1] One of the most important applications of this qualification is found when members of one class are also members of another class: they may not exercise votes at one class meeting to benefit themselves as members, perhaps to a greater extent, of the other class.

In all these cases the Courts will not interfere to restrain or set aside votes unless it is clear that the member was exercising the votes improperly. If there has been full explanation of the proposal, and it is supported by members with no different interest, the Courts will be slow to conclude that the votes of members who had other interests were not validly cast.

Articles normally contain restrictions on the power of directors to vote at board meetings on contracts or arrangements in which they are interested.[2] No such restrictions apply to them when they vote in their capacity as members at general meetings,[3] but their duty as directors requires full disclosure to the members of any different interest which they may have.

The method of voting by a corporation which is a member of a company has been explained (p. 95).

Articles usually contain regulations for voting by joint holders of shares, and in cases of members of unsound mind (Regulations 63 and 64 of Table A are examples).

Further, articles frequently provide that no objection may be raised to a voter except at the meeting at which he tenders a vote, and make the chairman of the meeting the person who decides upon any such objection (Regulation 66).

This is a rather tiresome and probably misleading provision: tiresome because very often other members who might wish to object may not be aware that a particular person has voted, or may not then know of the conflicting interest which he has: misleading because,

[1] *British America Nickel Corporation v. O'Brien*, [1927] A.C. at p. 373; *Goodfellow v. Nelson Line*, [1912] 2 Ch. 324. *Re Holders Investment Trust Ltd.*, [1971] 1 W.L.R. 583.

[2] See Regulation 84 of Table A and Section 199.

[3] *East Pant-Du United Lead Mining Co. v. Merryweather* (1864) 2 H. & M. 254.

if the member has voted for improper reasons, the Court will interfere, if asked, despite the wording of the article.

(1) *Show of Hands*

Unless the articles otherwise provide, voting will, in the first instance, normally be by show of hands.

Usually every member personally present and entitled to vote has one vote only, independent of the number of shares or proxies he holds. At a meeting of the members of a company the articles of which allow voting by proxy the chairman, in ascertaining the number of votes given on a show of hands, must count the vote of each member who holds proxies as a single vote, and not count a vote for each of the members whose proxies he holds.[1] The vote of a non-member, *i.e.* a person not entitled to vote on his own account but who was a proxy for a member, would not, unless the articles so provided, be counted on a show of hands. Regulation 62 of Table A does not so provide. A representative of a corporation, however, under Section 139 (*ante*, p. 95) would be entitled to vote on a show of hands by virtue of Sub-section (2) of that Section. It is desirable that if non-members are admitted to the meeting they should be known to the chairman to prevent them taking part in a show of hands. Similarly if members not entitled to vote are entitled to attend, the presence of such members should be brought to the attention of the chairman.

Regulation 58 of Table A provides that at any general meeting a resolution put to the vote of the meeting shall be decided on a show of hands, unless a poll is (before or on the declaration of the result of the show of hands) validly demanded and most articles contain a similar provision. In such a case it is not necessary to go through the sterile procedure of a show of hands: the chairman, or the appropriate number of members, may demand a poll as soon as the resolution is put, or may demand it beforehand. The virtue of a show of hands in such a case, *e.g.* where there is a bitter proxy battle, is that it enables those who have taken the trouble to attend in person to express their feelings, even though these may have no effect on the result of the motion. For the position where the articles make the chairman's declaration as to the result of the show of hands conclusive, see p. 102, *ante*.

(2) *Demanding a Poll*

The articles may contain provisions governing the way in which a poll must be demanded at any general meeting, but all such provisions

[1] *Ernest* v. *Loma Gold Mines Co.*, [1897] 1 Ch. 1.

will be subject to the provisions of Section 137 which is overriding. The effect of this Section is that

(a) Articles cannot exclude the right to demand a poll (except on the election of the chairman of a meeting or on the adjournment of a meeting), and
(b) Articles cannot make a demand ineffective if made by
 (i) five members entitled to vote; or
 (ii) members holding 10 per cent or more of the voting rights applicable; or
 (iii) members holding shares on which 10 per cent or more of the total paid-up capital has been paid.

The section also provides that a proxy may demand or join in demanding a poll. See also Regulation 72 of Table A.

Modern articles usually provide that the chairman of a meeting may demand a poll, and they sometimes provide that members fewer in number or smaller in holdings than the minimum specified in Section 137 may demand a poll.

They also frequently provide that unless a poll is demanded a declaration by the chairman that a resolution has been carried or lost and an entry to that effect in the minute book is to be conclusive evidence of the fact without proof of the number of votes for or against the resolution. See Regulation 58 of Table A.

If a poll is duly demanded it is the chairman's duty to grant it, and to fix the time and place for the poll in accordance with the articles. This power is a fiduciary power and must be exercised in a reasonable way to enable the members to record their votes. It would not, for example, be reasonable or proper to direct that the poll be taken at midnight on a Saturday, or in a place where shareholders could not conveniently attend.

If the demand is challenged it must, of course, be justified, but it need not be justified if the chairman knows privately that the demand is, in fact, supported by the requisite number.[1] In such a case it is usually simpler and preferable for the chairman to resolve the point by himself making the demand. If a poll is not taken after a proper demand therefor, the resolution which has been challenged is void.[2]

(3) *Taking a Poll*

Articles frequently provide that a poll demanded on the election of a chairman or a question of adjournment is to be taken forthwith, but that a poll on any other question is to be taken at such time as

[1] *Re Phoenix Electric Light Co.* (1883) 48 L.T. 260.
[2] *R. v. Cooper* (1870) L.R., 5 Q.B. 457.

the chairman directs, and that business other than that on which the poll is demanded may proceed in the meantime. See, for example, Regulation 61 of Table A. By Regulation 59 a poll is to be taken in such manner as the chairman directs (except as provided in Regulation 61) and the result of the poll is to be deemed to be the resolution of the meeting at which the poll was demanded.

It is under Section 137 competent for articles to provide that no poll may be demanded on the election of a chairman or on a question of adjournment. Accordingly articles sometimes provide that the election of the chairman or a motion for an adjournment be determined on a show of hands of those members present at the meeting. In such cases numbers present, and not shares held, are decisive. More usual are articles providing, on these two questions, for any poll to be held immediately. On motions on which the articles provide that the chairman shall decide when and how the poll be taken, the chairman's power of decision is a fiduciary one. If he thinks that, in order to obtain the considered views of shareholders, the poll should be fixed for a future date, of which notice can be given, he should follow this course. If on the other hand, he feels that the matter is too urgent for that course, or that shareholders have already had the opportunity to express their considered views, he should hold the poll as soon as possible.[1] The decision is his, not the board's.

The usual method for taking a poll is to require every member who is entitled to vote to sign a paper (in order to prevent personation) headed "for" or "against" the motion; the number of votes to which each member is under the articles entitled is inserted against the signature of the member, and these having been added, the chairman declares accordingly. Where the articles provide that a poll shall be taken within seven days of the meeting, at a time and place to be fixed by the directors, such time and place must be fixed after a poll has been demanded and cannot be fixed in advance.[2]

A member may vote personally at a poll, though not present when the poll was demanded,[3] or if, as is usual, the articles provide that a proxy is effective if deposited a certain number of hours before the taking of a poll, a shareholder who had not previously attended or appointed a proxy may appoint one for this purpose.

Resolutions must be put to the poll separately and not *en bloc*, otherwise the poll is invalid.[4] All the resolutions may, however, be included on one sheet of paper, to be separately marked by the voters.

[1] See *re Chillington Iron Co.* (1885) 29 Ch. D. 159.

[2] *Re British Flax Producers Company* (1889) 60 L.T. 215.

[3] *Campbell v. Maund* (1836) 5 A. & E. 865.

[4] *Patent Wood Keg Syndicate Ltd. v. Pearse* (1906) W.N. 164.

Scrutineers are often appointed to be present at the counting. Where the articles do not provide for the appointment of scrutineers they may be appointed by the chairman. Unless the articles require scrutineers, it is not obligatory to have any: but it is an advisable step for two reasons: first, the presence of independent scrutineers reduces the danger of a poll being subsequently challenged by a dissident shareholder, and secondly, because if, as is usual, the auditors are appointed, they have the staff and experience necessary for conducting the poll. Sometimes where there is a dispute, scrutineers representing the warring parties are appointed jointly, but dissident shareholders have no right to insist on the presence of scrutineers appointed by themselves.

The chairman should fix the hours during which the poll is to take place; if he does not do so, he cannot close the poll so long as votes are coming in. After waiting a reasonable time, if no more voters present themselves, the chairman may declare the poll closed. The improper exclusion of a voter may invalidate a poll.[1]

The right to vote and the number of shares held are determined by reference to the register of the members. "The register of shareholders, on which there can be no notice of a trust, furnishes the only means of ascertaining whether you have a lawful meeting or a lawful demand for a poll, or of enabling the scrutineers to strike out votes."[2] Where there is a limitation of the number of votes which any member may exercise, he may transfer some of his shares to trustees on his behalf, and if they are duly registered, increase his voting power.[3]

A poll is regarded as part of the proceedings of the original meeting. "The taking of a poll is a mere enlargement of the meeting at which it was demanded."[4]

Under Table A, or under the common form of articles, a poll cannot be taken by sending voting papers to the members, to be lodged with the company. They or their proxies must attend and give the votes personally.[5]

Section 138 provides that on a poll a member entitled to more than one vote need not use all his votes or cast all the votes he uses in the same way. The object of this provision is to enable a person who holds some shares as trustee for one person and some as trustee for

[1] *R. v. Rector &c. of St. Mary, Lambeth*, 8 A. & E. 356.

[2] *Pender v. Lushington* (1877) 6. Ch. D. 70, at 78.

[3] *Re Stranton Iron and Steel Co.* (1873) L.R. 16 Eq. 559.

[4] *R. v. Wimbledon Local Board* (1882) 8 Q.B.D., at p. 464; see also *Shaw v. Tati Concessions, post*, p. 117.

[5] *McMillan v. Le Roi Mining Co.*, [1906] 1 Ch. 331.

another to cast the votes belonging to those shares as the persons beneficially entitled individually direct, even if they require the votes to be used in different ways.[1]

A poll is complete as from the day on which it is taken, even if the declaration of the result is delayed.[2]

(4) *Proxies*

The word "proxy" is used confusingly to describe a person appointed in the place of another to represent him, and also the instrument by which a person is so appointed. A right to appoint a proxy is conferred by Section 136(1). Under that Sub-section a member entitled to attend and vote at a meeting is entitled to appoint another person, who need not himself be a member of the company, as his proxy, to attend and vote instead of himself. The Sub-section does not apply to a company not having a share capital, and in that case the right, if any, to appoint a proxy must still be conferred by the articles. Unless otherwise provided by the articles a proxy may vote only on a poll. Table A does not otherwise provide and consequently under Part II the position arises that a proxy may count towards a quorum under Regulation 4 (*ante*, p. 94), but may not vote unless a poll is demanded. A proxy has under Section 137(2) (*ante*, p. 108) the same right to demand or join in demanding a poll as the person who appointed him would have had.

Further under Section 136(1) a proxy at a meeting of a private company has the same right to speak at the meeting as his appointor would have had. The Sub-section also provides that a member of a private company is not entitled, unless the articles so provide, to appoint more than one proxy to attend on the same occasion. In public companies the right is to appoint one or more proxies. This means what it says, so that a member could in theory appoint one proxy for each share that he holds. It does not have the restricted meaning of appointing one person, or, failing him, another, and so on.

The expenses incurred by a Board in sending out proxies are properly payable by the company: indeed the Listing Agreement of the Stock Exchange requires companies whose shares are listed to send out proxies for all Resolutions to be proposed. In *Peel v. London and North Western Railway Co.*[3] it was held that it was the

[1] The Act does not say how, in such circumstances, the majority for the purpose of numbers is calculated under Section 206, where the same position may arise.

[2] *Holmes v. Keyes*, [1958] Ch. 670.

[3] [1907] 1 Ch. 5.

duty of the directors to inform the shareholders of the facts of their policy, and the reason why they considered that this policy should be maintained and supported by the shareholders, and that they were justified in trying to influence and secure votes for this purpose, and accordingly that expenses which had thus been *bona fide* incurred in the interest of the company were properly payable out of the funds of the company, *e.g.*, issuing of stamped proxy papers, containing the names of three directors as proposed proxies, with a stamped envelope for return. This is an important decision in relation to "take-over" bids and in cases where a group of shareholders is attacking the directors, for it enables directors to use the company's funds to defend their policy. By virtue of Sub-section(4) of Section 136 invitations to appoint a person or persons as proxy, if issued at the company's expense, must be sent to all members entitled to vote at the relevant meeting. Failure to observe this rule lays every officer of the company knowingly or wilfully authorising or permitting the default open to a fine not exceeding £100.

The Act does not specify any particular form of proxy. Table A offers two types: one where there is an open discretion to the appointee as to how he is to vote; the other where he is directed how to vote. The Stock Exchange requires, for quoted companies, the latter form.

Proxy battles have increased in England in recent years, and some of the difficulties which arise could be avoided by a more carefully worded form of proxy. For example, the form should make clear whether the proxy may exercise any discretion on an amendment, or on a motion to adjourn the meeting. These points can be important if, as is usually the case, the proxy appointed is one of the directors, who may represent a large number of shareholders and may be uncertain as to his powers: in some cases his course of conduct will be easy to decide,[1] but on other occasions he may be unclear as to what he can and what he should do.

He may even find himself in a position where he believes that he should, in the interests of his appointor, vote in a way different from the direction given him in the form of proxy. For example, he may have been directed to vote in favour of a scheme which the directors had recommended, but finds that a more favourable scheme is now offered. In such a case the proxy can, in the editors' view, vote as he thinks fit, and is entitled to ignore the original instructions, by treating them as given on the basis of a set of circumstances which no longer apply.

A more difficult problem can be the position of the company where

[1] See *Waxed Papers, Ltd.* (1937) 2 All E.R. 481.

a proxy holder purports to vote in a manner contrary to the instructions given in the proxy form, without any apparent justification for so doing. If this happens, the chairman or scrutineers should note specifically the proxies concerned, and if the figures affect, or could affect, the result of the resolution, application should be made to the Court to determine whether the votes be accepted as cast, accepted as the form of proxy directed, or rejected.[1]

Two conflicting principles of law arise in connection with proxies, and a chairman may sometimes find it difficult to decide whether to accept or reject a vote which a person claims to exercise as a proxy. The first principle is that it is the duty of the chairman to obtain, if he can, the decision of the shareholders: the second is that since the right to appoint a proxy is given by contract (*i.e.* the contract constituted by the articles) any member who seeks to exercise his right must carry out and comply with whatever requirements the articles specify.

In accordance with the first principle, it has been decided[2] that where articles prescribed that proxies must be in a specified form or as near thereto as circumstances should permit, and the specified form was a proxy applicable to a single meeting, general proxies were permissible.

On the other hand where particular formalities are prescribed they must be followed. If they are not, it is not merely the chairman's right, but his duty, as representing the shareholders, to reject them.

Articles usually require that forms of proxy be deposited with the company in advance of the meeting. The usual requirement is for the deposit to be made not less than 48 hours before the meeting: the Act prohibits a longer period being specified (Section 136(3)).

Any formalities specified in the articles as to place or time of deposit or the form of address on an envelope, must be followed. In *Burnett v. Gill*[3] the articles provided that no person should be entitled to vote as a proxy unless the instrument appointing him should be deposited at the office of the company 48 hours before the meeting. The company's registered office was the office of the secretary, a chartered accountant. It was held that a proxy addressed to "the chairman of the meeting", care of the secretary whose name only was mentioned, was not duly deposited at the office.

In *Harben v. Phillips*[4] Cotton L.J. explained the principle. "The right of a shareholder to vote by proxy depends on the contract

[1] As to proxies on adjournments see *post*, p. 117.
[2] *Isaacs v. Chapman* (1915) 32 T.L.R. 183.
[3] *The Times*, 13th June, 1906, p. 4.
[4] *Harben v. Phillips* (1883) 23 Ch. D. 14, at 32.

between himself and his co-shareholders, and where parties have a right depending upon the contract between them and the other parties, there, in my opinion, all the requisitions of the contract as to the exercise of that right must be followed." In that case it was held that the proxy papers which were not attested as required by the articles were improperly admitted by the chairman. Presumably even though the right is now conferred by the Act the articles may still validly require attestation. In off share funds the requirement of attestation or some form of verification is commonly found. The person appointed a proxy cannot act as an attesting witness.[1]

Most articles provide that a vote given in accordance with the terms of an instrument of proxy is to be regarded as valid notwithstanding the death or insanity of the principal or revocation of the proxy or authority under which it was executed or the transfer of the share under which it was given unless notification of the event giving rise to the invalidity is received at the registered office before the meeting or adjourned meeting at which the proxy is to be used.

In *Cousins v. International Brick Co.*[2] the articles contained a similar provision, but it was held that a shareholder who had given a proxy and had not revoked it could attend the meeting personally and vote, in which case his proxy could not vote for him. The provision for revocation by a transfer is a dangerous one: in order to give it any meaning, the word "transfer" must mean something less than registration. If so, sending of a transfer form to the company constitutes notice of the transfer; the result will be that until the transfer is registered the shares concerned may be disenfranchised. The transferor remains on the register but is treated as having revoked any proxy which he had given previously. The transferee may find himself unable to obtain a fresh proxy from the transferor, who by that time will probably not be concerned as to whether the votes are exercised or not.

Forms of proxy do not require a stamp unless they are for more than one meeting.[3] If they are, even if the meetings are for the same day, they will require a 50p stamp.[4] A proxy for a specified meeting is not available for a different meeting. This will be so even if the specified meeting never takes place, and another meeting is called instead, perhaps for identical business. This happens not infrequently where inadequate notice of the first intended meeting is given.

[1] *Re Parrott*, [1891] 2 Q.B. 151.

[2] [1931] 2 Ch. 90.

[3] This applies even if the date of the meeting is not specified, *e.g.* "the next general meeting of the company".

[4] Stamp Act 1891. First Schedule.

Difficult problems frequently arise as to which of two or more proxies is valid. It is sometimes thought that a later proxy automatically revokes an earlier one, but this is not so. There are two facets to the problem: the first, what was the intention of the appointor; the second, what is the evidence of the intention.

As to intention, it will normally be the intention of a person who makes a new appointment that a former appointment be revoked and replaced by the new one, but this will not necessarily be the case. He may forget that he has given an earlier one; he may intend that both appointments should be effective, or that his chances of voting are doubled; he may think that he is required to fill up the form sent to him; or (and it is a happy state of affairs which finds this happening) he may wish to confuse the matter for the sake of confusion.

As to the evidence of the intention, there is usually none except perhaps a date on the form of proxy or the date when it is received. But with modern post delays, date of receipt is little guide: and dates on the forms themselves are by no means conclusive.

The matter may be further complicated if an earlier proxy is stated to be irrevocable, or if the company is on notice that it was given, irrevocably, for valuable consideration.

In the opinion of the editors, the problem should be avoided as far as possible by some provision in the articles, but in the absence of that, the following guidelines are offered to enable a chairman or scrutineer to decide on proxy problems, where the problem is not covered by the articles:

(1) if there are two or more proxies for the same shares, the later in date (if given) should be accepted to the exclusion of the earlier.
(2) if there is no date, the one which appears on the evidence to have been signed later should be accepted to the exclusion of the others.
(3) if there is no sufficient evidence, and both proxy holders claim the right to vote, they should both be excluded since neither can establish his right.
(4) if a later proxy is received too late to be used at the meeting, it will, nevertheless, constitute notice of revocation of the earlier proxy: if the meeting is adjourned, or a poll is held later, the later proxy may be valid for that purpose.
(5) if the earlier proxy, in any of the above cases, was made irrevocable for valuable consideration and the proxy holder claims that he is still entitled to the vote, that claim should be recognised as being the valid compliance with the requirements

of the articles for voting by proxy: a shareholder must not be assumed to intend to commit a breach of his contract with the earlier proxy holder, and any later proxy should be rejected so long as the first proxy holder claims the right to vote.

(6) If the shareholder himself is present at the meeting, his presence will not of itself revoke the authority given to his proxy: if the shareholder seeks to vote, he thereby displaces his proxy on that resolution, but the authority revives for subsequent purposes unless, once again, the shareholder acts to displace his authority.

It has been decided that if the articles provide that a proxy shall be valid, notwithstanding that it has been revoked, unless notice of revocation is received before the meeting then that provision shall mean what it says: accordingly a revocation notice received after the commencement of the meeting but before a poll is taken is ineffective.[1] If, however, the shareholder himself votes, this will constitute valid revocation.[2]

In *Oliver v. Dalgleish*[3] forms of proxy were given to X by a number of shareholders for a meeting to be held on a particular day. The forms described the meeting as an Annual General Meeting whereas it was in fact an Extraordinary General Meeting. Some of the forms instructed X to vote against the resolutions. X simply marked his voting paper "for" the resolutions without stating how many votes he cast. The chairman rejected all his votes. It was held (a) that the misdescription of the meeting did not invalidate the forms of proxy, (b) that the failure to obey the instructions of some of those who gave the proxies did not invalidate all the votes cast by X.

An adjourned meeting, as regards notice, is regarded in law as a continuance of the original meeting.[4] Consequently where the articles require proxies to be lodged before the meeting this means the original meeting.[5] Normally articles require the lodging before the meeting or adjourned meeting at which the votes are sought to be cast. In that case lodging by the specified time before the adjourned meeting meets is effective; but this is only effective if the meeting is in fact adjourned. If all that happens is that directions are given for a poll to be taken at a later time, but the meeting itself is not adjourned, the provision does not take effect so as to validate the

[1] *Spiller & Mayo* (1926) W.N. 78.
[2] *Cousins v. International Brick Company Ltd.*, [1931] 2 Ch. 90 C.A.
[3] [1963] 1 W.L.R. 1274.
[4] *Scadding v. Lorant* (1851) 3 H.L.C. 418.
[5] *McLaren v. Thomson*, [1917] 2 Ch. 261.

proxy.[1] The mere postponement of the poll is not an adjournment *ad hoc* of the meeting within the meaning of an article allowing the lodgment of proxies 48 hours before a meeting or adjourned meeting. The original meeting continues for the purpose of the poll, and no fresh proxies may be lodged.

The problem of *Shaw v. Tati Concessions* will not arise where the articles permit lodging of proxies before the taking of a poll. Articles frequently provide that they may be so lodged not less than 24 hours before a poll. If this is so there may be proxies which were too late (within 48 hours before the meeting) for effect in full at the meeting (*e.g.* to join in demanding a poll) but which are in time for being used if a poll is demanded and held.

[1] *Shaw v. Tati Concessions*, [1913] 1 Ch. 292.

CHAPTER 17

Types of Resolutions

There are three types of resolution: Ordinary, Extraordinary and Special. The Act mentions Ordinary Resolutions only once (Section 184) but frequently refers to resolutions by "the company in general meeting"; such resolutions are Ordinary Resolutions. On the other hand the Act specifically defines Extraordinary and Special Resolutions. It is to be hoped that any new Companies Act will abolish Extraordinary Resolutions, which have been an anachronism since 1907. Their sole use is to provide examiners with an easy question.

(1) *Ordinary Resolutions*, usually referred to in the Act as resolutions of the company in general meeting, are those which are passed by a bare majority of those voting at any kind of general meeting.

As has been pointed out (*ante*, p. 69), a company may delegate certain of its powers to its directors in such a way that those powers can no longer be exercised by the company in general meeting. Apart from acts which the company by such delegation has abandoned its powers to perform, a company may carry out by ordinary resolution all such acts as are not required by the Act or by its articles to be effected by special or extraordinary resolution. There are, however, a number of things which a company is expressly empowered by the Act to carry out by a resolution of the company in general meeting, *i.e.* by an ordinary resolution.

The Act provides in certain cases that the company in general meeting may, if so authorised by its articles, do certain things—for example, various changes (not including reduction) of capital, under Section 61. If the articles do not so authorise, an *ad hoc* Special Resolution to carry out the proposal will be effective.

The fact that the Act gives such power does not mean that the articles may not require something more stringent, and in private companies articles frequently provide that changes in capital require a special resolution (see below).

The one case in the Act where there is specific reference to an Ordinary Resolution is Section 184, which, subject to a minor exception,[1] provides that a company may by ordinary resolution remove a director before the expiration of his period of office, notwithstanding anything in its articles or in any agreement between it and him. Special notice is required of any resolution to remove a director under the section or to appoint somebody instead of a director so removed at the meeting at which he is removed, and on receipt of notice of an intended resolution to remove a director under this section the company is bound forthwith to send a copy thereof to the director concerned, and the director (whether or not he is a member of the company) is entitled to be heard on the resolution at the meeting (Sub-sections (1) and (2)).

Although the Section requires that special notice be given of such a resolution, it does not require that the resolution be proposed by the person who gave the special notice. Once someone has given special notice, he or any other shareholder entitled to vote may propose the resolution.

It is to be noted that the Section does not itself authorise the appointment of some other person in place of a director removed in this way: that is left to the articles: all that the Section provides in this respect is special notice of any intention to appoint someone else, and (Sub-section (4)) that if a vacancy caused by a removal is not filled at the meeting it may be filled as a casual vacancy, which again takes one back to the articles to find who has the power to fill and how.

The special notice referred to is described below. The Section also provides that when a notice is given of an intended resolution to remove a director under the Section, the director in question may require his representations as to the intended resolution to be circulated to the members of the company, or, if that cannot or has not been done, to be read out at the meeting at which the resolution is proposed. If, however, the company or any other person who claims to be aggrieved satisfies the Court that the rights conferred by the Section are being abused to secure needless publicity for defamatory matter, the representations need not be sent out or read at the meeting (Sub-section (3)).

A director appointed at the same meeting in place of one removed under Section 184 is for the purpose of working out which directors are to retire by rotation deemed to have been appointed on the day the removed director was last appointed a director (Sub-section (5)).

The Section is not to deprive a removed director of compensation or damages payable to him in respect of the termination of his

[1] The exception is the case of a director who on 18th July, 1945, held office for life. S. 184(1).

appointment as director or of any appointment terminating with his appointment as director, *e.g.* as managing director, and is not to interfere with any other power that the company may have of removing a director (Sub-section (6)).

The provisions of Section 184 override anything to the contrary in the articles, but the articles may themselves contain provisions for the removal of a director. They frequently provide for removal by Extraordinary Resolution, and it is generally thought that if this is so no special notice is required and the other provisions of Section 184 do not apply. If this is correct (as the editors believe) the articles could equally effectively provide for removal, without Section 184 provisions, by Ordinary Resolution. The power would be additional to that conferred by the Section.

In private companies, or companies of special types, the provisions of Section 184 are sometimes contrary to what the shareholders want or what is in their true interests. In such cases special articles are often incorporated, which by one means or another give special protection to the directors, *e.g.* by giving extra votes on any removal resolution to the director under attack; see *Bushell v. Faith.*[1] Despite what Lord Morris said in that case, such articles are sometimes important or even essential in order to safeguard the interests of persons, who, perhaps, incorporate a company to be operated as a quasi-partnership.

The special notice required in this case is required in the case of two other kinds of resolution. Under Section 160 it is required for a resolution directed against the re-election of the retiring auditor (see *ante*, p. 75). In the event of such a notice being given, that Section gives the retiring auditor a like right of making and having circulated or read out his representations as to the proposed resolution as is given to a director by Section 184, subject to similar provisions regarding defamatory matter.

Under Section 185 special notice is also required for the appointment of a director over the age limit imposed on directors by this Section or for the appointment of a director who is not to retire on attaining that age limit. The provision as to age limit may, however, be excluded by the company's articles (Sub-section (7)) and does not normally apply to a private company (Sub-section (8)).

All these resolutions for which special notice is required are ordinary resolutions and only differ from other ordinary resolutions by reason of the necessity for special notice of them being given.

The special notice required in the case of resolutions of these three kinds mentioned above is dealt with by Section 142, which

[1] [1970] A.C. 1099.

provides that, where special notice is required of a resolution, the resolution shall not be effective unless notice of the intention to move it has been given to the company not less than 28 days before the meeting at which it is moved, and the company shall give its members notice of any such resolution at the same time and in the same manner as it gives notice of the meeting or, if that is not practicable, shall give them notice, either by advertisement in a newspaper having an appropriate circulation or in any other mode allowed by the articles, not less than 21 days before the meeting.

A proviso lays down that if, after notice has been given to the company, a meeting is called for a date 28 days or less after the notice has been given, the notice though not given within the time required by the Section shall be deemed to have been properly given for the purposes thereof. This achieves the dual purpose of ensuring that the directors cannot frustrate the proposal by promptly calling a meeting without the removal resolution, and of making effective a resolution for removing a director even if, for convenience or to save expense or by necessity, the meeting is called for holding within the specified 28 days.

It will be noted that the requirements as to special notice are two-fold. First, notice of the intention to move the resolution must be given to the company not less than 28 days before the meeting at which it is to be moved, and consequently even if the board desire to put forward a resolution for which special notice is required, they must arrange for someone to give this notice to the company. This notice should be given by a person who, being entitled to do so, intends to propose the resolution, but provided that such notice has been duly given any member may in fact propose the resolution. Secondly, on receipt of this notice the board must, subject to the proviso, give notice of the proposed resolution to the members in the same way as it gives notice of the meeting.

Mere receipt by the company of notice of an intention to move a resolution under this Section does not compel the company to hold a meeting. If the notice signifies the intention to move the resolution at the next meeting they need not give notice of it until the next annual general meeting is held unless an extraordinary general meeting is either convened in the ordinary way or requisitioned under Section 132 before the date for the annual general meeting. If, therefore, the next meeting is not an annual general meeting it will be sufficient to give 14 days' notice of the resolution. If, however, it is impracticable for notice of the intended resolution to be given in the same way as notice of the meeting is given, then in any case, subject, again, to the proviso, 21 days' notice thereof must be given either by advertisement in a newspaper or in any other way allowed by the articles.

As stated (*ante*, p. 82), the unanimous consent of all the members entitled to vote, even though given separately, may in some cases be equivalent to the passing of an ordinary resolution. But where special notice is required this must, in fact, be given.

(2) *Extraordinary Resolutions*.—The Act provides that certain things may be done by Extraordinary Resolution. This is a right of the members, and cannot be excluded by the articles. These, which are all connected with the voluntary winding up of a company, are as follows: resolving that a company shall be wound up on the ground that it cannot by reason of its liabilities continue its business (Section 278); sanctioning the exercise by the liquidator of certain powers in a voluntary winding-up (Section 303); for making a scheme of arrangement between the liquidator and the company's creditors binding on the company and the creditors (Section 306); and for disposing of the books and papers of the company and the liquidator in a members' voluntary winding-up (Section 341).

In addition articles sometimes provide that certain things, *e.g.* the removal of a director without going through the formalities of giving special notice, may be effected by extraordinary resolution.

An extraordinary resolution is one which has been passed by a majority of not less than three-fourths of such members, as being entitled so to do, vote in person or, where proxies are allowed, by proxy at a general meeting of which notice specifying the intention to propose the resolution as an extraordinary resolution has been duly given (Section 141(1)).

This Sub-section is dealing only with voting on a show of hands. Unless the articles otherwise provide, which they will very seldom do, on a show of hands only members present are counted, not those present by proxy.

The position on a poll is dealt with by Sub-section (4) of Section 141, which provides that in computing the majority on a poll demanded on the question that an extraordinary resolution or a special resolution be passed, reference shall be had to the number of votes cast for and against the resolution.

In Sub-section (1) the words "a majority of" are redundant. If 100 votes are cast, 75 will secure the passing of an extraordinary resolution.

Consequently, for a special or extraordinary resolution to be passed on a show of hands at least 75 per cent of the members voting must vote in its favour and on a poll 75 per cent of the total votes validly cast, which will include votes cast by proxies, must be in favour of the resolution.

It is generally considered that the notice of the meeting at which it is intended to propose a resolution as an extraordinary resolution, must set out the exact words of the resolution, and also that it is intended to propose the resolution as an extraordinary resolution.[1] In *re Oxted Motor Company*[2] it was held that an extraordinary resolution for voluntary winding-up might be passed by the unanimous consent of all the members even though no notice had been given. Since all the members could, under Section 141, consent to short notice, this decision does not involve any departure from principle but conforms with the Section as with common sense. In addition, it is supportable, in the view of the editors, on the principle that all the shareholders can consent to any proposal unless the Act imposes any outside restriction, *e.g.* consent of the Court. Section 141 is an enabling Section, by which certain things can be done by less than all the members, subject to certain safeguards.

Under Section 133 (*ante*, p. 83) the length of notice of a meeting for passing an extraordinary resolution by a company other than an unlimited company is 14 clear days unless a shorter notice is agreed to in the manner specified in Sub-section (3) of that section.

(3) *Special Resolutions* are required by the Act for various purposes, the most usual of which are as follows: Altering articles (Section 10), making alterations in the objects clause of the memorandum (Section 5), and of certain other matters in the memorandum (Section 23), changing the name of the company (Section 18), and reducing the capital of the company (Section 66). In certain circumstances a special resolution is required to bring about a winding-up of the company. In addition the articles may provide that the company shall only be able to do certain things by special resolution.

To pass a special resolution involves the same requirements as for an extraordinary resolution except that instead of 14 days' notice 21 are required, and the resolution must be specified in the notice as a special resolution. The majority required is the same as for an extraordinary resolution. A proviso to the Sub-section permits the passing of a special resolution at a meeting of which less than 21 days' notice has been given if it is so agreed by a majority in number of the members having the right to attend and vote at any such meeting, being a majority together holding not less than 95 per cent in nominal value of the shares giving that right, or, in the case of a company not having a share capital, together representing not less than 95 per cent of the total voting rights at that meeting of all the members.

[1] *McConnell v. Prill & Co.*, [1916] 2 Ch. 57.

[2] [1921] 3 K.B. 32.

There is no limitation to the shortness of the notice provided the specified number of members attend and agree to the notice in fact given. If all the shareholders are gathered together and it is decided to pass a special resolution, the correct procedure is to write out a notice convening a meeting, set out the resolution and at the foot set out words for shareholders to agree to the convening of the meeting at short notice. The meeting is then held and the resolution passed.

A special (or extraordinary) resolution cannot be passed otherwise than at a meeting: accordingly it is sometimes thought that a resolution will not be effective as a special or extraordinary resolution if merely signed by all members (see Table A, Part II, Regulation 5). In the editors' view this is a wrong conclusion, since it ignores the principle that all the members can agree to anything, so as to bind themselves, their successors and the company, unless the Act imposes some outside requirement. Such a resolution would fall to be delivered to the Registrar of Companies for filing under Section 143(4).

(4) *Matters common to both Special and Extraordinary Resolutions.*—Section 141 Sub-section (3) provides that at any meeting at which an extraordinary resolution or a special resolution is submitted to be passed, a declaration of the chairman that the resolution is carried shall, unless a poll is demanded, be conclusive evidence of the fact without proof of the number or proportion of the votes recorded in favour of or against the resolution.

The statutory provision as to the effect of the declaration by the chairman where no poll is demanded is extended by Table A and often by other forms of articles.

The notice of the meeting for the purpose of passing a special or extraordinary resolution must be given in the same way as is required by the articles for notice of other meetings of the company, or if the meeting is directed to be held by the Court in manner directed by the Court (Sub-section (5)).

The demand for a poll on resolutions of this kind is governed by the same provisions as demanded on an ordinary resolution (see *ante*, p. 108).

A printed copy of every special and extraordinary resolution must under Section 143 be forwarded to the registrar of companies.

If the Act provides that a particular thing may be effected by the passing of an extraordinary or special resolution the articles cannot require a different kind of resolution for that purpose,[1] either more stringent or less. If the Act contains no requirements as to the way

[1] *Ayre & Skelsey's Adamant Cement Co.* (1904) 20 T.L.R. 587.

in which a company is to do any particular act it is competent for the articles to require for such act a resolution passed by a greater majority than that necessary for a special or extraordinary resolution.

(5) *Amendments to proposed Ordinary Resolutions.*—The amendment to an ordinary resolution must be within the scope of the notice convening the meeting. This principle has been interpreted surprisingly broadly so that where notice was given of a resolution to appoint three named directors an amendment to appoint two additional directors was held to be valid.[1] In that case, however, notice was given of the resolution with the addition of the words "with such amendments as shall be determined on at the meeting". Similarly in *Choppington Collieries v. Johnson*[2] the articles provided that the election of directors in place of those retiring by rotation was not special business. Notice was sent out of an annual general meeting stating that the business was (*inter alia*) to elect directors (in the plural) and also stating that one retiring director offered himself for re-election. It was held that the meeting could appoint persons other than the retiring director to be directors up to the maximum number allowed by the articles. An amendment should not impose a greater burden on the company than the original motion.

A proposed amendment need not be in writing unless the articles expressly provide, but they should be sufficiently definite.[3]

Every amendment must be put to the meeting. A proposed amendment need not be seconded unless the articles specifically require this. "If the chairman put the question without its being proposed or seconded by anybody, that would be perfectly good."[4] A chairman is not justified in refusing a motion or amendment because there is no seconder unless the articles or rules expressly provide that all motions or amendments shall be seconded.

If the mover of the amendment does not challenge the chairman's ruling, that is not a waiver of his right to impeach the resolution. "When a chairman deliberately rules that a certain amendment cannot be put it would be improper and indecent for any shareholder to proceed to discuss the propriety of the chairman's ruling. Of course I am assuming that he gives his ruling deliberately, and having the matter sufficiently before him."[5]

Where there are more amendments than one they should be put

[1] *Betts v. Macnaghten,* [1910] 1 Ch. 430.
[2] [1944] 1 All E.R. 762.
[3] *Henderson v. Bank of Australasia* (1890) 45 Ch. D. 330.
[4] *Re Horbury Bridge Coal Co.* (1879) 11 Ch. D. 109, at 118.
[5] *Henderson v. Bank of Australasia* (1890) 45 Ch. 9 330, at 350.

to the meeting in the order in which they affect the main question and then the main question in its original form or as finally amended. Strict adherence to the formality of putting motions and amendments is not essential, provided they are put to the meeting in such a way that those present understand what it is that they are called upon to decide.[1]

[1] *Ex parte Stevens* (1852) 16 J.P. 632.

CHAPTER 18

Business of Meetings

Articles usually provide that all business conducted at extraordinary general meetings, and all except certain specified matters to be conducted at annual general meetings, is to be special business: and they further provide that notice of a general meeting is, in the case of special business, to specify the general nature of that business.

In Table A these provisions are found in Regulations 50 and 52. The business specified in Regulation 52 as not being special business of an annual general meeting consists of the consideration of the accounts, balance sheets and reports of the directors and auditors, the election of directors in place of those retiring, and the appointment of, and the fixing of the remuneration of, the auditors.

In the absence of any such provisions in the articles all the business to be transacted must be specified in the notice, but most articles have provisions corresponding to Regulations 50 and 52 of Table A. Thus when the company's articles contain these or similar provisions, the matters declared not to be special business may be transacted at an annual general meeting but not at other general meetings, although not specified in the notice convening the meeting.

(1) *Reading the notice convening the meeting and the auditors' report.*—Meetings are usually opened by the secretary reading the notice convening the meeting, or the chairman asking the meeting to agree that the notice be taken as read. Even the latter is a somewhat pompous formality, and quite unnecessary. If the meeting is an annual general meeting, or other meeting at which the accounts are to be considered, the auditors' report must be read, not taken as read, for Sub-section (2) of Section 162 provides that the auditors' report on the company's accounts shall be read before the company in general meeting and shall be open to inspection by any member. There is no statutory requirement for reading the notice.

Far more sensible than reading the full notice, is for the chairman or proposer of each resolution to read the proposed resolution when its turn comes, so that shareholders are aware at the right time of what they are considering. Sometimes the minutes of the previous meeting are then read and formally verified as correct, but, unless required by the articles, this proceeding at a general meeting is unnecessary, and generally, a waste of time.

(2) *Consideration of accounts, etc.*—Under Section 148, the directors must once at least in every calendar year lay before the company in general meeting a profit and loss account for the period since the preceding account made up to a date generally not more than nine months before the meeting and a balance sheet as at that date, and this is almost invariably done at the annual general meeting. If the company has subsidiaries, group accounts must at the same time be laid before the company in general meeting (Section 150).

In addition, there is to be attached to the balance sheet laid before the company in general meeting the directors' report. Section 157, which lays down two requirements, provides that there shall be attached to every balance sheet laid before a company in general meeting a report by the directors with respect to the state of the company's affairs, the amount, if any, which they recommend should be paid by way of dividend, and the amount, if any, which they propose to carry to reserves. The report must deal, so far as is material for the appreciation of the state of the company's affairs by its members and will not in the directors' opinion be harmful to the business of the company or of any of its subsidiaries, with any change during the financial year in the nature of the company's business, or in the company's subsidiaries, or in the classes of business in which the company has an interest, whether as member of another company or otherwise. The Companies Act 1967 imposes certain other requirements.

Under Section 158 copies of the balance sheet to be laid before the company and of the documents required to be annexed thereto, together with a copy of the auditors' report, must in the case of a company having a share capital, be sent to every member of the company, every debenture holder of the company whether they are entitled to receive notices of meetings or not, and to all persons other than members or debenture holders who are entitled to receive notices of general meetings of the company, *e.g.* the auditors. They need not be sent to a member or debenture holder who is not entitled to receive notices of meetings if the company does not know his address, and if joint holders of shares and debentures are not all entitled to notice of meetings the copies need only be sent to those joint holders who are entitled to notices or, if none is entitled, to one such joint holder. In the case of companies not having a share capital these documents need not be sent to members or debenture holders who are not entitled to receive notices of meetings of the company.

There is no need to read the accounts or directors' report and no purpose in doing so.

The chairman usually proceeds to make some comments on the accounts, explains the position of the company, gives such further information concerning its affairs as he thinks may properly be made known, and concludes by moving that the report and accounts be adopted. This is usually seconded by another director with a few remarks, and then members present at the meeting are free to comment upon or criticise the report, the accounts, and the chairman's speech.

So far as it can be done without injury to the interests of the company, the directors should answer freely all inquiries as regards the accounts and the company's affairs. But they are not bound to answer in general meeting any questions that they consider it undesirable in the best interests of the company to answer.

Usually at an annual general meeting, unless steps have been previously taken by dissatisfied members, there is very little that the members can do if dissatisfied with the directors' report or the conduct of the directors. They can vote against the resolution for the adoption of the report, but even if the resolution is lost that has no effect other than indicating the disapproval of a majority of the meeting. If it is lost an attempt is sometimes made by the dissatisfied members to appoint a committee of inspection from among their number to look into the affairs of the company, but this cannot be done without proper notice of a resolution therefor having been given. Such a procedure is, in any case, valueless, since the resolution does not give the committee any powers of investigation for requiring information. So long as the directors remain the directors of the company they retain their powers as such, and the company cannot remove the control of the company's affairs from them.[1]

In some cases, however, where the meeting proves hostile, the directors may agree to give certain information to a committee appointed by the dissatisfied members and to adjourn the meeting until that has been done. They are not, however, bound to do so.

Under Section 165, the Department of Trade is required to appoint one or more competent inspectors to investigate the affairs of a company and to report on them in such manner as the board direct if the company by a special resolution or the Court by order declares that its affairs ought to be so investigated, and may do so of its own motion in certain circumstances.

[1] *Automatic Self-Cleansing Filter Co. v. Cunninghame*, [1906] 2 Ch. 34.

Under Section 164 the Department may also appoint such inspectors on the application of a specified proportion of the members of the company. The Department is always very difficult to stir under this section, and, indeed, the number of ill-judged applications that have been made justifies the Departments' reluctance to act. Where, however, the majority of the members of a company disapprove of the conduct of the directors they will presumably avail themselves of the power conferred by Section 184 of removing the directors by ordinary resolutions and appointing others in their places by like resolutions (see *ante*, p. 119). This, however, can only be done if the requisite notices have been given, and if they have not been given in time for an annual general meeting a subsequent meeting will have to be requisitioned for the purpose.

(3) *Declaring a dividend.*—Assuming the report is adopted, one of the directors usually then moves the payment of the dividend recommended therein. Articles usually provide that the company in general meeting may declare dividends, but that no dividend shall exceed the amount recommended by the directors.

(4) *Election of directors.*—The articles generally contain provisions relating to the retirement and election of directors. For example, Table A provides that at the first annual general meeting all the directors shall retire from office and at subsequent annual general meetings one-third of the directors (being those who have been longest in office) shall retire, that a retiring director is eligible for re-election and that the company may at the meeting at which a director retires fill the vacated office, but that if it is not filled the retiring director, if offering himself for re-election, is deemed to be re-elected unless it is resolved not to fill the office or a resolution for his re-election is lost.[1] Table A also contains provisions whereunder notice of the intention to propose any person (other than a retiring director or a person recommended by the directors) for election to the board must be given to the company with notice of the willingness to act of the person proposed to be elected. If the articles require such notice to be given by a certain time, the board is bound to refuse to accept the motion unless it is prepared itself to recommend the nominee.

In the case of a public company the appointment of each director must, to be valid, be effected by a separate resolution unless the meeting agrees without a dissentient to a motion for the appointment of two or more directors being made by a single resolution (Section 183).

A resolution moved in contravention of that section is void and

[1] See *Grundt v. Great Boulder Proprietary Gold Mines Ltd.*, [1948] Ch. 145 (C.A.).

the persons thereby intended to be appointed directors will not be so appointed. The section also provides that if an election is thereby avoided and the office of a retiring director is in consequence not filled, no provision for the retiring director's automatic reappointment such as in Regulation 92 of Table A referred to above is to apply (Sub-section (2)(*b*)).

It should be noted that though the election of directors is generally ordinary business of which notice is not required, if the articles contain a provision similar to Regulation 93 of Table A and it is desired to move the appointment of a person who is neither a retiring director nor recommended by the directors, notice will have to be given to the company of that intention in accordance with the article.

(5) *Appointment and remuneration of auditors.*—Usually a firm of accountants is appointed as auditors. If the composition of that firm changes, then technically it is the old firm which remains as auditors. In practice no point is ever taken on this technicality: but with the current tendency for firms to amalgamate and merge, it is probably prudent, and certainly correct, for a resolution to be proposed at the next annual general meeting appointing the new firm. The statutory provisions relating to this matter are contained in Section 159.

Sub-section (1) provides that every company shall at each annual general meeting appoint an auditor or auditors to hold office from the conclusion of that, until the conclusion of the next, annual general meeting.

Thus the appointment of the auditor must be made at the annual general meeting. As has already been stated, the accounts are usually laid before the annual general meeting, but may under the provisions of Section 148 be laid before any general meeting held in the appropriate calendar year.

Section 159(2) provides that at any annual general meeting a retiring auditor, however, appointed shall be reappointed without any resolution being passed unless (a) he is not qualified for reappointment; or (b) a resolution has been passed at that meeting appointing someone instead of him or providing expressly that he shall not be reappointed; or (c) he has given the company notice in writing of his unwillingness to be reappointed.

The proviso to this Sub-section provides that where notice has been given of an intended resolution to appoint some other person in place of the retiring auditor, but the resolution cannot be proceeded with by reason of the death, incapacity, or disqualification of that person, the retiring auditor shall not be automatically reappointed.

Special notice (see *ante*, p. 120) must be given of any resolution for the appointment of some person other than the retiring auditor as auditor or of any resolution providing expressly that a retiring auditor shall not be reappointed (Section 160(1)).

If no auditor is appointed or reappointed the Department of Trade may fill the vacancy (Section 159(3)). The directors may appoint the first auditors subject to the company's power of removal (Section 159(5)), and they may also fill casual vacancies (Section 159(6)).

Section 159(7) provides that the remuneration of the auditors of a company in the case of an auditor appointed by the directors or by the Department of Trade may be fixed by the directors or by the Department as the case may be, and except in those cases shall be fixed by the company in general meeting or in such manner as the company in general meeting shall determine. For the purpose of Sub-section (7) any sums paid by the company in respect of the auditors' expenses are to be included in the expression remuneration.

Unlike the appointment of auditors the determination of their remuneration need not be made at the annual general meeting, but it will clearly be generally convenient to fix it then.

(6) *Special business* can be transacted at an annual general meeting provided due notice thereof has been given. There is no need to transact special business at an extraordinary general meeting, although this is often done.

CHAPTER 19

Adjournments

Where no provision is made by the articles as to the adjournment of a meeting, the power of adjourning is vested in the meeting.[1] Motions for adjournment can generally be brought forward at any period of the meeting, and take precedence over any matter then under consideration.

Usually, however, the question of adjournments is provided for by the articles, in which case the provisions of the articles must be followed. In the special situation that the meeting is in total disorder, the chairman has an inherent power (whatever the provisions of the articles) to adjourn the meeting for a short time, taking steps, so far as possible, to ensure that all present know of the adjournment.[2]

Table A provides a common set of provisions. Regulation 57 provides that the chairman of the meeting may, with the consent of a meeting at which a quorum is present (and shall if so directed by the meeting), adjourn the meeting from time to time and from place to place, but that no business is to be transacted at any adjourned meeting other than the business left unfinished at the meeting from which the adjournment took place. When a meeting is adjourned for 30 days or more, notice of the adjourned meeting is to be given as in the case of an original meeting but that in any other case no notice is necessary.

This gives the power on the question of adjournment absolutely to the meeting. Sometimes, however, the articles only provide that the chairman may adjourn with the consent of the meeting. In that case he cannot adjourn without such consent but cannot be compelled to adjourn the meeting against his wishes.[3]

The power given to the chairman is a fiduciary one: he is not entitled to adjourn a meeting capriciously before the business of the meeting has been transacted, and if he purports to do so without good reason, the meeting may appoint another chairman and

[1] Cf. *R. v. Grimshaw* (1847) 11 Jur. 965.
[2] *John v. Rees*, [1970] Ch. 345.
[3] *Salisbury Gold Mining Co. v. Hathorn*, [1897] A.C. 268.

proceed with the business.[1] Similarly he may not adjourn to a place or time which would be unreasonable for shareholders.

Since his power is fiduciary, it will sometimes be his duty to adjourn: if, for example, he believes that shareholders should be given an opportunity to reconsider a proposal, or to consider an alternative, or to review the matter in the light of changed circumstances, he should exercise his power to adjourn and should explain why. If he takes such a decision in good faith he will not be open to challenge and the decision will be effective.

The power is given to him personally, not to the board.

More usual are cases where the articles permit a poll to be called for a proposal to adjourn. In that event the articles will provide that the poll be taken immediately, or, if they do not so provide in express terms, there must be an implied requirement for the purpose in order to give effect to the obvious intention. If a poll is taken, proxy holders may be in doubt whether or not they can exercise their proxy votes, and, if so, how. Sometimes it will be plain how they should exercise them, as being in the best interests of their appointors:[2] sometimes they will have been given specific directions for this purpose: but in other cases they may be in doubt. In the opinion of the editors the principles upon which a proxy holder should act are that he is an agent for the appointor, and, in the absence of express instruction, is entitled to act in whatever way he feels is in the interests of the appointor or accords with what he would wish. If he takes a decision in accordance with that view, held in good faith, it will not be open to successful challenge by the appointor or the company or anyone else. If he feels unable to decide, he may take no action.

The agency is in the proxy holder personally: even if the proxy was canvassed by the board, it is he, and not the board, who has the right and duty to decide.[3]

Business at adjourned meetings.—Section 144 provides that where a resolution is passed at an adjourned meeting of a company, the holders of any class of shares in a company, or the directors of a company, the resolution shall for all purposes be treated as having been passed on the date on which it was in fact passed, and shall not be deemed to have been passed on any earlier date.

The articles usually provide what business may be conducted at an adjourned meeting. Usually only such business can be transacted at the adjourned meeting as has been left unfinished at the original meeting.

[1] *National Dwellings Society v. Sykes*, [1894] 3 Ch. 159.
[2] See *Re Waxed Papers Ltd.* (1937) 2 All E.R. 481.
[3] See further on proxies, *ante*, p. 111 *et seq.*

Sometimes it is possible to transact business which could not have been transacted at the original meeting. Thus in *Catesby v. Burnett*,[1] the articles provided that a member should not be qualified to be elected a director unless 14 clear days' notice of the intention in that behalf were given to the company before the day of election. At the date of the annual general meeting there were two directors due for retirement, but the meeting was adjourned without any election of directors. Notice had been given 14 clear days before the adjourned meeting, and the two new directors elected thereat were held to be validly appointed, since the date of adjourned meeting was the day of election. If the articles had provided for 14 days' notice before the meeting at which they were elected, this would not have been so.

For similar reasons, proxies will sometimes be available for use at an adjourned meeting where they would not have been available at the earlier meeting, as, for example, where they have to be deposited not less than 48 hours "before the meeting or adjourned meeting": see Regulation 69 of Table A.

An adjourned meeting is in law the continuance of the original meeting,[2] and a fresh notice is not therefore necessary,[3] unless the articles require such a notice to be given. Most articles do so provide where the adjournment is of some length, cf. Regulation 57 of Table A.

The directors of a company, in the absence of express authority in the articles of association, have no power to postpone a general meeting of the company properly convened.[4] If they endeavour to exercise such a power, the shareholders can, if they think fit, meet at the place, time and day appointed by the notice, and transact all the business which could properly be put before the meeting as convened. If the directors wish to postpone a meeting, the only way is to meet formally and get the meeting to adjourn itself to a more suitable and convenient time.

It is not uncommon for directors to wish to postpone a meeting, either because circumstances have already changed or changes are expected. In such circumstances they should, if time permits, inform shareholders of their intention and the reason, either by circular or, where time is too short, by newspaper advertisement. The purpose of notifying shareholders is to indicate that the meeting

[1] [1916] 2 Ch. 325.
[2] *Scadding v. Lorant* (1851) 3 H.L.C. 418.
[3] *Wills v. Murray* (1850) 4 Ex. 843.
[4] *Smith v. Paringa Mines*, [1906] 2 Ch. 193.

will be a mere formality and it will be a waste of shareholders' time to attend it.

A meeting may in certain circumstances be continued on a later date without any adjournment in the strict sense having taken place.[1]

[1] *Jackson v. Hamlyn*, [1953] 1 Ch. 577.

CHAPTER 20

Minutes

Section 145(1) provides that every company shall cause minutes of all proceedings of general meetings, and all proceedings at meetings of its directors to be entered in books kept for that purpose.

Section 146 requires the minutes of proceedings of general meetings of a company to be kept at the registered office of the company, and during business hours (subject to such reasonable restrictions as the company may by its articles or in general meeting impose, so that no less than two hours in each day be allowed for inspection) to be open to the inspection of any member without charge. The section also entitles any member to be furnished within seven days after he has made a request to the company with a copy of any such minutes at a charge not exceeding sixpence for every hundred words. The company and every officer in default under the section is liable to a default fine, and the Court may make orders for inspection or directing copies to be sent to the persons requiring them.

There is no requirement that minutes of directors' meetings be available for inspection by members of the company: a director is, by virtue of his office, entitled to see minutes of directors' meetings, but, in the absence of an express provision in the articles, shareholders have no such right: the reasoning behind this was expressed in 1859 as follows:

> "It is highly proper that an inspection of the books containing the proceedings of directors should be obtained on special occasions and for special purposes: but the business of such companies could hardly be conducted if anyone, by buying a share, might entitle himself at all times to gain a knowledge of every commercial transaction to which the directors engage, the moment that an entry of it is made in their books . . . the proposed daily and hourly inspection and publication of all their proceedings . . . would probably ere long be found very prejudicial to shareholders."[1]

But they should be accessible to directors and the secretary; auditors

[1] *R. v. Mariquita Mining Co.* (1859) 1 E. & E. 289.

also are entitled under Section 162 to see them for the purposes of audit.

In addition, minutes should be kept of committees of the board. These, like minutes of board meetings, must, in the opinion of the editors, be available for inspection by all the directors, whether or not they were members of the committee. Even if the matter discussed was concerned with a particular director, or affairs in which he was concerned, and he was excluded from the committee for that very reason, he is entitled as a director to know what decision was taken. The editors are aware of cases where a so-called "secret" minute book is kept; this is not only improper but, because it generates suspicion, rather silly.

As the minutes of general meetings are required to be open for inspection of the members and those of directors' meetings are not, separate books for each class of minutes are generally kept.

Section 436 provides that any register, index, minute book or book of account required by the Act to be kept by a company may be kept either by making entries in bound books or by recording the matters in question in any other manner, and that where any such register, index, minute book or books of account is not kept by making entries in a bound book, but by some other means, adequate precautions must be taken for guarding against falsification and facilitating its discovery. The company and every officer of the company who fails to take adequate precautions is liable to a fine. Consequently, with proper precautions, minutes may now be kept in loose-leaf books.

Section 145(2) provides that minutes of any meeting required to be kept by Section 145(1) shall be evidence of the proceedings if purporting to be signed by the chairman of the meeting at which the proceedings were had, or by the chairman of the next succeeding meeting.

Further, by Section 145(3), where minutes have been made in accordance with the provisions of the section of the proceedings at any general meeting of the company or meeting of directors or managers, the meeting is, until the contrary is proved, to be deemed to have been duly held and convened, and all proceedings had thereat to have been duly had, and all appointments of directors, managers or liquidators are to be deemed to be valid.

It is essential, therefore, that the minutes should contain an accurate record of all proceedings transacted and appointments made.

"Directors ought to place on record, either in formal minutes or otherwise, the purport and effect of their deliberations and conclusions; and if they do this insufficiently or inaccurately they cannot reasonably complain of inferences different from those which they allege to be right."[1]

A clear distinction should be carefully drawn between a report and a minute. The former chiefly consists of what was said, the latter consists of what was done or agreed upon, and its place of record is the minutes. Speeches and arguments at a general meeting may form the material of a newspaper report, but the resolutions and decisions are the only proper material for the minutes. The minutes will only be evidence of those matters properly entered in them.

Though not required by the Act, minutes are sometimes read, or if previously circulated to the members, taken as read, at the next following meeting, and submitted for verification of their correctness. If regarded as a correct report of the proceedings by those members present at that meeting, they are signed by the chairman. If considered incorrect, they may be modified and then signed.

The chairman of the meeting, or more usually of the succeeding meeting, whether present or not at the previous meeting, may, under Section 145, sign the minutes.

They need not, unless required by the articles, be signed at, or with the approval of, a meeting, and may be signed even after a winding-up order has been made.

A decision in 1864 (before the present series of Companies Acts) was concerned with an article which provided that a minute signed by any person purporting to be chairman of any meeting of directors was to be receivable in evidence without further proof. An entry was made in a minute book stating the names of parties and number of shares subscribed for, the name of the chairman who signed the minute being set down for one hundred shares. The minute was signed, not at the next meeting, but after the proceedings to wind up the company. It was held that the minute was *prima facie* evidence against all who were present at the meeting, and in the absence of counter evidence showing the incorrectness of the minute, the chairman was liable as a contributory for one hundred shares.[2]

The signature of the chairman to minutes which embody the terms of a contract may be sufficient to satisfy the Statute of Frauds.[3]

It is generally desirable that the minutes of directors' meetings should not be signed until approved by a subsequent meeting. If a succeeding meeting of any kind requires the minutes of a previous

[1] *Re Liverpool Household Stores* (1890) 59 L.J.Ch. at p. 619.
[2] *Ex parte Stock* (1864) 33 L.J.Ch. 731.
[3] *Jones v. Victoria Graving Dock* (1877) 2 Q.B.D. 314.

meeting to be altered before approving them as correct, some reference to this should be made in the minutes of the later meeting.

Once minutes have been signed they should not be altered or corrected internally. "I trust I shall never again see or hear of the secretary of a company, whether under superior directions or otherwise, altering minutes of meetings, either by striking out anything or adding anything."[1] If they are found to be incorrect the proper procedure is to add a further minute or note correcting the mistake, and to have the chairman sign that addition. In this way anyone who reads them will know the correct position, whereas a minute with alterations in it renders it uncertain whether the alterations were authorised. If the original minutes were approved at a later meeting, the addition should also be approved and a record made of it.

Pages should not be removed from the minute book, the pages of which should be numbered consecutively.

The Act merely makes the minutes when signed *prima facie* evidence, *i.e.* the burden of showing that they are wrong is on those who say so. "The minutes in the books are to be received, not as conclusive, but as *prima facie* evidence of resolutions and proceedings at general meetings: and also it may be added, and I think correctly, that inasmuch as the chairman who presides at such meetings, and has to receive the poll and declare its result, has *prima facie* authority to decide all emergent questions which necessarily require decision at the time, his decision of those questions will naturally govern, and properly govern, the entry of the minute in the books; and, though in no sense conclusive, it throws the burden of proof upon the other side, who may say, contrary to the entry in the minute book, following the decision of the chairman, that the result of the poll was different from that there recorded."[2]

Evidence may be given to show what in fact was done even if this contradicts the minutes.[3] "As they were directors, the minute is admissible against them; but none the less does other evidence appear admissible though the existence of the minute is a circumstance to be considered in judging of its weight."[4]

Articles sometimes provide that the minutes of a meeting if purporting to be signed by the chairman shall be "conclusive evidence without any further proof of the facts therein stated". According to the only reported decision on such an article, evidence cannot be

[1] *Re Cawley & Co.* (1889) 42 Ch. D. 209 at 226.
[2] *Re Indian Zoedone Co.* (1884) 26 Ch. D. 70 at 77.
[3] *Re Fireproof Doors*, [1916] 2 Ch. 142.
[4] *Re Pyle Works, No.* 2, [1891] 1 Ch. 173 at 184.

given in such a case to contradict minutes so signed unless it can first be shown that the minutes have been written up fraudulently.[1] The editors very much doubt whether this decision is correct, and in their view an article so framed is most inadvisable. The secretary should make the necessary notes as each meeting, whether general or of the board, proceeds and subsequently write up the minutes in the minute book.

The secretary should take care that the record is absolutely impartial and free from ambiguity, that the exact account of what was actually agreed upon and nothing more is minuted, and that it is sufficiently detailed and complete, so that an absent member can fully understand from the record what was done at the meeting. In the case of board meetings the names of directors present should be recorded; the names of other persons if recorded, should be stated as being "in attendance".

A director who is present at a meeting of the board at which the minutes of a previous board meeting are confirmed, even though he be a party to their confirmation, is not thereby made responsible for what was resolved upon at such previous board meeting if the resolution has been acted upon before the minutes are confirmed.[2] He is, however, thereby given notice that such resolution was passed.

In the case of resolutions of directors not carried unanimously, it is desirable to record the names of those who voted for and against the resolution, if there is a request for such a record. A director is not entitled to have his protest recorded in the minutes, but if he votes against a motion he is entitled to have that fact noted in the minutes if he so desires.

It is not essential to the validity of the exercise of power of directors that they should be formally embodied in formal resolutions, provided that the minutes record the substance of the decision arrived at.[3]

[1] *Kerr v. John Mottram Ltd.*, [1940] Ch. 657.

[2] *Re Lands Allotment Co.*, [1894] 1 Ch. 616, at p. 635; *Burton v. Bevan*, [1908] 2 Ch. 240.

[3] *Re Land Credit Co.* (1869) L.R., 4 Ch. App. 460 at 473.

CHAPTER 21

Meetings of Directors

Section 176 provides that every company registered on or after the 1st November, 1929 (other than a private company), shall have at least two directors, and every company registered before that date and every private company, shall have a director.

Normal day-to-day management decisions are taken by directors and others with responsibility in that field delegated by the board. Some matters require to be dealt with in a more formal way, with a record kept of the decisions: for this purpose board meetings are held.

Almost invariably the articles contain provisions relating to board meetings. For example, Regulation 98 of Table A provides that the directors may meet together for the despatch of business, adjourn, and otherwise regulate their meetings, as they think fit; that questions arising at any meeting shall be decided by a majority of votes; that in case of an equality of votes, the chairman shall have a second or casting vote; that a director may, and the secretary on the requisition of a director shall, at any time summon a meeting of the directors; and that it shall not be necessary to give notice of a meeting of directors to any director for the time being absent from the United Kingdom.

Most articles allow decisions to be come to by a majority of the directors present, but in certain types of companies (*e.g.* where there are special classes of shares each with rights to appoint directors, or companies which are, in effect, incorporated partnerships) articles frequently provide that all or some matters require an affirmative resolution from all directors, or from a specified majority, or from a majority including directors of both classes or factions.

Directors hold their powers in a fiduciary capacity and must exercise them *bona fide* for the benefit of the company, not for their own ends.[1]

(1) *Board Meetings*

To constitute a valid board meeting the following conditions must be complied with:

[1] *Piercy v. S. Mills & Co.*, [1920] 1 Ch. 77.

(i) *The proper person must be in the chair.*—His appointment is generally governed by the articles. Regulation 101 of Table A, for example, provides that the directors may elect a chairman of their meetings and determine the period for which he is to hold office, and that if no such chairman is elected, or if at any meeting the chairman is not present within five minutes after the time appointed for holding the same, the directors present may choose one of their number to be chairman of the meeting.

An appointment of a chairman of directors made in contravention of the articles is void and is not regularised by mere acquiescence, and consequently resolutions carried by the casting vote of such a chairman are inoperative.[1]

(ii) *The board must be properly constituted.*—Except as mentioned below, acts done as directors by persons who have not been validly elected do not bind the company;[2] it is otherwise if the fact that they were not properly elected is only discovered afterwards, for Section 180 provides that the acts of a director or manager shall be valid notwithstanding any defect that may afterwards be discovered in his appointment or qualification. This Section is merely intended to cure slips in the appointment of directors and cannot in any case be relied on by a person who in fact knew of the invalidity even if its discovery was not general, or when there was no appointment at all.[3]

Outsiders are, the absence of knowledge to the contrary, entitled to assume that the domestic affairs of a company are properly conducted; the basis for this principle is known as the Rule in *Royal British Bank v. Turquand.*[4] It is outside the scope of this work to consider this Rule in any detail, but broadly its effect is that directors acting irregularly will bind the company to outsiders unless for any reason the outsiders were put upon inquiry.

Where the articles provided that the quorum at directors' meetings should be fixed by the directors and it was properly fixed at three, and at a meeting of two the secretary was instructed to affix the seal to a mortgage, it was held that as between the company and the mortgagees who had no notice of the irregularity the execution of the deed was valid.[5]

Since 1925 this decision could also be upheld under Section 74 of the Law of Property Act 1925.

[1] *Clark v. Workman*, [1920] 1 I.R. 107.

[2] *Garden Gully United Quartz Mining Co. v. McLister* (1875) 1 App. Cas. 39.

[3] *Morris v. Kanssen*, [1946] A.C. 459.

[4] (1856) 6 El. & Bl. 327. See also European Communities Act 1972 Section 9(1).

[5] *County of Gloucester Bank v. Rudry Merthyr &c. Co.*, [1895] 1 Ch. 629.

Sometimes articles provide for alternate or substitute directors to act for directors going abroad. Under normal articles one person may be alternate for more than one director, but in the opinion of the editors it is desirable for the outsider to exclude such a possibility by expressly stating that one person may not be alternate for more than one director. In such cases an alternate director is counted as a director, and if the alternate is a director in his own right he counts as two persons, both for the purposes of quorum and of voting. In such a case it may be possible for one person to constitute a meeting, if he is duly appointed alternate for a sufficient number of directors to form a quorum.

(iii) Where board approval is required, directors must either act at a duly constituted meeting or by unanimous decision arrived at informally.[1]

This requirement of a board meeting was illustrated starkly in one case.[2] The articles provided that no person not recommended by the board of directors for election as a director should be eligible unless at the time he had held twenty shares for two months. B, who was not a shareholder, was elected unanimously at a general meeting, six out of seven directors, who were then the only shareholders, being present. It was held that B's election was void. "Six directors out of seven met in a different capacity and for a different purpose, and such a meeting does not make them a board of directors."

A board meeting can be held under informal circumstances, but the casual meeting of the only two directors at a railway station cannot be treated as a board meeting at the option of one against the will of the other.[3] The dividing line is, however, narrow. Where one of the only two directors did not attend a meeting, proper notice of which had been given, but was met by the other shortly after in the passage, that other proposed a resolution and, on the first director objecting, declared it passed by virtue of his casting vote, and this resolution was held to have been duly passed.[4]

Articles, however, frequently allow the directors, if unanimous, to act without holding a meeting. Regulation 106 of Table A provides that a resolution in writing, signed by all the directors entitled to receive notice of a meeting of the directors, shall be as valid and effectual as if it had been passed at a meeting of the directors duly convened and held.

[1] *Collie's Claim* (1871) 12 Eq. 246, 258: *exp. Kennedy* (1890) 44 Ch. D. 472, at 481.
[2] *Re East Norfolk Tramways Co., Barber's Case* (1877) 5 Ch. D. 963, at p. 967.
[3] *Barron v. Potter*, [1914] 1 Ch. 895.
[4] *Smith v. Paringa Mines*, [1906] 2 Ch. 193.

A director need not attend every meeting, though he should attend as often as circumstances permit. He is bound to use fair and reasonable diligence in the management of his company's affairs and to act honestly.[1]

A director is not liable for misfeasance committed by co-directors without his knowledge at a board meeting at which he is not present.[2]

A subsequent meeting can ratify the business done at an informal meeting,[3] and can ratify an unauthorised act of an agent of the company.[4]

(2) *Notice of Meetings*

Directors of a company can at any meeting of the board deal with all the affairs of the company then requiring attention so far as the powers conferred on them by the articles extend; previous notice of special business is not necessary[5] unless the articles so require.

Reasonable notice must be given of the meeting, but it need not be in writing unless the articles so provide.[6] Even in the absence of such a provision as is contained in Regulation 98 of Table A, presumably any director may summon a meeting. What is a reasonable notice will depend on the facts in any particular case and may depend on a course of conduct. In *re Homer Gold Mines*[7] a shorter notice than any previously given was held invalid, since the Court came to the conclusion that the notice had been so given with a view to excluding certain directors. A notice may, however, be extremely short if all the directors are able to attend and if any director wishes to object to the shortness of the notice he should make that objection at once.[8] If a proper notice be not given, the proceedings are invalid unless all the directors are present.[9] There is, however, no need to send notice when the directors have decided to hold meeings at regular intervals, *i.e.* when there is a fixed day and time of which all directors have knowledge, and, therefore, notice (*e.g.* weekly meetings on Fridays, at 3 p.m. or every first Thursday in the month at 11 a.m.). Even in the absence of a provision as to directors out of the United Kingdom similar to Regulation 98

[1] *Re Forest of Dean Coal Mining Co.* (1878) 10 Ch. D. 450; *Re City Equitable Fire Insurance Co.*, [1925] Ch. 407.

[2] *Perry's Case* (1876) 34 L.T. 716.

[3] *Re Portuguese Consolidated Copper Mines* (1889) 42 Ch. D. 160.

[4] *Molineaux v. London, Birmingham, &c. Co.*, [1902] 2 K.B. 589.

[5] *La Compagnie de Mayville v. Whitley*, [1896] 1 Ch. 788.

[6] *Browne v. La Trinidad* (1887) 37 Ch. D. 1.

[7] (1888) 39 Ch. D. 546.

[8] *Browne v. La Trinidad, supra.*

[9] *Harben v. Phillips* (1883) 23 Ch. D. 14.

of Table A in certain circumstances notice need not be given to a director who is abroad and out of reach.[1] A director cannot, however, waive his right to notice and even if he says, "I shall not be able to come; you need not summon me," he must be given notice.[2]

Directors are entitled to take the business at a board meeting in any order they may think proper.[3]

(3) *Quorum*

Business can only be validly transacted by the majority of the directors at a meeting properly convened[4] and held and at which there is the quorum as prescribed by the articles.

Regulation 99 of Table A provides that the quorum necessary for the transaction of the business of the directors may be fixed by the directors, and unless so fixed shall be two.

Where such a provision is found, an outsider is entitled under the rule in *Turquands case*,[5] to assume, in the absence of indication otherwise, that the quorum is two: in principle he might even be entitled to rely on a decision where only one director is present, but since one person cannot normally constitute a "meeting" this would put the outsider on inquiry.

Nevertheless one director who is also alternate for another could constitute a meeting.

If no provision is made by the articles a majority of the directors will constitute a quorum, but under certain circumstances apparently the necessary number may be determined by the practice of the board.[6]

A quorum of directors means a quorum competent to transact and vote on the business before the board; and therefore, in a case where the articles prohibited interested directors from voting, a resolution passed at a meeting of three directors, two of whom were interested in the subject-matter of the resolution, was held invalid.[7] In another case articles provided that directors could contract with the company, but should not vote in connection with such contracts, and that until otherwise determined three should be a quorum. Four directors were present at a meeting. At that meeting a resolution was passed for the issue of a debenture to one of the directors present who did not vote on that resolution and a similar resolution was

[1] *Re Halifax Sugar Co.* (1890) 62 L.T. 564.
[2] *Re Portuguese Consolidated Copper Mines* (1889) 42 Ch. D. 160.
[3] *Re Cawley & Co.* (1889) 42 Ch. D. 209.
[4] *York Tramways Co. v. Willows* (1882) 8 Q.B.D. 685.
[5] *Royal British Bank v. Turquand* (1856) 6 E. & B. 327.
[6] *Regent's Canal Ironworks* (1867) W.N. 79.
[7] *Yuill v. Greymouth Point Elizabeth R. Co.*, [1904] 1 Ch. 32.

passed to issue another debenture to another director who was present, but did not vote on this latter resolution. It was held in the circumstances of the case that the issue of both debentures was part of one entire transaction in which the directors to whom the debentures were issued were jointly interested and that there was therefore no quorum and the debentures were not validly issued. It was subsequently resolved that in future a quorum should be two so as to enable the difficulty to be got over. One of the directors interested in the transaction was one of the three directors present when that resolution was passed and being interested was unable to count towards a quorum. The purported reduction of the quorum was consequently ineffective.[1]

One director may be a quorum if the articles so provide.[2]

In *re Copal Varnish Co.*,[3] where one director out of a board of two refused to attend meetings summoned to consider transfers of shares in order to prevent a quorum being formed, it was held that the transferees were entitled to an order directing the company to register the transfers, since a shareholder has a property in his shares which he has the right to dispose of subject only to any express restriction in the articles. Even if the articles give directors a power to decline to register a transfer, such a power is not exercised where the directors have not passed a resolution declining so to register.[4]

Failure to keep quorum.—Where there is a quorum at the beginning of a meeting, but some of the directors leave the meeting, so that a number less than the quorum remain, any subsequent acts are invalid. This would not be the case if the articles provided that "the quorum shall be two directors present when the meeting proceeds to business", as was found in relation to general meetings in *re Hartley Baird*,[5] but such a provision would be most unusual. The normal provision is similar to that found in Regulation 99 of Table A referred to above.

Minimum number.—Articles usually fix what is to be the maximum and minimum number of the directors. Where a minimum is fixed, and the number of the directors has never reached the minimum, they cannot act even though they are sufficient to form a quorum.[6] But if there have been sufficient directors to satisfy the requirement of the minimum number, and their number falls below the minimum

[1] *Re North Eastern Insurance Co.*, [1919] 1 Ch. 198.
[2] *Re Fireproof Doors*, [1916] 2 Ch. 142.
[3] [1917] 2 Ch. 349.
[4] *Hackney Pavilion*, [1924] 1 Ch. 276.
[5] [1955] Ch. 143.
[6] *Re Sly, Spink & Co.*, [1911] 2 Ch. 430.

but there are nevertheless sufficient directors to form a quorum, most articles provide that in such a case the continuing directors may act for limited purposes, usually for calling a general meeting or for filling the vacancies in their number: see Regulation 100 of Table A.

Under such an article a single director may be entitled to act for those purposes.[1]

(4) *Directors' Votes*

Unless the articles otherwise provide, each director has only one vote at a board meeting, and in the event of a disagreement the majority view will prevail, though the chairman is usually given a casting vote, cf. Regulation 98 of Table A.

Votes of directors in matters in which they are interested.—Directors stand in a fiduciary relation to the members of the company, and under the general rules relating to such a relationship a director cannot, in the absence of express provision in the articles, contract with the company without the sanction of the company in general meeting. A director is precluded from dealing on behalf of the company with himself and from entering into any engagements in which he has a personal interest conflicting or which may possibly conflict with the interests of those whose interests it is his duty to protect. This rule extends not only to contracts with the director himself but to contracts with any firms or companies in which that director has an interest either as director or shareholder and even if he holds the shares in the other company as a trustee. The smallest conceivable conflict of interest will be sufficient to bring this rule into operation.[2] Even the allotment of shares or the issue of debentures by directors to themselves will fall within this rule.[3] Most articles specify exemptions from this strict rule but frequently provide that in the case of any such contract the interested director is not to vote. In that case a director prohibited from voting does not count towards a quorum.[4] Such a prohibition will not, however, prevent a director from voting as a shareholder at general meetings of the company upon contracts in which he is interested,[5] and a director is entitled to attend board meetings even when he is not entitled to vote thereat.[6] It is, however, perfectly competent for the articles

[1] *Dover &c Light Railway Co.*, [1914] 1 Ch. 568, 2 Ch. 506.
[2] *Transvaal Lands Co. v. New Belgium Land Co.*, [1914] 2 Ch. 488.
[3] *Neal v. Quinn* (1916) W.N. 223.
[4] See Regulation 84 of Table A.
[5] *North-West Transportation Co. v. Beatty* (1887) 12 App. Cas. 589.
[6] *Grimwade v. B.P.S. Syndicate* (1915) 31 T.L.R. 531.

not only to permit such contracts but to allow the interested directors to vote on matters connected therewith.

When any such contracts are permitted the provisions of Section 199 must be observed. That Section declares that it is the duty of a director who is in any way, whether directly or indirectly, interested in a contract or proposed contract with the company to declare the nature of his interest at a meeting of the directors of the company and provides for a fine not exceeding £100 on non-compliance with the Section. It is to be noticed that it is not sufficient for a director merely to declare that he is interested: he must declare the nature of his interest. This does not mean the full extent or quantum of his interest: so that if the interest that he has is, say, 100 shares in the other contracting company, he has to declare that he holds shares but need not disclose the number. If, however, his shareholding in the other company were a controlling one, this fact would alter the nature of his interest and he would have to disclose not merely that he is a shareholder, but the controlling shareholder.

The principle to be observed, in deciding what has to be disclosed, is that any aspect of the interest which could or might affect the attitude of the director or of his colleagues, is part of the "nature" of the interest and has to be disclosed.

The fact that a director discloses the nature of his interest and does not vote does not absolve him from responsibility with regard to the proposal. He is entitled to speak on the proposal and if he feels it is against the interests of the company he must, of course, say so. He is not entitled merely to sit back and wash his hands of the matter.

The Section also provides that in the case of a proposed contract the declaration required by the Section is to be made at the meeting of the directors at which the question of entering into the contract is first taken into consideration, or if the director is not at the date of that meeting interested in the proposed contract, at the next meeting of the directors held after he becomes interested, and in a case where the director becomes interested in a contract after it is made, the declaration is to be made at the first meeting of the directors held after the director becomes interested.

Under the Section, a general notice given to the directors of a company by a director to the effect that he is a member of a specified company or firm and is to be regarded as interested in any contract which may, after the date of the notice, be made with that company or firm, is deemed to be a sufficient declaration of interest in relation to any contract so made, but no such notice is of any effect unless it is given at a meeting of the directors or the director takes reasonable steps to secure that it is brought up and read at the next meeting of the directors after it is given.

Apart from any specific exemptions found in the articles, which permit a director to vote despite his other interests, articles usually provide in addition that the prohibitions may at any time be suspended or relaxed to any extent, and either generally or in respect of any particular contract, arrangement or transaction, by the company in general meeting: see Regulation 84 of Table A. Even if the articles permit a director to vote on a resolution in which he is interested, this does not absolve him from disclosure, under Section 199 of the nature of his interest. That disclosure has to be made so that the other directors can give due weight to the opposing interest while assessing the directors' views.

Articles frequently permit a director to hold any other office or place of profit under the company (other than the office of auditor) in conjunction with his office of director for such period and on such terms (as to remuneration and otherwise) as the directors may determine; see Regulation 84 of Table A. The articles usually go on to provide that no director or intending director shall be disqualified by his office from contracting with the company either with regard to his tenure of any such other office or place of profit or as vendor, purchaser or otherwise, and that no such contract, or any contract or arrangement entered into by or on behalf of the company in which any director is in any way interested, shall be liable to be avoided, and that no director so contracting or being so interested shall be liable to account to the company for any profit realised by any such contract or arrangement, by reason of such director holding that office or of the fiduciary relation thereby established. In addition, the articles usually permit a director, notwithstanding his interest, to be counted in the quorum present at any meeting at which he or any other director is appointed to hold any such office or place of profit under the company or at which the terms of any such appointment are arranged, and allow him to vote on any such appointment or arrangement other than his own appointment or the arrangement of the terms of his appointment.

Finally it is usually provided by the articles that a director may act by himself or his firm in a professional capacity for the company, and that he or his firm shall be entitled to remuneration for professional services as if he were not a director; but these provisions are stated not to authorise a director or his firm to act as auditor to the company.

Thus in certain circumstances under an article such as Regulation 84 of Table A a director may vote though interested, and in other circumstances he may not. Many articles (particularly those of private companies) do not contain such an elaborate provision, but it is often useful to permit the restrictions imposed by the articles to be relaxed by the company in general meeting, especially where there are only two or three directors of the company.

It will be observed that Section 199 refers only to contracts with the company whereas Regulation 84 refers to contracts or arrangements. In principle a director, because of his fiduciary position, should disclose any interest which he has in any matter which the board considers, whether or not it be technically a contract with the company. Section 199 is declaratory but not exhaustive.

(5) *Committees*

The directors may, if the articles contain the necessary authority, delegate their powers to committees. The articles generally provide for this, as does Table A, in Regulations 102 to 104.

When a board of directors delegate their powers to a committee without any provision as to the committee acting by a quorum, all acts of the committee must be done in the presence of all the members of the committee, and the committee have no power to add to their number or supply a vacancy.[1]

In all cases of delegation of powers to a committee its powers and authority should be clearly stated by the resolution effecting the delegation. Where a company is regulated by an article in form of Regulation 102 of Table A, directors may delegate their powers to a committee of one.[2]

Committees are usually appointed for one of three main purposes: either to deal with a matter which requires speedy decision, where the whole board could not be contacted quickly enough: or to deal with a matter where it is desirable to have discussion free from the embarrassing presence of a director who is personally concerned in the matter: *e.g.* for the appointment or removal of a director to or from executive office. Nevertheless the minutes (as distinct from a report on the discussions) are open to inspection by directors who were not on the committee, including the one being discussed. Thirdly, standing committees are often appointed for routine matters, such as transfer.

The power to delegate to a committee is, like all directors' powers, a fiduciary one. It cannot be exercised for an improper purpose; for example to exclude one or more directors from the forum where the board's decisions are taken.

[1] *Re Liverpool Household Stores* (1890) 59 L.J.Ch. 616.
[2] *Re Fireproof Doors*, [1916] 2 Ch. 142.

CHAPTER 22

Meetings in Winding Up

This Part has hitherto been concerned with meetings held in relation to the affairs of a company while it is a going concern. In this chapter are noticed the main provisions dealing with meetings held in connection with the winding up of companies.

Various classes of meetings are required to be held by the Act and, in addition, the Companies (Winding-Up) Rules, 1949 (S.I. 1949, No. 330) contain provisions dealing with meetings of creditors and contributories in a winding up by the Court and of creditors in a creditors' voluntary winding up.

(1) *Meetings of Creditors and Contributories in a Winding Up by the Court*

The first meetings held in a winding up of this kind are governed by Section 239.

Under this section the official receiver (who becomes provisional liquidator until he or some other person becomes liquidator) is required to summon separate meetings of the creditors and contributories of the company. These meetings decide whether or not application is to be made to the Court for appointing a liquidator in place of the official receiver: if the two meetings choose different persons for appointment as liquidator, the Court decides the difference and makes such order as it thinks fit.[1]

If no appointment is made by the Court, the official receiver becomes the liquidator. He also becomes liquidator if there is at any time a vacancy.

"Contributory" is defined by Section 213 to mean every person liable to contribute to the assets of a company in the event of its being wound up, and for the purposes of all proceedings prior to the final determination of the question of who are the contributories, includes any person alleged to be a contributory. A holder of fully paid shares is included in the term.[2]

[1] Compare a creditors' voluntary winding up, Section 294, where the creditors' choice is decisive.

[2] *Anglesea Colliery Co.* (1866) L.R., 1 Ch. 555; *Consolidated Goldfields of New Zealand Ltd.*, [1953] Ch. 689.

It is also the business of these first meetings to determine whether or not application is to be made to the Court for the appointment of a committee of inspection to act with the liquidator and who are to be members of the committee if appointed (Section 252).

Rules 121 to 126 of the Winding Up Rules contain detailed provisions relating to the convening and holding of these meetings. They provide that the official receiver may require the attendance of directors and officers of the company at the first meetings and must send to each creditor and contributory a summary of the company's statement of affairs together with his observations thereon.

Subsequent meetings of creditors and contributories may also be called, and the liquidator is bound to have regard to any directions given by such meetings, which, in case of conflict, override directions given by the Committee of Inspection (Section 246).

Section 246 also provides that the liquidator may summon general meetings of the creditors or contributories for the purpose of ascertaining their wishes, and that it is his duty to summon meetings at such times as the creditors or contributories, by resolution, either at the meeting appointing the liquidator or otherwise, may direct, or whenever requested in writing to do so by one-tenth in value of the creditors or contributories as the case may be.

Under Section 346, which applies to all classes of winding up, the Court may, as to all matters relating to the winding up of a company, have regard to the wishes of the creditors or contributories of the company, as proved to it by any sufficient evidence, and may, if it thinks fit, for the purpose of ascertaining those wishes, direct meetings of the creditors or contributories to be called, held and conducted in such manner as the Court directs, and may appoint a person to act as chairman of any such meeting and to report the result to the Court. The section provides that in the case of creditors, regard shall be had to the value of each creditor's debt and that in the case of contributories, regard shall be had to the number of votes conferred on each contributory by the Act or the articles.

Rules 127 to 156 of the Winding Up Rules deal with meetings of creditors and contributories in a winding up by the Court and also with meetings of creditors in a creditors' voluntary winding up (see below). These rules provide (among other things) for seven days' notice of meetings by advertisement in the London Gazette and a local paper and by post to those entitled to attend, the appointment of a chairman, the passing of resolutions when a majority in number and value of those present vote in favour,[1] adjournment, quorum, voting and the appointment of proxies.

(2) *Meetings of Creditors and the Company in a Voluntary Winding Up*

A voluntary winding up is either a creditors' or a members' voluntary winding up. Under Section 283 the winding up will be a members' voluntary winding up where before the day on which the resolution for winding up is passed the directors have made and filed with the Registrar of Companies a statutory declaration that they have made a full inquiry into the affairs of the company and have formed the opinion that the company will be able to pay its debts in full within a specified period not exceeding twelve months from the commencement of the winding up. If this declaration is not made the winding up will be a creditors' voluntary winding up.

The Section makes it an offence to make this declaration without reasonable grounds therefor, and further provides that if the opinion expressed therein turns out to be unfounded the onus is on the persons making the declaration to show that they had reasonable grounds for making it.

Further, by Section 288, if the liquidator is at any time of the opinion that the company will not be able to pay its debts in full within the period stated in the declaration of solvency, the liquidator must summon forthwith a meeting of the creditors and lay before them a statement of the assets and liabilities of the company. By this means the creditors are brought into a winding up which commenced as a members' voluntary winding up but should have commenced as a creditors' voluntary winding up. Section 291 requires that when the liquidator takes this step, the annual and final meetings thereafter to be called will be those applicable to a creditors' voluntary winding up.

In both kinds of voluntary winding up, meetings of the company continue to be held after the commencement of the winding up and these meetings are not referred to as meetings of contributories but as meetings of the company.

(*a*) *Provisions applicable to a Members' Voluntary Winding Up.*— Sections 284 to 291 deal exclusively with members' voluntary winding up.

The following provisions (in addition to those already noticed) are of importance:

[1] Where a majority in value differs from a majority in number, the Court normally favours the majority in value: *re Bloxwich Iron & Steel Co.* (1894) W.N. 111.

(i) The company in general meeting appoints the liquidator and fixes his remuneration (Section 285) and fills any vacancy in the office (Section 286); in the latter case the requisite meeting may be convened by any contributory or the continuing liquidator (if more than one was appointed).

(ii) If the winding up lasts more than one year the liquidator must summon a general meeting of the company to be held at or within three months after the end of each year and must lay before the meeting an account of his acts and dealings and of the conduct of the winding up during the preceding year (Section 289).

(iii) When the affairs of the company have been fully wound up the liquidator must, by advertisement in the London Gazette, call a general meeting of the company and lay before it his final account. Within one week thereafter he makes a return to the Registrar of Companies of the holding of the meeting (or that there was no quorum at the meeting) and the company is automatically dissolved three months after the return is registered (Section 290).

Under Secion 303(1)(*e*) the liquidator has the power in a voluntary winding up of any kind to summon general meetings of the company. In an ordinary members' voluntary winding up where it is clear that the company's debts will be paid within the time stated in the declaration of solvency there will first be the meeting at which the resolution for winding up is passed and this meeting will generally also appoint the liquidator. There will then be the yearly meetings required by Section 289 if the winding up so long continues, any meetings the liquidator may choose to call and the final meeting. These meetings will be called and conducted in accordance with the company's articles (save that the final meeting is to be called by advertisement in the Gazette) and are not affected by the Winding Up Rules.

(*b*) *Provisions applicable to a Creditors' Voluntary Winding Up.*— As might be expected, the greatest difference between members' and creditors' voluntary winding up is that in the latter the creditors, in the main, have control of the proceedings. In particular:

(i) A meeting of the creditors must be convened for the same day as or the day after that on which the meeting of the company to consider the resolution for voluntary winding up is to be held. Notice of this meeting is to be sent by post to the creditors simultaneously with the sending of the notices of the company meeting and the meeting must also be advertised in the London Gazette and two local newspapers circulating in the district where the registered office or principal place of business is situated. A full statement of the company's affairs and a list of creditors must be laid before the meeting and a director of the company must preside thereat (Section 293).

(ii) At their first meetings mentioned above the creditors and the company may nominate a person to be liquidator. If there are different nominations the creditors' nominee is appointed unless the Court orders otherwise (Section 294). If the holding of the creditors' meeting is delayed, any liquidator nominated by the company will be the properly appointed liquidator until the creditors' meeting is held and some other person is nominated by them.[1]

(iii) The creditors may at any meeting appoint a Committee of Inspection of not more than five persons. If this is done the company may also nominate not more than five persons to act as members of such committee; but if the creditors resolve that all or any of the persons nominated by the company ought not to be members of the committee, they shall not be members unless the Court otherwise directs (Section 295).

(iv) The creditors fill any vacancy in the office of liquidator (Section 297).

(v) Annual and final meetings of the company are held as in the case of a members' voluntary liquidation and annual and final meetings of the creditors are called at the same time (Sections 299 and 300).

Rules 129 to 156 of the Winding Up Rules referred to above will apply to meetings of creditors called in accordance with these provisions except where the rules themselves otherwise provide and in addition to these meetings a liquidator in any creditors' voluntary winding up may from time to time summon, hold, and conduct meetings of creditors for the purpose of ascertaining their wishes (Rule 127(2)).

In the rare event of an order being made for a winding up under supervision, the first meetings will usually have been already held. The subsequent meetings will generally be held as if the winding up was a winding up by the Court (Section 315(2)).

(*c*) *Meetings under Section* 306 *of the Act.*—Section 306 of the Act provides that any arrangement between a company about to be or in the course of being wound up and its creditors shall be binding on the creditors and the company if acceded to by three-fourths in number and value of the creditors and sanctioned by extraordinary

[1] *Re Centrebind Ltd.*, [1967] 1 W.L.R. 377.

resolution of the company. By Sub-section (2) any creditor or contributory may within three weeks of the completion of the arrangement appeal to the Court against it and the Court may amend, vary or confirm it.

The Section only applies in relation to voluntary winding up and only when such a winding up is in being or pending.[1]

Whilst the Section requires a meeting of the company it appears unnecessary to hold a meeting of the creditors. If acceded to by the requisite majority it becomes binding on all even if they were not aware of it.

The Section is almost never used in practice, the procedure under Section 206 of the Act (see Chapter 13) being more clear and convenient.

(3) *Meetings of Committees of Inspection*

The Act makes provision for the appointment of committees of inspection in the case of a winding up by the Court at the first meetings of creditors and contributories (Section 252). The committee of inspection, if there is one, exercises a measure of control over the winding up and its consent is required to the exercise by the liquidator of certain powers. Section 253 provides that a committee of inspection shall consist of creditors and contributories or persons holding general powers of attorney from creditors or contributories in such proportions as may be agreed on by the meetings of creditors and contributories or as, in case of difference, may be determined by the Court; there are special provisions relating to Scotland.

Under the Section the committee is to meet at such times as they appoint or, failing appointment, at least once a month. The liquidator or any member of the committee may call a meeting when he thinks necessary. The committee may act by a majority of those present but the necessary quorum is a majority of the committee.

A member of the committee may resign and may be removed by those (creditors or contributories) by whom he was appointed; his office becomes vacant if he becomes bankrupt, compounds with his creditors or is absent from five consecutive meetings without the leave of the other members appointed by those by whom he was appointed. A vacancy on the committee is filled by resolution of those by whom the retiring member was appointed unless the Court, on the application of the liquidator, orders that the vacancy should not be filled. The continuing members of the committee, if not less than two, may act notwithstanding any vacancy.

[1] *Re Contal Radio*, [1932] 2 Ch. 66.

As mentioned above, Section 295 of the Act also provides for the appointment of a committee of inspection in the case of a creditors' voluntary winding up. To such a committee the provisions of Section 253, except those as to the appointment of the original members, will apply (Section 295(2)).

PART FOUR

Meetings of Local Authorities

CHAPTER 23

Meetings of Local Authorities

Introduction

The Local Government Act 1972 almost wholly replaces the Local Government Act 1933 and it incorporates, with amendments, the provisions of the London Government Act 1963 relating to the constitution of the London authorities. It will be referred to in this Part as "the 1972 Act".

The 1972 Act created new structures for local government in England and Wales and allocated local government functions to them. In outline, the local government structure is as follows:

(a) England and Wales is divided into counties and districts. All counties, including Greater London, and all districts, including the London Boroughs, have councils. These councils are known as Principal Councils. Although some counties and districts are called metropolitan counties and metropolitan districts, the distinction lies in their different functions. Constitutionally, they are indistinguishable from non-metropolitan counties and districts.

(b) Below the level of the Principal Councils, there is a distinction between England and Wales:

(i) In some parts of England, some districts are sub-divided into parishes, all with Parish Meetings. In addition, some parishes have Parish Councils.

(ii) In Wales, all districts are sub-divided into communities, each of which has a Community Meeting. Some communities have Community Councils.

Neither Parish nor Community Meetings are local authorities, and the constitutions of the English Parish and the Welsh Community Meetings differ, reflecting the fact that Welsh Community Meetings have no executive powers.

Meetings

The 1972 Act contains the main statutory provisions relating to the constitution and meetings of the local authorities, including

London. The 1972 Act also provides for meetings of the English Parish Meetings and the Welsh Community Meetings. In addition to the statutory provisions, all local authorities have power to make bye-laws or standing orders not inconsistent with the statutory provisions. Subject to the statutory provisions and to any such bye-laws or standing orders, the general principles governing meetings which have been discussed in Part I of this book apply to meetings of Councils, to committees of Councils, and to Parish and Community Meetings.

The statutory provisions are set out in Parts I to IV of the Twelfth Schedule to the 1972 Act. This chapter deals in general terms with the provisions common to all and summarises the main differences between different types of Councils. Part I of the Twelfth Schedule refers to Principal Councils, Part II of the Twelfth Schedule to Parish Councils, and Part IV of the Twelfth Schedule to Community Councils. Part VI of the Twelfth Schedule relates to local authorities generally, and Parts III and V of the Twelfth Schedule refer to English Parish Meetings and Welsh Community Meetings respectively.

Annual Meetings

(a) *Councils.*—Meeting of all Councils are of two types: Annual and other Meetings. All Councils are required to hold an Annual Meeting. The date for the Annual Meeting is fixed in accordance with provisions set out for each type of Council in the appropriate Part of the Twelfth Schedule (see table below under Dates and Times of Meetings).

(*b*) *Parish and Community Meetings.*—All Parish Meetings are required to assemble annually. There is no statutory requirement for Community Meetings to assemble annually.

Other Meetings: Who may Convene

(*a*) *Councils.*—In addition to the Annual Meeting, Councils may hold such other meetings as they may determine. Parish Councils are required to hold three other meetings in addition to their Annual Meeting (Twelfth Schedule, Part II, paragraphs 7 and 8).

Extraordinary meetings of Councils can be called by:

(i) the Chairman at any time (Parts I, II and IV, paragraphs 3(1), 9(1) and 25(1)), or

(ii) any five members of a Principal Council (twenty in the case of the Greater London Council) or any two members of a Parish or Community Council who requisition the Chairman to call a meeting. If the Chairman refuses or does not call a meeting within seven days, a specified number of members may call a meeting themselves; the specified number being twenty for the Greater London Council, five for every other Principal Council and two for a Parish or Community Council. Those members who call the meeting are not required to be the same as those who make the requisition.

(*b*) *Meetings.*—In addition to the annual assembly of the Parish and Community Meetings, Parish Meetings may hold such other meetings as the Parish Council, or, if there is no Parish Council, the Chairman of the Parish Meeting may determine. A Parish without a Parish Council is required to assemble at least twice in every year. Community Meetings may be convened at any time.

A Parish or Community Meeting may be convened in the following ways:

(i) In the case of a Parish or Community possessing a Parish or Community Council, a meeting may be convened by:
1. the Chairman of the Parish or Community Council, or
2. any two Parish or Community Councillors; or

(ii) In a Parish without a Parish Council, by the Chairman of the Parish Meeting, who is chosen at the Annual Parish Meeting and holds office until his successor is elected (Section 15(10)); or

(iii) By any six local government electors for the Parish or Community.

Place of Meetings

The place for all Council Meetings is fixed by the Council. The place, surprisingly, may be either within or without the area of the authority.

All Parish and Community Councils and Meetings are prohibited from holding their meetings in premises licensed for the sale of intoxicating liquor, except in cases where no other suitable room is available for such meetings either free of charge or at a reasonable cost (Parts II, III, IV and V, paragraphs 10(1), 14(5), 26(1) and 32(2)).

Date and Times of Meetings

The 1972 Act contains provisions as to the dates and times for holding meetings; these provisions vary according to the type of Council and according to the type of meeting and are found in the Parts of the Twelfth Schedule of the 1972 Act which relate to the respective types of local authority or Council.

(1) The time for the Annual Meeting of Councils is fixed by the Council, or if no time is fixed, at twelve noon for Principal Councils and six o'clock in the evening for Parish and Community Councils. The dates and times for holding the other meetings of the Councils are fixed by the Councils as they may determine.

(2) The dates for the annual meetings of Councils are as follows:

(a) Principal Councils other than the Greater London Council:

(i) In an election year for councillors, on the eighth day after the day of retirement of councillors or such other day within the 21 days immediately following the day of retirement as the Council may fix; and

(ii) In any other year, on a day fixed by the Council in March, April or May.

(b) The Greater London Council:

(i) In an election year for councillors, on the eighteenth day after the election day or on such other day within the seven days immediately following that eighteenth day as the Council may fix; and

(ii) In any other year, on a day fixed by the Council in March, April or May.

(c) Parish and Community Councils:

(i) In an election year for councillors, on, or within, 14 days after the day on which the councillors elected take office; and

(ii) In any other year, on a day fixed by the Council in May.

(d) Parish Meetings:

Between 1st March and 1st June (both inclusive); the date and time to be fixed by the Parish Council, or if there is no such Council, by the Chairman of the Parish Meeting.

Summoning of Meetings

(1) The Twelfth Schedule specifies two separate steps to be taken for the proper summoning of every Council Meeting:

(a) Notice of the time and place of the intended meeting has to be published as follows:

(i) At the Council Offices for Principal Councils, and

(ii) At some conspicuous place in the parish or community for Parish and Community Councils.

When the meeting is called by members of the Council, this notice must be signed by them and must specify the proposed business.

(b) A summons to attend the meeting must be left at or sent by post to the usual place of residence of every Council member, or, in the case of a member of a Principal Council, at some other address notified by the Councillor (Twelfth Schedule, Part I, paragraph 4(3)). The summons need not be sent by registered post. The summons must be signed by the proper officer of the council (defined in s. 270 of the 1972 Act), *i.e.* the Clerk, for example, and must specify the business proposed to be transacted at the meeting.

The Schedule provides in each Part that want of service of the summons on any member of the Council does not affect the validity of the meeting. This provision appears superficially to be of much wider effect than the like provision in Regulation 51 of Table A in the First Schedule to the Companies Act 1948 which is concerned with accidental omission to give notice of a meeting. But it would probably be construed similarly, so that non-service, if accidental, would be excused, but if deliberate, *e.g.* not sent because the person to be served was known to be away or ill, or had asked not to be sent the notice, or because earlier notices had been returned by the Post Office, would not be excused under this provision. For cases concerned with the Table A and similar provisions, see *Harben v. Phillips,*[1] *Young v. Ladies Imperial Club,*[2] *re West Canadian Colleries,*[3] *Musselwhite v. Musselwhite & Sons Ltd.*[4] (and see p. 7 *supra*).

The notice required to be published and the summons required to be left or sent must be so published and left or sent three clear days at least before the meeting. For the purpose of calculating three clear days, the date on which the notice is published or the summons left or sent and the date of the meeting are excluded, and there must be three whole days in between these two dates: three clear days means three whole days clear, not merely 72 hours, see *re Hector Whaling Ltd.,*[5] *R. v. Herefordshire Justices*[6] (and see p. 83 *supra*).

(2) For Parish and Community Meetings, a public notice specifying the time and place of the intended meeting must be given by posting a notice in some conspicuous place or places in the Parish or Community, and by giving notice in any other

[1] (1883) 23 Ch. D. 14. [2] 2 K.B. 523. [3] [1962] Ch. 370.
[4] [1962] Ch. 964. [5] [1936] Ch. 208. [6] (1820) 3 B. & Ald. 581.

manner that appears desirable to the person convening the meeting.

The notice must be published, with one exception, at least seven clear days before the meeting. At least fourteen clear days' notice is required if the business proposed to be transacted relates to either:

(a) the establishment or dissolution of a Parish or Community Council, or
(b) the grouping of the parish with another parish or parishes under a common Parish Council or the grouping of the community with another community or communities under a common Community Council.

Business at Meetings

The 1972 Act specifies business which is to be transacted at Annual Meetings of Councils: apart from this, and one major exception, no business may be transacted at any meeting other than specified in the summons or notice convening the meeting. See *Longfield Parish Council v. Wright*[1] where a resolution which did not comply with such a regulation failed. The major exception, previously often allowed in practice, enables urgent business to be brought before Principal Councils in accordance with such Councils' standing orders (Twelfth Schedule, Part I, paragraph 4(5)). The exception only applies, therefore, if the Councils' standing orders make provision for urgent business.

Procedure at Meetings

Part IV of the Twelfth Schedule contains general provisions relating to procedure at meetings for all local authorities. Subject to statutory provisions, standing orders may be made by the local authority for the regulation of proceedings (Twelfth Schedule, Part VI, paragraph 42).

In a parish with a Parish Council, the Parish Council may make standing orders for the regulation of proceedings and business at Parish Meetings. In the absence of a Parish Council, the Parish Meeting may regulate its own proceedings and business subject to statutory provisions.

Chairman of Meeting

The 1972 Act specifically provides who is to preside at meetings of Councils and Parish and Community Meetings.

[1] [1918] 88 L.J.Ch. 119.

(1) The Chairman,[1] or failing him the Vice-Chairman, presides at all meetings of Councils. In Greater London, the deputy chairman, if any, of the Greater London Council presides in the absence of the Chairman and the Vice-Chairman, and in London Borough Councils, the deputy mayor, if chosen, presides in the absence of the mayor. In the absence of all of the above, the members of the Council are entitled to choose one of their members to preside.

(2) The Chairman, or failing him, the Vice-Chairman, of the Parish Council presides at Parish Meetings in the case of a parish having a Parish Council. In a parish without a Parish Council, the Parish Meeting is chaired by the Chairman elected by the Parish Meeting at its annual assembly. The Parish Meeting may appoint a person to take the chair in the absence of the Chairman and Vice-Chairman of the Parish Council, or the Chairman of the Parish Meeting, as the case may be.

(3) The Chairman of the Community Council presides at Community Meetings in the case of a community having a Community Council. In any other case, a Community Meeting appoints a person to be Chairman at that Meeting. Thus, there is no permanent Chairman for such Community, unlike Parish, Meetings.

Attendance at Meetings by Non-members

(1) *By Members of the Public.*—The Public Bodies (Admission to Meetings) Act 1960 provides that all Local Authority meetings and meetings of committees consisting entirely of Council members, are normally open to the public. This right of access is extended by Section 100 of the 1972 Act, and to six types of statutory committees (excluding education committees).

Whenever publicity would be prejudical to the public interest by reason of the confidential nature of the business to be transacted, or for other special reasons arising from the nature of the business or of the proceedings, a Local Authority may resolve that the public be excluded. The "special reason" must be stated in the resolution. The exclusion may be for the whole or part of the proceedings. The receiving of advice from an outside person, not on the Council or a committee, may be a sufficient reason.

[1] Any Parish or Community Council can request to be called a Town Council and their Chairman and Vice-Chairman are called Town Mayor and Town Deputy Mayor (Local Government Act 1972 ss. 245–6). These are changes of title only and have no effect upon the powers or functions of such councils.

In practice, the right of the public to access to committees of Local Authorities may be defeated in two ways:

(a) Section 100 of the 1972 Act does not confer the right of access to sub-committees of Local Authorities. Committees have power under Section 101(2) of the 1972 Act to arrange for their functions to be discharged by sub-committees, and thus, exclude the public.

(b) Decisions may be taken without discussion at committee meetings whilst the discussion may take place at unofficial meetings to which the public have no right of access.

Where the meeting is open to the public, three days' notice must be given by posting it at the Council offices; if the meeting is called at less than three days' notice, the public notice must be posted when the meeting is convened.

(2) *Press.*—In addition, newspapers may require a copy of the agenda and other information regarding a proposed meeting to be supplied to them, and publication of such agenda and information is privileged unless published with malice (Section 1(5), The Public Bodies (Admission to Meetings) Act 1960). See also as to qualified privilege, Schedule to the Defamation Act 1952, which is amended by Section 2(2) of the Public Bodies (Admission to Meetings) Act 1960.

(3) The Chairman of a Parish Council or Community Council is entitled to attend a Parish or Community Meeting for the Parish or Community, even if he is not a local government elector for that Parish or Community. If he attends in such circumstances, the only vote to which he is entitled is his casting vote in the event of an equality of votes on a poll (Twelfth Schedule, Parts III and V, paragraphs 16 and 31).

Quorum

(1) A quorum must be present in order to empower a Council Meeting to conduct business. The quorum is one-fourth of the members of the Council for Principal Councils, and one-third for Parish and Community Councils.

The quorum must be a disinterested quorum, so that no member can be counted who is disabled from voting (see below under heading "Disability to Vote").

If more than one-third of the members of a Local Authority are disqualified then the quorum is to be one-fourth of the remaining qualified members for a Principal Council, and one-third of the remaining qualified members for a Parish and

Community Council until the number of qualified members is increased to not less than two-thirds of the whole number of members of the authority. In no case can the quorum be less than three at a Parish or Community Council (Twelfth Schedule, Parts II and IV, paragraphs 12 and 28).

(2) Council decisions are made by a majority of the members of the Local Authority present and voting at meetings. In the case of equality of votes the person presiding has a casting vote. A show of hands is the prescribed method of voting in Parish and Community Councils, for other Local Authorities, the method is not prescribed, so that standing orders may provide for voting by means of division.

The names of members present at meetings are required to be recorded. Moreover, a member of a Parish or Community Council may request that on a particular question, how each member gave his vote shall be recorded. These records can be made conveniently in the minutes of the meeting.

(3) Decisions of Parish and Community Meetings are made by a majority of those present and voting at the meeting. The person presiding at the meeting has a casting vote in the case of an equality of votes. Unless a poll is duly demanded, the decision of the person presiding as to the result of the voting is final.

A poll may be demanded at any time before the conclusion of the meeting upon any question arising during the meeting: it need not be demanded at the time when the question is dealt with.

For a demand to be effective, the person presiding must consent, or it must be made by not less than ten, or one-third of the electors present, whichever is the less. A poll is taken of those entitled to attend the meeting and it is taken by ballot in accordance with rules made by statutory instrument. In effect, a poll is conducted in much the same way as if it were a poll for the election of parish or community councillors.

Disability to Vote

Any member of a Local Authority, who has any pecuniary interest, direct or indirect, in a contract or proposed contract or other matter and who is present at a meeting at which it is to be considered, must disclose the fact as early as possible in the meeting. He may not discuss nor vote upon it (Section 94(1)). The same rule applies to committees.

Standing orders may, moreover, provide for the exclusion of a member whilst a matter is being considered in which he is interested (Section 94(4)).

(1) The scope of "pecuniary interest" is restricted, *inter alia*, in the following ways:
  (a) It does not include the receipt by the Chairman, Vice-Chairman or a member of a Local Authority of an allowance or payment from that Authority (Section 94(5)).
  (b) A member of a Local Authority having an indirect pecuniary interest in a contract, proposed contract, or other matter by reason only of a beneficial interest in shares or securities not exceeding a nominal value of £1,000 or one-hundredth of the total nominal value of the issued share capital or of any one class of shares in the case of a company with more than one class of share capital, whichever is the less, is not prohibited from taking part in the discussion or voting. Even so, the duty to disclose the interest remains (Section 97(6)).
  (c) An interest of a member which is so remote or insignificant that it cannot reasonably be regarded as likely to influence a member in discussing or voting on the matter is not treated as a pecuniary interest (Section 97(5)).
(2) Penalties are imposed for breach of the Sections. Section 95(3) makes the interest of a spouse of a member the interest of that member. General notice of employment with a specified employer may be made to the proper officer of the Authority, and this constitutes adequate notice (Section 96(1)). The proper officer is required to record any disclosure in a book which is open to inspection by members of the Council (Section 96(2)).
(3) Where such disabilities would apply to so great a proportion of the Council as to impede business, or in any other case where it is in the interests of the inhabitants of the area that the disabilities should be removed, they may be relaxed by a District Council as respects a member of a Parish or Community Council, and by the Secretary of State for the Environment as respects a member of any other Local Authority (Section 97(1)).
  (a) A member may apply to the Secretary of State if he wishes to obtain permission to speak in a discussion and vote on matters in which he has a pecuniary interest. For convenience, such an application is normally made through

the Clerk of the Council, but an individual member may apply directly to the Secretary of State.

(i) Permission to speak will normally be given for any matter in which a member has a pecuniary interest so long as it is not an interest which is peculiar to that member.

(ii) Permission to vote will not normally be given unless the number of members disabled would be at least half of the Council, or committee, or the effect of the disability on the Council or committee would be such as to enable the minority members to adopt policies opposed by the majority, disabled, members.

(b) Under Section 97(2), the Secretary for State has removed the disability on council house tenants and tenants (whether controlled or statutory) of unfurnished accommodation considering, discussing and voting on matters of general housing policy at meetings of Local Authorities, committees, sub-committees or joint committees. Each member must still decide whether he has a pecuniary interest in the matter under consideration by his Council despite this general dispensation.[1]

In addition to the disabilities imposed under Section 94, Section 93 precludes a councillor on the Greater London Council voting on any matter involving only expenditure on account of which his electoral area is not, for the time being, liable to be charged.

Minutes

(1) *Councils.*—Minutes of all the proceedings of a meeting of a Local Authority are required to be kept (Twelfth Schedule, Part VI, paragraph 41(1)). Notwithstanding any statute or rule of law to the contrary, these minutes may be recorded on loose leaves consecutively numbered (Twelfth Schedule, Part VI, paragraph 41(2)).

The minutes are signed by the persons presiding at the meeting which they record, or the next meeting, and any minutes purporting to be so signed is to be received in evidence without further proof (Twelfth Schedule, Part VI, paragraph 41(2)).

By Section 228, minutes are to be open to the inspection of any Local Government elector for the area, on payment of a fee of 10p; he may also make a copy thereof or an extract therefrom. This also includes minutes of committees if they have been submitted to the

[1] See Department of the Environment Circular No. 40/72.

Council.[1] Minutes may be inspected by an agent of a Local Government elector.[2]

Where minutes have been so signed, then unless the contrary is proved, the meeting is deemed to have been duly convened and held, and all the members present at the meeting shall be seemed to have been duly qualified (Section 41(3)).

Minutes of the last previous meeting are either read, or, if they have been circulated, taken as read. They are usually confirmed, that is to say verified as a correct record.[3]

A member does not make himself liable for any illegal act done at a meeting at which he was not present, merely by voting subsequently for the confirmation of the minutes recording the act.[4]

(2) Similarly, minutes must be kept of the proceedings of a Parish Meeting, or a Parish Meeting committee, or a Community Meeting (Twelfth Schedule, Parts III and V, paragraphs 19 and 35).

Committees

The 1972 Act gives wide discretion to Local Authorities to discharge their functions through committees, sub-committees, officers and other Local Authorities (Sections 101–10). Certain statutory committees are preserved.

The quorum, proceedings and place of meeting of committees, sub-committees and joint committees are determined by the committees themselves, subject to any standing orders made by the Local Authorities (Section 106). Generally, the rules already set out governing Council Meetings also govern such committees.

In a parish not having a Parish Council, the Parish Meeting may arrange to discharge its functions through a committee of the Parish Meeting (Section 108). This provision does not apply to Wales where Community Meetings have no executive functions.

[1] *Williams v. Manchester Corporation* (1897) 45 W.R. 412.

[2] *R. v. Glamorgan C.C.*, [1936] 1 All E.R. 168, following the principle of *R. v. Bedwelty U.D.C.*, [1934] 1 K.B. 333, where it was held that the acounts of a Local Authority might be inspected by the agent of an elector.

[3] *R. v. Mayor of York* (1853) 1 E. & B. 594.

[4] *Burton v. Bevan*, [1908] 2 Ch. 240.

APPENDIX

Forms of Notices of Meetings of Companies, Agenda Papers and Minutes

APPENDIX

Forms of Notices of Meetings of Companies, Agenda Papers and Minutes

(1) *Notices of board meetings*

Clause 98 of Table A, and the Articles of most companies, provide that "the directors may meet together for the dispatch of business, adjourn, and otherwise regulate their meetings as they think fit".

This, of course, leaves it open to the directors to instruct the secretary from time to time as to their wishes in the matter of notices; or to *Resolve*—as is often done—that meetings of the board are to be held at regular intervals, "of which no additional notice shall be given".

Apart from such special instructions, the usual practice is to send a simple notice in the following form without specifying the business to be transacted:

JOHN JONES & COMPANY, LIMITED

370 Lombard Street, EC2 5BX.
10*th December*, 19—,

Sir,

I beg to give you notice that a meeting of the directors will be held at the registered office of the company on next, the day of , at a.m.

ANDREW ARMSTRONG,
Secretary

, Esq.

If the directors have given instructions that when any special business is to be brought up for consideration, a brief intimation of its nature is to be included in the notice, an addendum to the foregoing would take this form:

"Business to be transacted:
"General business, and the proposed purchase of further premises in Street, N.E."

(2) *Agenda of board meeting*

Held on , 19 , at the company's registered office.

AGENDA	CHAIRMAN'S NOTES
Present	*A. B. in the chair.* *C. D.* *E. F.* *G. H.* *directors.*

Agenda—*continued*	Chairman's Notes
In attendance	*M. N., solicitor of the company.* *O. P., Secretary.*
Read Minutes of last meeting ...	*Read and signed.*
Submit Bank Pass Book, with adjustment account to agree same with cash book ... ... And statement of cash flow ...	*Examined, and secretary instructed to request bank to transfer* £500 *from deposit to current account.*
Report Cheques (if any) signed since last meeting...	*Approved*
Produce List of Accounts for payment, and submit cheques in payment of same for signature ...	*All except P. T.'s account approved and cheques signed.* *Secretary to write to P. T. regarding shortage of delivery.*
Submit Transfer Deeds, Nos. to	*Passed for registration. Certificates ordered to be signed and sealed.*
Seal Certificates Nos. to , in place of Certificates Nos. cancelled	*Cancelled certificates examined. New certificates signed and sealed.*
Allot 1000 Ordinary Shares at per share applied for by the following: 700 to of 300 to of	*Allotted, and secretary ordered to send notice of allotment forthwith*

[The foregoing and any kindred formal matters are generally disposed of *first*, so as to leave time for any special matters to be discussed fully and without interruption.]

Consider Report of Managing Director [*or* of committee, *or* sub-committee, *as the case may be*] ...	*Proposed engagement of Mr. L. K. at a salary of* £5,000 *per annum, and the erection of a new storage shed as recommended. Approved.*
Examine Trading Account and cost and work details	*Examined: Reduction of* 2 *per cent. in cost noted.*
Read Letter from A. Z. dated ....19 ...	*Secretary instructed to reply that* ....
Consider Draft Directors' Report to be submitted to general meeting. *Fix* date of general meeting	*Approved with amendments. Secretary instructed to have this printed and sent with notice of general meeting for the , at* 3 *p.m.*
Next meeting	*at* 11 *a.m.*

[It is, of course, impossible to enumerate the many special questions that may arise for consideration; but in constructing agenda it is, as stated above, the approved plan to arrange for taking the formal business first, and routine correspondence is generally considered after the signing of the minutes.]

(3) *Minutes of board meeting*

The "notes" of the chairman appended to the foregoing agenda will, when recorded in minutes, appear in the following form:

Board meeting held at the registered office of the company on ,
19 .

Present: Mr. A. B. in the chair.
,, C. D.
,, E. F.
,, G. H. directors.

In attendance: Mr. M. N., the company's solicitor, Mr. O. P., Secretary.

(1) *Minutes.*—The minutes of the board meeting held on were read and approved and signed by the chairman.

(2) *Finance.*—The bank pass book was compared with the cash book, showing, with adjustments, available cash balance of £

A further statement of cash flow was produced showing:

Accounts falling due and payable by the company within the next month, £	Falling due and payable to the company within the next month, £

The secretary was directed to request the bankers to transfer £500 from deposit account to current account.

Details of cheques drawn since last meeting were submitted and approved.

Lists of accounts due for payment, with their corresponding vouchers, were submitted, and cheques for all these, except the account of P. T. & Co., were signed.

The secretary was instructed to write to P. T. & Co. respecting an alleged shortage of delivery in their last consignment.

(3) *Transfers.*—Transfer deeds numbered to inclusive, as appearing in the transfer register, were submitted and passed by the board. It was resolved that the transferees be entered in the register of members and that certificates for the shares transferred be signed and sealed.

Share certificates, Nos. for shares, were thereupon *Cancelled* by the board and new certificates for shares, Nos. to , were signed and sealed.

Applications received from:

Mr. , of , for 700 Ordinary Shares
Mr. , of , ,, 300 ,, ,,

at per share were submitted and approved, and it was *Resolved* that the shares applied for be allotted, and that the secretary be instructed to send to the applicants notice of allotment forthwith.

(4) *Report of managing director.*—The report of the managing director was read, and the engagement of Mr. L. K. at a salary of £5,000 per annum, and also the erection of a new storage shed at a cost not to exceed £ as recommended, were approved.

"Trading account" and "cost and work details" to date were examined, and a reduction of 2 per cent in the cost of production noted by the board.

(5) *Correspondence.*—A letter dated , from A. Z., with reference to , was read, and the secretary was instructed to reply that ....

(6) *Annual general meeting.*—A draft notice convening the annual general meeting, together with a draft report of directors, were *Considered* and with some alterations approved, and ordered to be printed and sent to the shareholders, the date of the meeting being fixed for 3 p.m. on the , at

(7) *Next meeting.*—The next meeting of the board was fixed for the at 11 a.m., at the registered office, and the secretary was instructed to have proofs of the report and notice of general meeting ready for the use of the board by that date.

....

Chairman.

(*Date.*)

(4) *Notice of statutory meeting*

THE COMPANY, LIMITED.

NOTICE IS HEREBY GIVEN that in accordance with the provisions of Section 130 of the Companies Act, 1948, the statutory meeting of the above-named Company will be held at
on day the day of 19 , at two o'clock in the afternoon.

A copy of the report required by the above-named section to be sent to the members accompanies this notice.

Dated this day of 19 .

By Order of the Board,

ANDREW ARMSTRONG,
Secretary.

370 Lombard Street,
London, EC2 5BX.

* NOTE. A member entitled to attend and vote at the above meeting may appoint one or more proxies to attend and vote instead of him. A proxy need not be a member of the Company.

(5) *Agenda of statutory meeting*

[As the contents of the report to be presented to the shareholders fourteen days before the statutory meeting are fully set out in Section 130 of the Companies Act, 1948, and cover the whole ground, the agenda of such a meeting is very simple:]

THE COMPANY, LIMITED.

Statutory meeting, held at
on , 19 , at o'clock.

	CHAIRMAN'S NOTES
[*Read* notice convening the meeting]	*Read*
Ask the meeting whether the statutory report may be taken as read, or whether it shall be read	*Taken as read*

	CHAIRMAN'S NOTES
Chairman to direct the attention of the meeting to the fact that a list of the shareholders in the company is, in accordance with Section 130 of the Act, open to the inspection of members during the continuance of the meeting	*List produced and shown*
Chairman to make short statement of the company's position and prospects, supplementing to some extent the statutory report, and invite inquiries from members who do not understand any of the contents of the report	*Statement made*

* There must appear with reasonable prominence in every notice calling a meeting of a company having a share capital a statement to this effect 136(2) of the Companies Act 1948).

[After the chairman has answered such questions to the best of his ability, the members are at liberty to discuss any matter relating to the formation of the company, or arising out of the statutory report, whether previous notice has been given or not; but no resolution of which notice has not been given in accordance with the articles may be passed; or the meeting may adjourn from time to time.

When such discussion has ceased, if no adjournment has been determined upon by the meeting, the chairman will declare the meeting closed.]

(6) *Minutes of statutory meeting*

Reproduced in minutes the foregoing will appear as follows:

Statutory meeting of THE
COMPANY, LIMITED, held at , on
Mr. in the chair.

15 shareholders present in person or by proxy.

The notice convening the meeting was read; the statutory report being, with the consent of the meeting, taken as read.

The chairman directed the attention of the meeting to the fact that a list of the shareholders in the company was, in accordance with the provisions of the Act, placed on the table and would remain open to the inspection of members during the continuance of the meeting.

The chairman then made a short statement on the company's position and prospects, supplementing to some extent the information contained in the statutory report, and invited inquiries from those members who had any difficulty in understanding the report.

After answering all the questions addressed to him, a discussion arose respecting the formation of the company, in which members A and B and C took part, on the conclusion of which—as there was no business to transact—the meeting closed, with a vote of thanks to the chairman.

....

Chairman.
(*Date.*)

(7) *Notice of annual general meeting*

THE COMPANY, LIMITED.

NOTICE IS HEREBY GIVEN that the [second] annual general meeting of the above-named company will be held at , on day, the day of , 19 , at two o'clock in the afternoon, for the following purposes:

To receive and consider the report of the directors, the accounts and balance sheet, and the auditors' report thereon;

To declare dividends, to elect directors, and to transact the other ordinary business of the company.

Mr. W. retires from the Board by rotation but offers himself for re-election.

Notice is also hereby given that the transfer books of company will be closed from the to the , 19 , both days inclusive.

Dated this day of 19 ,

By Order of the Board

....

Secretary

370 Lombard Street,
London, EC2 5BX

[The note relating to proxies must be inserted.]

When it is desired to transact any special business at an annual general meeting the notice must also contain the words "And to transact the following special business, *viz.*:"]

(8) *Agenda for annual general meeting*

THE COMPANY, LIMITED.

[Second] annual general meeting, to be held at on 19 , at o'clock.

AGENDA	CHAIRMAN'S NOTES
[Read notice convening the meeting]	*Read*
Read report of auditors	*Read*

[The auditors' report *must be read* at the general meeting at which the balance sheet is submitted, and be open to inspection by any shareholder (Section 14 (2) of the Companies Act, 1967).]

Ask the meeting whether the directors' report and the accounts as submitted shall be read or taken as read	*Taken as read*
Chairman to make statement of the company's position and general prospects, and	*Statement made*
Move that the report and accounts as audited and certified, now before the meeting, be approved and adopted	*Moved*
Call on to second the motion	*Seconded by*

Agenda—*continued*	Chairman's Notes
Ascertain whether the shareholders have any points to discuss or questions to ask, arising out of this *motion*	*Discussion and questions asked*
Reply to any questions	*Questions answered*
Put the motion to the meeting and declare the result	*Put and carried unanimously*
Move that the dividends recommended by the directors in their report, *viz.* 6 per cent on the preference shares and 7½ per cent on the ordinary shares, be approved and paid to shareholders appearing on the register of members at the closing of the books on *inst.*	*Seconded by Mr. C. Carried*
Elect a director in place of Mr. W., retiring by rotation	*Proposed by Mr. A.; seconded by Mr. B. Mr. W. re-elected*
Invite a shareholder to move that the remuneration of Messrs R. and Son, as auditors of the company for the current year, be £	*Moved by Mr. M.; seconded by Mr. N. Carried*
Declare proceedings at an end.	

(9) *Minutes of annual general meeting*

The [second] annual general meeting of THE COMPANY LIMITED, held at on
Mr. in the chair.

(1) *Reports and accounts.*—The notice convening the meeting and the auditors' report were *Read.* The directors' report and accounts were, with the consent of the meeting, taken as read.

After the chairman had addressed the meeting and replied to all the questions addressed to him, it was, on the motion of the chairman seconded by Mr. , unanimously *Resolved* "that the report and accounts to , 19 , as audited and certified by the company's auditors, be approved and adopted."

(2) *Dividend.*—It was then on the motion of the chairman, seconded by Mr. C., unanimously *Resolved* that the dividends recommended by the directors in their annual report, *viz.* 6 per cent on the preference shares and 7½ per cent on the ordinary shares, be approved and that the dividends be paid to those members whose names appeared in the register of members at the close of business on 19 .

(3) *Directors.*—On the proposition of Mr. A., seconded by Mr. B., it was *Resolved* that Mr. W., the director retiring by rotation, be re-elected.

(4) *Auditors.*—It was proposed by Mr. M., seconded by Mr. N., and *Resolved* that the renumeration of Messrs. R. & SON, as the auditors of the company for the current year, be £ .*

The meeting then terminated with a vote of thanks to the board.

(Signed),

....

Chairman.
(*Date.*)

* The re-election of the retiring auditors is not essential.

(10) *Notice of extraordinary general meeting*

....LIMITED

NOTICE IS HEREBY GIVEN that an Extraordinary General Meeting of the above-named Company will be held at on day the day of , 19 , at o'clock' in the afternoon, for the purpose of considering and if thought fit passing the following resolution, which will be proposed as a [special] [extraordinary] [ordinary] resolution.

[Special] [Extraordinary] Resolution
[set out resolution]

By order of the board,
Dated this day of , 19
....
Secretary.

370 Lombard Street,
London, EC2 5BX

[The note relating to proxies must be inserted.]

(11) *Agenda of extraordinary general meeting*

THE COMPANY, LIMITED.

Extraordinary general meeting to be held at on 19 , at o'clock.

AGENDA	CHAIRMAN'S NOTES
Chairman to make statement as to the circumstances which have arisen rendering it advisable for the company to pass the following resolution	*Statement made*
Move the resolution specified in the notice	*Moved*
Call on to second the motion	*Seconded by*
Reply to any questions that may be addressed to him respecting the matter	*Mr.* .... *Questions replied to*
Put the resolution to the meeting [if appropriate as a special or extraordinary resolution] and declare result	*Passed*
Declare the meeting closed.	

(12) *Minutes of extraordinary general meeting*

Extraordinary general meeting of THE COMPANY, LIMITED, held at on the day of 19 , at o'clock.

Mr. in the chair.

15 shareholders present in person or by proxy.

The following resolution was duly passed as a [special] [extraordinary] [ordinary] resolution:

The proceedings then terminated.

INDEX

INDEX